CONTRIBUTIONS BY: JIM WALLIS, TONY CAMPOLO, SHANE CLAIBORNE, JOHN PERKINS, LARRY ACOSTA, JEREMY DEL RIO, NOEL CASTELLANOS

W9-DEU-051

DEEP JUSTICE IN A BROKEN WORLD

HELPING YOUR KIDS SERVE OTHERS AND RIGHT THE WRONGS AROUND THEM

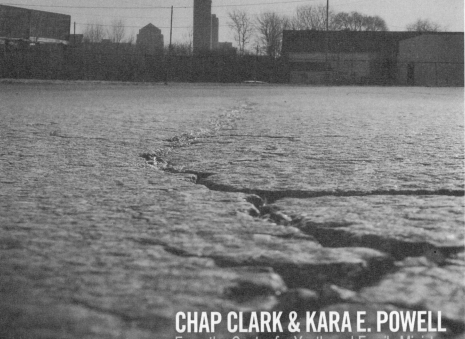

CHAP CLARK & KARA E. POWELL
From the Center for Youth and Family Ministry

ZONDERVAN®

ZONDERVAN.com/
AUTHORTRACKER
follow your favorite authors

youth
specialties

**youth
specialties**

Deep Justice in a Broken World: Helping Your Kids Serve Others and Right the Wrongs Around Them
Copyright 2007 by Chap Clark and Kara E. Powell

Youth Specialties resources, 300 S. Pierce St., El Cajon, CA 92020 are published by Zondervan, 5300
Patterson Ave. SE, Grand Rapids, MI 49530.

ISBN-10: 0-310-27377-3
ISBN-13: 978-0-310-27377-6

Cover design by SharpSeven Design
Interior design by Mark Novelli, IMAGO MEDIA

Printed in the United States of America

07 08 09 10 11 12 • 20 19 18 17 16 15 14 13 12 11 10 9 8 7 6 5 4 3 2 1

ACKNOWLEDGMENTS

"If you want to travel fast...go alone.
If you want to travel far...go together."

The African proverb above captures the 18-month journey of writing this book. So many of you have traveled together with us, and we hope the book's message travels far.

Thanks to the members of the executive committee at the Center for Youth and Family Ministry (CYFM) for giving your hearts and souls to translating research into resources that transform youth and family ministry.

Thanks to Cheryl Crawford, David Fraze, Eric Iverson, Dave Livermore, Mark Maines, Lowell Noble, Ginny Olson, J.R. Rozko, and Jude Tiersma Watson for reading part or all of the manuscript and sharing your justice insights.

Thanks to Brad Griffin, Rana Choi, Mike Hensley, and Melanie Lammers for being the best CYFM teammates we can imagine.

Thanks to everyone who shared their justice stories and kingdom wisdom with us—from students like Kristin, Marcus, and Demetrice to leaders like Jim Wallis, Glen Stassen, Bill Pannell, John Perkins, Tony Campolo, Efrem Smith, Lina Thompson, Anthony Flynn, Rudy Carrasco, Alexie Torres-Fleming, and Shane Claiborne.

Thanks to Larry Acosta, Noel Castellanos, and Jeremy Del Rio for the heroic justice work each of you does every day and for your chapters that help us move from reflection to action.

An enormous thank you from Kara to Dave for being one of my justice heroes and modeling kingdom love and sacrifice in our family, our church, and our world. Nathan, Krista, and Jessica, every day you inspire me by the way you receive the kingdom of God with childlike joy and wonder.

From Chap to my family, and especially to my new daughter-in-law, the *new* Katie Clark, thank you for helping me learn more deeply that loving Jesus means following and living for him as he brings in his kingdom. The way each of you has tutored me in the power and meaning of mercy, justice, and peace-making has made me a better man, husband, father, friend, and servant of Jesus Christ. May this book make you proud for how you have influenced it.

We also thank the family at Fuller Theological Seminary. You have shaped and challenged us to continue to ask hard questions about life in the kingdom of God. We will always be grateful for the opportunity to serve alongside such an incredible community of people.

CONTENTS

Section 1: Both/And Kingdom Thinking

Section 2: Both/And Kingdom Living

SECTION ONE
BOTH/AND KINGDOM THINKING

WHAT'S DEEP JUSTICE AND HOW DO I KNOW IF I'M DOING IT?

BY KARA POWELL

Ice cream has the power to bring deep justice to our broken world.

Guess how much money you, I, the kids in our ministries, and every other American spend each year on mint chocolate chip, strawberry, jamoca almond fudge, rainbow sherbet, just plain vanilla, and all other ice cream flavors?

Go ahead. Take a guess.

$20 billion.[1]

For those of you who like to see a lot of zeroes, that's $20,000,000,000.

Compare that $20 billion with other figures recently released by the United Nations.[2] Providing clean water and basic sanitation for the entire world would cost $7 billion a year for the next ten years.

An additional $4 billion a year for the next ten years could finance basic health care that would prevent the deaths of 3 million infants each year.

So for $11 billion a year for the next decade, just over half of what Americans spend on ice cream, we could give the world clean water and basic sanitation and prevent the deaths of millions of babies. But since there is no Give-Up-Ice-Cream-for-World-Health movement, odds are good that we'll keep eating our mint chocolate chip and much of the world will lack water and health care.

Does that seem just to you?

---

[1] State of the World 2004, Worldwatch Institute, http://www.worldwildlife.org/news/displayPR.cfm?prID=122.

[2] United Nations Development Program 2005 Human Development Report, http://hdr.undp.org/reports/global/2005/pdf/HDR05_chapter_3.pdf.

On September 11, 2001, the terrorists who hijacked four U.S. planes claimed 2,792 lives. Our entire nation—and much of the world—was glued to radios, televisions, and the Internet, desperate to find out why and how so many had been killed.

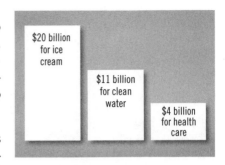

Yet on that same day nearly three times as many people were killed by HIV/AIDS worldwide. And that same number of people died from HIV/AIDS on September 12, 2001. And on September 13. And that many people have died because of AIDS every day since then. Yet as AIDS rips apart children, families, villages, and entire nations, the world remains disengaged. Tragically, so do our churches and youth ministries.

Does that seem just to you?

Many of us slept on comfortable mattresses last night, and with a flick of a thermostat switch, we kept our homes at temperatures we considered ideal. Last night, approximately 600,000 homeless people sought shelter on U.S. streets.[3] Making matters worse, an estimated 38 percent of those homeless persons were children.[4]

Does that seem just to you?

Perhaps the most alarming statistic of all is that this injustice and poverty is happening in a world in which 2.1 billion of us, or 33 percent of the world's total population, claim to be followers of Christ, who taught in Matthew 25:40 that whatever we do for the "least of these brothers and sisters," we are actually doing for him.[5]

Does that seem just to you?

It doesn't seem just to us either.

A growing number of youth ministries are alarmed by the brokenness of our world and are determined to restore justice.

Maybe you lead one of them.

---

[3] U.S. Department of Health and Human Services, "Ending Chronic Homelessness: Strategies for Action," March 2003.

[4] National Alliance to End Homelessness, "A Plan, Not a Dream: How to End Homelessness in Ten Years," 2000.

[5] "Major Religions of the World Ranked by Number of Adherents," http://www.adherents.com/Religions_By_Adherents.html.

Some of you are partnering with faith communities of different ethnic and economic backgrounds to create job centers, food co-ops, and college scholarship funds to counter the injustice in your town. Others of you are mobilizing kids and families to mentor under-resourced kids at your local school as well as serve as advocates at your school district for increased funding. Still others are raising up groups of kids who care about the AIDS pandemic—in the United States, in Africa, and in Asia (which is now being called the "new Africa" of AIDS).

> "The church should consist of communities of loving defiance. Instead it consists largely of comfortable clubs of conformity."
>
> RONALD J. SIDER,
> *RICH CHRISTIANS IN AN AGE OF HUNGER*

The good news is that our hearts are in the right place. The bad news is that many of us are novices who might be doing more harm than good.

This book is for youth workers—rookies and veterans—who don't want to waste another minute doing mediocre service.

It's for youth workers of all colors and classes who hunger to learn from one another, as well as from the people who are most in need of justice.

It's for youth workers—urban, suburban, small-town, and rural—who want to see and be a part of God's deep justice.

WHAT IS DEEP JUSTICE, ANYWAY?

One of the authors of this book, Jeremy Del Rio, wanted to tell his five-year-old son why he was spending so much time on the phone and at his computer, working on his chapters. So Jeremy described social justice to Judah in two very simple words: righting wrongs.

I don't think I've ever heard a better definition.

Deep justice is about righting wrongs.

Righting wrongs is only possible when we understand the difference between service and social justice. Service is vital to the life of faith, a high calling modeled for us consistently by Jesus. But his call to love is also a call to look for more lasting solutions.

God's doesn't extend his call only to the church in the U.S. or the West. In fact, we would all be wise to remember God is already at work in those who have needs. We don't have to muster up our own solutions and "go get 'em" in the name of justice. Often the keys to overcoming poverty and oppression lie within those communities that are the most broken and brokenhearted. Our primary role as youth ministries is simply to come alongside those who are struggling and remove the obstacles that hinder those solutions.

Enter deep justice.

THE PARABLE OF THE CRACKED ROADS

Once upon a time, three youth ministries decided to address an unusual—and dire—problem permeating their city. Somehow, their streets and sidewalks had fallen prey to alarming cracks that crisscrossed the entire town. These cracks were two-to-four inches wide and several feet long, making the roads danger-ous and virtually undriveable. No one knew the exact cause of the cracks, yet residents felt trapped in their homes and ventured to work, school, and church only when necessary.

In an effort to fix the town's problem, the first youth ministry surveyed the damage and came up with a Quick-And-Easy-Physical-Solu-tion. Their plan was to use a thin layer of topcoat to cover the cracks and render the roads driveable and the sidewalks walkable. Residents stood and watched as the adult leaders and kids poured out of their minivans, mixed up the topcoat, and spread it across the cracks like a layer of chocolate ic-ing on a cake. Pleased with the quick repair, the townfolk hugged the kids and cheered as the youth ministry drove off in minivans.

> Interestingly for we who care about jus-tice, 62 percent of the world's Christians live in Africa, Asia, and Latin America.

The topcoat worked.

For a few weeks.

But the weight of the cars, the heat of the sun, and the pounding of the rain soon eroded the topcoat. The cracks reappeared, and residents retreated again to their homes. Some thought the cracks were not as severe as they'd been before the topcoat, but no one could be sure.

The second youth ministry, upon examining the town's broken roads, ad-opted a different strategy. Recognizing that there was a lot they didn't know, the youth figured they'd better learn more about their town's needs and neigh-bors before making things right. They divided up into teams, some interviewing the residents and others visiting home improvement stores to learn about the type of cement that would best address the problem.

The neighbors had ideas for road repairs that the youth ministry never would have thought of. As a result, the youth ministry was able to develop a Warm-and-Fuzzy-Relational-Solution in which the youth ministry and the neighbors worked side by side filling in the cracks with a customized cement.

The cement worked. For six whole months. But to the students' chagrin, a new series of cracks began to crisscross the roads. Their new friends told them that even though the Warm-and-Fuzzy-Relational-Solution had fixed the old cracks, an entirely new set of cracks had emerged, rendering the roads almost as hazardous.

To find out some facts about U.S. poverty that will probably surprise your students, see page 205.

The third youth ministry, having heard about the first two well-intentioned-but-failed strategies, knew that neither topcoat nor a brand-new cement would make things right. Like those in the second youth ministry, these students spent several days interviewing neighbors and hearing stories and dreams about crack-free driving as well as the pain and fear caused by the unsafe driving conditions. Wanting to avoid the mistakes of the first two youth ministries, the third youth ministry adopted a more radical repair strategy.

The students decided to divide into two teams. The first team was tasked with repairing the current cracks. Recognizing that the very foundation of the city's roads was not right, the team members worked with their new friends to jackhammer large sections of road, dig up the resulting rubble, re-level the foundations, and then lay a brand-new asphalt surface for the roads.

In order to prevent the cracks from reappearing, the second team investigated a few deeper and more complex questions. First, the youth looked into why the faulty roads had been built in the first place, and lobbied at city hall to change the construction code so defective roads would never be built again. Second, they asked their neighbors why they'd been unable to fix their own roads, and raised funds to provide the construction and cement-laying training their neighbors would need to keep the roads shipshape in the future.

This Deep-Systemic-Solution did the trick. Thanks to the new stable foundation and the neighbors' new training, the broken roads were fixed—for good.

WHAT'S THE DIFFERENCE BETWEEN NOT-SO-DEEP SERVICE AND TRULY DEEP JUSTICE?

Have you ever noticed the pervasiveness of cracks throughout the streets and sidewalks of your own city or town? The heat of the sun, the wear and tear of cars, and the shifting soil all mean one thing: Pavement is going to crack.

The same is true of our social systems and our relationships. Due to sin, they crack. They break. As a result of this breakdown, our world experiences poverty, disease, oppression, racism, greed, and corruption.

Youth ministries doing only shallow service look at the world's brokenness, feel bad about it, and offer a few Band-Aids. They offer free turkeys to the homeless on Thanksgiving or send clothes to a child in Zambia at Christmas. The good news is that the turkey and clothes fix what's broken.

The bad news is that they fix brokenness for only a few hours.

Youth ministries engaged in deep justice take a different approach. Like their more shallow counterparts, they see the cracks, feel bad about them, and send turkeys and T-shirts. Yet they couple their service with deeper questions like, *How did these wrongs come to exist in the first place? How can we help the poor and marginalized fix their own problems? What does God want us to do that will make a difference beyond today?*

It's not that it's bad to give out turkeys and T-shirts. It's just that we'll never right the deep wrongs underlying class divisions, racism, and oppression in our world if that's all we do.

"On the one hand we are called to play the Good Samaritan on life's roadside; but that will be only an initial act. One day we must come to see that the whole Jericho road must be transformed so that men and women will not be constantly beaten and robbed as they make their journey on life's highway. True compassion is more than flinging a coin to a beggar; it is not haphazard and superficial. It comes to see that an edifice which produces beggars needs restructuring."

MARTIN LUTHER KING JR., "BEYOND VIETNAM: A TIME TO BREAK SILENCE," A SPEECH DELIVERED ON APRIL 4, 1967

THREE LAYERS OF DEPTH

Just like the first youth ministry facing the cracked roads, when we encounter something that's broken in our world, our first response is usually to respond with some sort of physical, tangible help. We send money, we distribute sandwiches, or we paint buildings.

Level 1: Physical Response

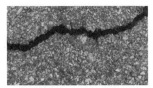

Recognizing that the money runs out, the sandwiches are eaten quickly, and the paint eventually fades, some youth ministries go a step deeper and offer a relational response. Like the second youth ministry fixing the cracked roads, they take the time to get to know those they are serving, try to learn from them, and even continue the friendship—in person or long distance—for months and years to come.

Level 1: Physical Response   Level 2: Relational Response

As we develop deep relationships with others, and as we see victims of injustice not *en masse* but as individuals with real names, faces, and stories, we will realize there is an even deeper level of response: a systemic response. But few youth ministries are willing to do whatever it takes—for however long it takes—until the systems that perpetuate the brokenness are fixed.

Level 1: Physical Response   Level 2: Relational Response   Level 3: Systemic Response

THE TOP OR THE BOTTOM OF THE CLIFF

Imagine one of your students runs into your youth room, shouting that some people who were walking in the hills near your church have fallen down a cliff and need help. You, your adult leaders, and all of your students drop whatever you're doing and race to help those who have fallen from the cliff. You call 911 and provide basic first aid until the paramedics arrive.

The next week, a different student races into your youth room, shouting that the same thing has happened. Again you all drop whatever you're doing and run to help the bruised and battered bodies lying at the bottom of the cliff.

It happens again the next week.

And the next week.

And the next.

Finally, you realize that while your first-aid efforts are helpful, maybe it's time for you to do more than race to the bottom of the cliff and bind up wounds. Maybe it's time for you to shift from a Level 1 or Level 2 response into the more rigorous, but longer-term, help of Level 3.

Maybe it's time for you to camp out at the top of the cliff and stop people from falling in—or maybe being kicked in—to begin with.

NOT-SO-DEEP SERVICE VS. TRULY DEEP JUSTICE

Throughout this book we'll be exploring ways we can move beyond shallow service so we can seek deeper justice for a broken world. But the table below provides a brief comparison.

Not-So-Deep Service	Deep Justice
Service makes us feel like a "great white savior" (or black or brown or some other skin color) who rescues the broken.	Justice means God does the rescuing, but often he works through the united power of his great and diverse community to do it.

Not-So-Deep Service	Deep Justice
Service often dehumanizes (even if subtly) those who are labeled the "receivers."	Justice restores human dignity by creating an environment in which all involved "give" and "receive" in a spirit of reciprocal learning and mutual ministry.
Service is something we do *for* others.	Justice is something we do *with* others.
Service is an event.	Justice is a lifestyle.
Service expects results immediately.	Justice hopes for results some time soon but recognizes that systemic change takes time.
The goal of service is to help others.	The goal of justice is to remove obstacles so others can help themselves.
Service focuses on what our own ministry can accomplish.	Justice focuses on how we can work with other ministries to accomplish even more.
Service is serving food at the local homeless shelter.	Justice means asking *why* people are hungry and homeless in the first place—and then doing something about it.

DEEP JUSTICE ASKS WHY

As the last row in the table above indicates, deep justice is not afraid to ask *why* the world is broken, and then take steps to fix it.

Why invites us to truly listen to and get to know the voiceless in our world.

Why requires a long-term perspective because poverty and powerlessness cannot be eliminated in weekend bursts of activism.

Why invites us to interact with social systems—because we cannot truly help individuals until we also change the systems that rob dignity.

Why forces us to face the truth about our own participation in the systems and structures that rob the poor of opportunities.

One word of warning: *Why* is not a popular question. Others may question you and your motives when you ask *why*. Bishop Oscar Romero, the martyred leader of the Nicaraguan church, once commented, "When I feed the poor, they call me a saint. When I ask *why* the poor are poor, they call me a communist."[6] Deep justice means not only asking *why*, but being prepared to do something about the answer.

DEEP JUSTICE IS MORE THAN A PROJECT

It's so tempting to try to distill deep justice into a "project," or maybe even two or three "projects" that we "go and do" with our kids. That's a little bit like saying a marriage basically boils down to a few overnighters and a handful of dinner dates each year. But justice, like marriage, is a daily commitment to be empowered by God's grace to love and serve others every day.

Like a fancy Valentine's Day dinner or an anniversary weekend, justice "projects" may play a part—perhaps even a significant part—in our justice journey. But the real reflection of our commitment to justice isn't whether we raise enough money to take kids on a weeklong spring break trip to serve in a Guatemalan orphanage; it's whether we are willing to view those we serve as "partners" instead of "projects" the other 51 weeks of the year.

DEEP JUSTICE IN REAL-LIFE KIDS

You may be wondering if 13- and 17-year-olds are capable of deep justice. We know they are. We've seen it with our own eyes.

When Kristin was a sophomore in our church's youth ministry, Sarah, her small group leader, started sending out monthly e-mail newsletters to Kristin and the other girls in her group. At the end of every newsletter, Sarah reminded the girls of our spring break trip to inner-city San Francisco, encouraging them to go.

When it came time to sign up for the trip, Kristin was the only one from her small group who signed up. She didn't know anyone else going on the trip, and she almost chickened out. But Sarah kept prodding her to go, and Kristin packed her bags and headed to San Francisco with the rest of the team.

[6] Tony Campolo, "Reflections on Youth Ministry in a Global Context," *Starting Right*, edited by Kenda Creasy Dean, Chap Clark, and Dave Rahn (Grand Rapids: Zondervan, 2001), 92.

During the trip, not only did Kristin fall in love with service, she fell in love with helping the homeless experience kingdom justice. Kristin's commitment to deep justice was crystallized when she and one of our adult leaders met J.R., a homeless man hanging out near the San Francisco Convention Center. Kristin offered her extra sack lunch to J.R. and started asking J.R. questions about his life, his family, and his life in San Francisco.

J.R. responded with a tirade against the government, the middle and upper classes, and Christians. While not a member of the government, Kristin is upper-middle class and a Christian. She remembers, "I left that lunch determined not to be the type of apathetic Christian J.R. hated."

She came back and dove into our church's Beverage Crew, a ministry in which high school students not only hit the streets to offer drinks to homeless persons, but also to build relationships with them and try to understand why they have ended up on the streets. As she's gotten to truly know people living out on the streets, she's realized "some of them choose to be there, but others just end up there. We don't know their stories until we talk to them. And we need to figure out how to help them help themselves."

> "We are God's demonstration community of the rule of Christ in the city. On a tract of earth's land purchased with the blood of Christ, Jesus the kingdom developer has begun building new housing. As a sample of what will be, he has erected a model home of what will eventually fill the urban neighborhood. Now he invites the urban world into that model home to take a look at what will be."
>
> HARVIE CONN,
> *PLANTING AND GROWING URBAN CHURCHES: FROM DREAM TO REALITY*

Over time, Kristin's commitment to justice on behalf of the homeless has grown deeper. Her junior year, not only did she join the team going to San Francisco during spring break, but she also served as the student shepherd and wrote morning devotionals for the entire group. The next year, Kristin was the student director for the San Francisco trip. She helped plan the trip, organized the training meetings ahead of time, and helped coach the teams in how to build relationships with those who are homeless.

Probably just as importantly, Kristin encouraged her friend, Brittany, to go on the San Francisco trip when they were both juniors. Like Kristin, Brittany loved it. In fact, she loved it so much that now Brittany is pursing a Global Studies major in college so she can right wrongs by learning about the economic, social, and political factors that compound our world's brokenness.

Or take Marcus, a high school senior in our church who received a Hi8 video camera as a Christmas gift when he was in sixth grade and has been making movies ever since. He started with freeze-frame animation with potatoes. "We didn't have any Mr. Potato Head toys around, so we used real potatoes," Marcus recalls.

Marcus' passion for and skills in moviemaking grew during the next several years. As a student at a Los Angeles public high school that is 80 percent Asian, Marcus was bothered by the friction he saw every day between students of different races and socioeconomic levels. In response, he and his friend decided to write, direct, and produce *Viola*, a full-length film about two students—one white American girl and one Chinese-American boy—and the lessons they learn about "fitting in" with people who are different from them.

"We got more than we bargained for," Marcus recalls. *Viola* involved ten months of pre- and post production and 300 high school students, including his entire school orchestra as the musicians who performed the score. But once it was completed, *Viola* was screened at a major Pasadena theatre and was also accepted at several film festivals. Even more importantly for Marcus, this justice movie made entirely by high school students has provoked great conversations about race at both his school and our church. As one junior at Marcus' high school commented, "The movie very realistically portrayed the stereotypes that are a part of our lives today. It wasn't sugarcoated like other movies. It was exactly like what my friends and I have gone through."

But when it comes to Marcus and deep justice, the show must go on. Since *Viola*, Marcus has worked on a number of other projects, all geared to spark conversation and insight about racial and economic injustices. He's even done a film in which, instead of casting an experienced actor to play the part of a homeless man, he cast an actual homeless man in the role.

Marcus' passion for deep justice isn't limited to filmmaking. He's also the vice president of "My Friend and I," a service organization at his school in which students with mental disabilities and students without mental disabilities are matched. Marcus has lunch with his buddy, Jeffrey, every week, and Jeffrey has even started having lunch with Marcus and his friends on other days too. "At first it was awkward when Jeffrey joined us. My friends even criticized me and made fun of both Jeffrey and me. But as they got to know Jeffrey, and he became a regular at our lunch table, they got to like him."

Marcus' small group leader, Jeff, has played a major role in Marcus' desire to change how others think about race, class, and disabilities. "It wasn't so much what Jeff has said about any of that; it's more how he has put us in positions that force us to think about it. The more I see and the more I serve, the more I realize how many wrongs need to be righted. We can't just meet people's needs short term; we have to help them learn how to meet their own needs long term."

Many youth workers realize that conceptions of "suburban" and "urban" aren't as fixed as they once were, as more and more towns are becoming blends of suburban and urban culture. While the poverty rate in U.S. large cities (18.8 percent) is still higher than in the suburbs (9.4 percent), because the suburbs are experiencing greater population growth, the suburban poor (a total of 12 million) now outnumber the inner-city poor (a total of 10.8 million).[7]

These stories confirm two things. First, God can use ordinary kids like Kristin and Marcus to bring about deep justice in a broken world. Second, God often works through us as youth workers to do it.

DEEP JUSTICE IS POSSIBLE IN YOUR SETTING WITH YOUR KIDS

Your setting is unlike any other. You may be working with kids whose allowances rival your own salary, or you may be working with kids who live on the streets. Your ministry may be out in the heartlands of rural America where the closest neighbor is a long walk away, or it may be in the hood where your closest neighbor is less than a foot away.

Either way, deep justice is for you. More importantly, it's for your students.

We've written this book with the hope that it will encourage and equip you to seek kingdom justice for our broken world regardless of your particular ministry setting. Suburban, urban, rural, or something in between, our prayer is that every chapter helps you dig deeper into the injustices in your community and your world so you can unearth the hope and freedom of the gospel.

---

[7] Alan Berube and Elizabeth Kneebone, "Two Steps Back: City and Suburban Poverty Trends 1999-2005" (Washington, D.C.: The Brookings Institution, December 2006).

WHY DEEP JUSTICE IS IMPORTANT IN YOUR YOUTH MINISTRY

Our mission at the Center for Youth and Family Ministry (CYFM) at Fuller Seminary is to turn research into resources that transform youth and family ministry. In our own experience and our conversations with youth leaders around the country, we're encountering revolutionaries who recognize that service and justice aren't just for adults. Not only are teenagers able to right the wrongs around them, but they are also like wet cement themselves. We want to make the right impression. Maybe a young Martin Luther King Jr. is sitting before you on Sunday. Perhaps you're giving a future Mother Teresa a ride home after church tomorrow night.

> For more on the mission and free resources offered by the Center for Youth and Family Ministry, including our free *CYFM E-Journal*, go to www.cyfm.net.

Even more likely, you are rubbing shoulders every day with kids who will some day be spouses, parents, bus drivers, administrators, teachers, business entrepreneurs, and political leaders. As philosopher and theologian Dallas Willard reminds us, "We are becoming who we will be—forever."[8]

That's true for that moldable 15-year-old you're taking out to coffee after school today. And it's just as true for us as adults.

So let's stop slapping Band-Aids on the gaping wounds of injustice around us. Instead, let's dig through the rubble of our broken world and experience the deep grace and hope of our Lord Jesus Christ.

> According to a study by the Corporation for National and Community Service, an estimated 15.5 million U.S. teenagers, or 55 percent of Americans between ages 12 and 18—participate in volunteer activities. This is close to twice the adult rate of 29 percent.[9]

---

[8] Dallas Willard, *The Divine Conspiracy* (New York: Harper Collins, 1998), 11.

[9] "First Lady Says More Teens Volunteering," *New York Times*, November 30, 2005.

DEEP JUSTICE APPLICATION QUESTIONS:

1. What signs of brokenness can you see in the kids and families in your youth ministry? How about in your city? In our country? Around the world?

2. In thinking about our broken world, Gary A. Haugen, president of the International Justice Mission, writes, "Over time I have come to see questions about suffering in the world not so much as questions about God's character but as questions about the obedience and faith of God's people." What do you think about that?

3. What have been some of your well-meaning, but shallow, adventures in service? Looking back, what would you have changed?

4. Of the three layers described on page 14 (physical response, relational response, systemic response), which is most common in your ministry? What's good about that? What's not so good about that?

5. What are the costs of shallow service—for you, for your students, for adults and volunteers, and for the poor and marginalized?

6. Why are you interested in deeper justice within your youth ministry? What are some of the barriers you might face as you pursue deep justice?

7. How would you describe your ministry setting—suburban, urban, rural, or something in between? How do the backgrounds of the students in your ministry influence the ways you seek deep justice for our broken world?

---

[10] Gary A. Haugen, *Good News About Injustice* (Downers Grove, IL: InterVarsity Press, 1999), 100.

WHAT STEPS DO I NEED TO TAKE TO RIGHT THE WRONGS AROUND ME?

BY KARA POWELL

Will anyone who feels a love-hate relationship with the infamous "CNN news crawl" please step forward?

Good. I'm glad I'm not alone.

Sure, we're all probably a bit better informed thanks to the news that scrolls across the bottom of our television screens. But is it possible these bite-sized nuggets also serve as some sort of placebo—causing us to think we're interacting with the brokenness in our cities, country, and world when in reality we've moved on as quickly as the next headline scrolls across the screen?

> "In the end there are only two possible attitudes which Christians can adopt toward the world. One is escape and the other engagement."
>
> JOHN STOTT, *ISSUES FACING CHRISTIANS TODAY*

Drive-by news watching, while efficient, isn't all that effective. I might feel a bit better about my world awareness, but I haven't really grappled with the tough and systemic issues that lie behind political turmoil, regional oppression, and worldwide poverty.

I can't help but wonder if we're replicating this shallowness in the justice opportunities we offer students. The two-hour, two-day, and two-week bursts of serving the poor that our ministries offer may soothe our collective conscience, but are we truly righting wrongs? Or do our current ministries, just like the CNN news crawl, make us think we're "world Christians" when in reality we're more like tourists passing through quickly before we return to life-as-usual?[11]

THE DEEP DESIGN: BIG PICTURE

To help us move past the shallow news crawl and seek God's justice for our broken world, we've developed a four-step process called Deep Design. Step One provides the opportunity to **discern** God's transforming justice work currently. Step Two allows you and your students to **reflect** upon fresh insights about justice from Scripture, historical leaders and thinkers, current research, and experience. Step Three invites you and your students to **observe** and hear the stories of others who are integrating these new insights into their justice work and then compare their journeys with your own. Step Four is the final culminating step that helps your ministry **apply** what you've learned from Steps 1, 2, and 3 to your efforts in seeking God's justice in the world around you.

> To read more about the Deep Design and what it means for your youth ministry, check out our free additional *Deep Justice* resources available at www.cyfm.net.

Each step in the Deep Design process can be represented in a simple, one-word question:

- Step One (Discernment): *Now?* By asking *Now?*, we're considering what type of justice work the King is already doing, as well as factors that are either hindering transformation or creating space for it.

- Step Two (Reflection): *New?* In Step Two, we reflect upon *New* insights that can help us create even more space for the King's justice work that we've identified in Step One.

- Step Three (Observation): *Who?* By looking at examples of other leaders and youth workers *Who* have already applied these *New* insights to their own settings, we can begin brainstorming some initial ways to translate those *New* understandings into tangible justice work.

- Step Four (Application): *How?* The fourth and final step gives us the chance to pick and choose from what we've learned in the first three steps to arrive at *How* we can best contribute to kingdom justice in the midst of the brokenness that surrounds us.

For you who like pictures (probably most of us), we've created a diagram of our Deep Design.[12]

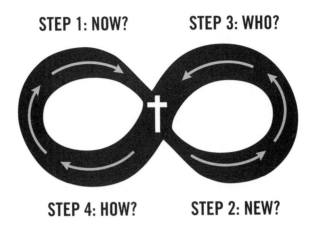

STEP 1: NOW?   **STEP 3: WHO?**

STEP 4: HOW?   **STEP 2: NEW?**

What's that cross doing in the middle of the Deep Design?

As we work through the Deep Design process, how do we know if our work is aligned with God's will and work? Although our finite brains prevent us from ever fully knowing, one way we understand God's activity is through his revelation, which we know primarily from Scripture. We have placed the cross at the heart of our Deep Design as a reminder that we want all of our justice to revolve around the model and grace of Christ.[13]

We first introduced the Deep Design in our previous book, *Deep Ministry in a Shallow World*. In that book, we provided specific sub-questions to ask at each step of the process. This book follows the same progression through the four steps with one major difference. Because of our commitment to engage with diverse authors who have unique experiences with God's justice in our broken world, we've simplified the four steps, giving each author freedom to dig through the four basic questions of **Now**? **New**? **Who**? and **How**? in ways that match his or her own passions, convictions, and stories.

---

[12] For more on the Deep Design, please see our previous book, *Deep Ministry in a Shallow World* (Grand Rapids: Zondervan, 2006).

[13] Had we been gearing this as an academic text, we would have labeled this filter "Christopraxis," meaning that our "praxis," or theologically grounded practices, is determined by God's activity as seen through Christ.

THE THEOLOGY THAT DRIVES OUR DEEP JUSTICE: THE KINGDOM OF GOD

The many diverse authors and youth ministry leaders we profile in this book are united in one strong message: We need a theology to both shape our motives and drive our methods for righting wrongs.

After all, most of us—whether we know it or not (and usually we don't)—have one or more theological themes in the driver's seat of our lives. For some of us, it's grace doing the steering. For others, it's love. Maybe for you it's hope. Or peace. Or freedom.

More and more church leaders are opening up the front doors of their thinking and ministries to the kingdom of God. According to theologian Stanley Grenz, "If we were to point to one topic that above all others has been the recipient of the labors of biblical scholars and theologians in the twentieth century, it would no doubt be the kingdom of God."[14]

> We use the terms "kingdom," "kingdom of God," and "kingdom of heaven" interchangeably. The only references to the "kingdom of heaven" in Scripture are in the book of Matthew.

What do we mean by the kingdom of God? We mean that which is under the rule of God, our King. The kingdom is not a geographical place but rather the order of perfect love, righteousness, justice, and peace that offers hope to our broken world.[15] As others are touched by the kingdom, they are transformed by the King's love and power.

What's our role in the kingdom? The kingdom is present and active in the world around us. Our role is to acknowledge it and participate in it as it advances and expands. Yet it is God, working in and through us, who is still the ultimate worker.

If the kingdom is already present, why is our world still broken? This is a theological question that has plagued Christ's followers ever since Jesus proclaimed, "The time has come, the kingdom of God is near. Repent and believe the good news!" (Mark 1:15). The best answer we can give is to join with a large number of scholars and leaders who believe in the "already/not yet" of God's kingdom. While

> "Scholars agree with what any of us can see in the Gospels: Jesus came announcing that the kingdom of God was at hand."
>
> GLEN H. STASSEN AND DAVID P. GUSHEE, *KINGDOM ETHICS*

---

[14] Stanley Grenz, *Theology for the Community of God* (Grand Rapids: Eerdmans, 1994), 492.

[15] Adapted from Grenz, *Theology for the Community of God*, 22.

> "Another image may help us understand this 'available' aspect of the kingdom...Think of visiting in a home where you have not been before. It is a fairly large house, and you sit for a while with your host in a living room or on the veranda. Dinner is announced, and he ushers you down a hall, saying at a certain point, 'Turn, for the dining room is at hand,' or more likely, 'Here's the dining room.' Similarly Jesus directs us to his kingdom."
>
> DALLAS WILLARD, *THE DIVINE CONSPIRACY*

the kingdom is already here, we are not yet experiencing the entirety of its power and presence. If you liken the kingdom to a banquet, we're getting plenty of delicious food already—but not the entire five-course meal.[16]

How does the kingdom relate to deep justice? Since the kingdom of God isn't just a way to be blessed but also a way to be a blessing, seeking the kingdom increases our desire to right wrongs. The kingdom invites all people—rich or poor, powerful or marginalized—to join in God's liberating gospel that is ever-revolutionary and ever-expanding.

Now let's look at how the four steps of the Deep Design can guide us as we seek to be part of God's bringing about his kingdom in our world.

STEP ONE IN THE DEEP DESIGN (DISCERNMENT):

How are we **NOW** living out the kingdom?

STEP 1: NOW?

---

[16] George Eldon Ladd, *The Gospel of the Kingdom* (Grand Rapids: Eerdmans, 1959), 41, 52-65.

As we use Step One of the Deep Design to assess what is happening in our youth ministries, it quickly becomes clear that we face choices about how we seek God's justice **Now**:

- Do we best let kids and adults know about the King by sharing about him with our words *or* showing him through our deeds?

- Do we best accomplish God's will on earth by working to right wrongs *or* praying for God to do it himself?

- Does God want us to work through existing organizations and ministries *or* launch new and more entrepreneurial approaches to serving the poor?

- Does the freedom God intends start with individuals *or* with social systems and structures?

- Do we know we've been successful when people have their spiritual need for Christ fulfilled *or* their physical needs for food and shelter met?

- Where do we first try to fix brokenness—in our own towns *or* in the nations of the world where the poverty is even greater?

> "The kingdom of God is a culture that takes form in world culture... [Yet] the kingdom of God is not primarily a religious culture but a power that liberates and frees persons within their existing culture to experience the 'human' culture that belongs by right of God's creation to each person. No longer are individuals oppressed by impersonal and tyrannical world powers; they are liberated (as in the exodus) to become a new people whose social relationships become the source of personal identity, and power is transformed into covenant love."
>
> RAY S. ANDERSON, *THE SHAPE OF PRACTICAL THEOLOGY: EMPOWERING MINISTRY WITH THEOLOGICAL PRAXIS*

These are all great questions that must be considered. But each of them contains a trap we can easily fall into. It's that little word *or*.

Often unknowingly, most of us have **Now** adopted "either/or" views about the kingdom.

Either the kingdom is about social change *or* it's about individual salvation.

Either this world is under God's reign *or* it is under Satan's.

Either we live in denial of the injustice and sin that surrounds us *or* we are paralyzed by our despair.

These simplistic *either/or* choices are no match for the complexity of the kingdom. Whether it's because we don't understand the kingdom complexity or because we just like to keep things "simple," the more our youth ministries **Now** try to slice the kingdom into narrow *either/or* categories, the more we miss out on the God-sized beauty of the whole.

Unfortunately, we are passing this *either/or* kingdom thinking on to our students. As we'll unpack throughout the rest of this book, most youth groups have 20/20 vision when it comes to certain aspects of Jesus' teachings but are blind to others. In our justice work **Now**, we too often invite into our youth ministries a few of our "favorite" commandments from the King, but kick out the rest.

STEP TWO IN THE DEEP DESIGN (REFLECTION): WHAT ARE NEW WAYS WE CAN EMBODY THE KINGDOM?

STEP 2: NEW?

The Jesus we serve was and is a revolutionary. Just as he kicked over the moneychangers' tables in the first century, Jesus kicks aside our tendency to perpetuate our incomplete—and often comfortable—views of kingdom justice in the twenty-first century.

Part of what made Jesus so provocative was the way he embodied not a narrow *either/or* kingdom, but God's *both/and* kingdom.

Jesus himself lived with the daily tension of being *both* fully God *and* fully human.

He offered people *both* physical healing *and* spiritual forgiveness.

He came *both* to fulfill the law *and* to usher in a new understanding of grace.

He understood *both* the depravity of human sin *and* the potential within each of us to participate in kingdom work and living.

He lived knowing *both* that the future of Christianity rested with his disciples *and* that they (and we) would betray him.

His death and resurrection makes salvation a gift *both* available to all *and* accepted by only some.

We've already introduced one big *both/and* of the kingdom of God: The kingdom is *both* already *and* not yet.

Given the stakes, the ways Jesus was able to live out justice in the midst of these *both/and* tensions is mind-blowing. Which might just mean it's kingdom-sized too.

BACK TO THE CRACKED ROADS

So with this *both/and* nature of the kingdom in mind, let's take another look at the story of the town with the cracked roads that we considered in chapter 1. Imagine that your youth ministry is located in this town. Upon hearing of your interest in justice work, the mayor invites you to help fix the roads. Always eager to engage your students in deeper justice, you accept her invitation.

To read more about the *both/and* tensions of the kingdom, check out our free *Deep Justice* resources available at www.cyfm.net

When you arrive at the cracked roads, full of both ideas and pickaxes, the mayor warns you of a peculiar local construction tradition that you're expected to obey. In your town, work is done using one hand, but not the other. Left or right, it doesn't matter. What matters is that you and your students can only dig up broken roads, stir up asphalt, and lay down new roads using one hand.

The result? Your work is slow. And frustrating.

Unfortunately, our *either/or* views of the kingdom resemble this bizarre construction ritual. For centuries, we believers have chosen one approach to the kingdom and proclaimed it the best. We've mastered our one kingdom strategy while our other hand hangs at our side—useless. We've even criticized others for their slow, one-handed, justice work without noticing how similarly our own work crawls forward.

What the *Both/And* Kingdom Does Not Mean...

Right about now we can hear the "heretic alarms" going off in some of your brains. As we talk about moving from the *either/or* to the *both/and* kingdom, let us clarify a few things that kingdom justice does not mean.

- *Both/and* kingdom justice does not mean Jesus is one of many ways to relationship with God. Call us conservative (believe us, we've been called way worse), but we take Jesus seriously when he proclaims himself the way, the truth, and the life (John 14:6). There might be many ways to experience Jesus, but fundamentally, Jesus is the path to real life in the present and eternal life in the future.

- *Both/and* kingdom justice does not mean we take Scripture's commands any less seriously. We aren't saying that it's time to water down Scripture so it's less extreme and less demanding. Instead, it's time to understand exactly how demanding it is by embracing all of its teachings.

The reality is that no single hand, no single approach, can contain the fullness of the kingdom to heal a broken world. Not even our favorite.

The hand of truth needs the hand of love.

The hand of holiness needs the hand of grace.

The hand on the right needs the hand on the left.

It's when these individually valid, but incomplete, hands work together that we can experience the full—and often mysterious—power of the King to heal our world's brokenness. Usually this means not just trying to combine the two ends of the *either/or* spectrum, but rather embracing a **New** more grand, more holistic kingdom perspective.

STEP THREE IN THE DEEP DESIGN (OBSERVATION): WHO IS APPLYING THESE KINGDOM INSIGHTS THAT WE CAN LEARN FROM?

STEP 3: WHO?

In figuring out how to go deeper in our kingdom justice, it's helpful to have examples of other leaders and activists who are already partnering with the broken and brokenhearted. The goal of the **Who** step is to observe other ministries and leaders who have come up with **New** insights about the *both/and* kingdom and are already trying to go deeper.

In this book, we've invited some of our nation's top justice thinkers and leaders to share their best ideas about bringing God's deep justice to a broken world. We've intentionally invited a diverse group to share their experiences and expertise—urban, small-town, and suburban; church and parachurch; male and female; white, black, and brown; serving in places like Los Angeles, Seattle, Chicago, Minneapolis, Philadelphia, Mendenhall, Memphis, and Washington, D.C. These people aren't perfect, but their willingness to try new ideas and dig, kick, and pickaxe their way into deeper justice can pave the way for our own kingdom work.

One important warning: You and your youth ministry will never be successful if you try to follow someone else's justice journey exactly.

If you don't get that warning, you should stop reading this book. It will mess you up. Seriously. Please put the book down and walk away.

The truth is that you live in a different community, you work with different students, your students have different parents, your community has different needs, your ministry has its own history, and you have your own leadership style. So view the experiences of those profiled in the **Who** section of each chapter not as a blueprint to follow precisely, but a springboard you use to plunge into your own deeper justice.

STEP FOUR IN THE DEEP DESIGN (APPLICATION): GIVEN EVERYTHING, HOW CAN WE GO DEEPER IN OUR JUSTICE?

STEP 4: HOW?

Once we've reflected on **New** depth in Step Two of our Deep Design and studied the examples of others in Step Three, we are well equipped to answer the final synthesizing question: Given all that we've learned, **How** is God prodding our ministry into deeper justice?

The fourth step is where we invite you to wade through the material from **Now**, **New**, and **Who** and prayerfully design your own youth ministry plan to right wrongs. To do this, we've included at the end of each chapter a short list of Deep Justice Application Questions for you to use with your own ministries and leadership teams. We've also given you some Deep Justice Recommended Action Steps that will help you figure out **How** to move into deep justice in your own life as well as in your youth ministry.

It might help if you think of each chapter like a jigsaw puzzle. Studying **Now**, **New**, and **Who** is a bit like dumping a box of puzzle pieces on a table. In the final section, by mulling over some strategic questions and practical recommendations, your youth ministry gets to figure out **How** to put those pieces together into a puzzle that helps you right wrongs. Sure, we'll give you some strong hints, but we believe the best "kingdom picture" for your students is something God can show you and your team.

A TALE OF TWO SECTIONS

We're applying this four-step Deep Design in both sections of this book. The first section, *Both/And Kingdom Thinking*, helps us peel back the layers of inadequate *either/or* theologies and philosophies that keep our youth ministries from the deep core of the *both/and* kingdom. The second section, *Both/And Kingdom Living*, helps us apply what we've discovered in the first section to three areas crucial to deep justice: race, money, and class.

Regardless of the topic, you'll note from the shape of the diagram (which resembles the mathematical sign of "infinity") that every time your youth ministry reaches one of its goals, you've basically created a new **Now** for yourself. This means the Deep Design process never ends. It's a constant loop of discernment, reflection, observation, and application. This feedback loop means that the CNN news crawl will never be enough to help us seek hope and healing for our broken world. Since the *both/and* kingdom is always evolving, our justice must also be constantly on the move.

DEEP JUSTICE APPLICATION QUESTIONS:

1. The best way to experience the Deep Design is with a team. What students, parents, adult volunteers, church leaders, and community members would you like to invite to discuss **Now**, **New**, **Who**, and **How** with you?

2. Of the list of kingdom *either/ors* given on page 29, which phrases best describe your approach to justice **Now**? What's good about that? What's not so good about that?

3. What **New** changes would be introduced into your justice if the *both/and* kingdom of God was in the driver's seat?

4. **Who** do you admire for their work in service and social justice? What have you already learned from these people? What else do you think they can teach you?

5. After reading these first two chapters, what initial ideas do you have about **How** to go deeper in kingdom justice with your students?

6. What types of resistance might you meet from parents, other pastors, or your church as you and your students try to right wrongs around you? How can you network with key leaders and parents in your church so that you have the support you need to seek deep justice?

HOW CAN MY TEACHING MOTIVATE KIDS TO DEEP JUSTICE?

BY KARA POWELL

NOW? (DISCERNMENT)

STEP 1: NOW?

It's one thing to read what the Bible says about the poor and broken and understand it. It's an entirely different thing to read what the Bible says about the poor and broken and actually live it.

For the last two decades, I've experimented with strategies to teach kids what the Bible says about the poor so they'll want to seek God's hope for our broken world. As I look back over those years, I've found that I seem to have evolved through two phases of shallow teaching about justice.

Phase 1: Pack Your Bags for a Guilt Trip

My first phase of teaching kids about justice went something like this: Others are living in hell now, and going to hell when they die, so how can you just sit there?

Kids, pack your bags. We're going on a guilt trip.

Granted, I camouflaged the guilt trip by talking about the difference between the sheep and the goats in Matthew 25:31-46, and the Great Commission's command to "go" and "make disciples" in Matthew 28:18-20.

But what I was really after was making students feel so bad about the poverty and power imbalances around them both locally and globally that they would get up and right some wrongs.

The good news is that kids did act. They visited kids in the children's hospital, they raked leaves for senior adults on Saturdays, they pooled their money to sponsor a few kids overseas, and some even spent their spring breaks or summer vacations sharing the gospel with people in Africa and Asia.

But any movement toward deep justice was short-lived. When I didn't constantly remind them of their responsibility to God and others, they reverted to life as usual. When it came to righting wrongs, most kids took 3 steps forward and 2.93 steps backward. Not a very big net gain.

> "The King will reply, 'I tell you the truth, whatever you did for one of the least of these brothers of mine, you did for me.' "
>
> MATTHEW 25:40

> "Therefore go and make disciples of all nations, baptizing them in the name of the Father and of the Son and of the Holy Spirit, and teaching them to obey everything I have commanded you."
>
> MATTHEW 28:19-20A

Using guilt to motivate kids to serve did work with a kid named Jason. He definitely got the message that there were problems in the world, and that he needed to do something. He decided to give his life away. The problem was that he didn't give his life to Jesus, he gave it to Communism.

Seriously.

Jason felt like Communism was more about helping the poor than Christianity. When I saw my kids choosing Karl Marx over Jesus Christ, that's when I knew I had a problem.

Phase 2: Less Than Amazing Grace

One of my life mottos—and a great slogan for the *both/and* kingdom—is "Balance is something we swing through on our way to the other extreme."

> "He has shown all you people what is good. And what does the Lord require of you? But to act justly and to love mercy and to walk humbly with your God."
>
> MICAH 6:8

Once I realized guilt wasn't working, I swung to the other extreme. After all, I told myself, Christianity is the only religion in the world that revolves around grace. We don't have to *earn* our way into heaven; we simply *receive* the gift of salvation extended to us by God the Father through Jesus the Son.

So I talked about *grace*. Amazing grace. I didn't want to turn kids away from their faith by forcing them to right wrongs if they didn't want to. So I didn't talk much about "going" or "doing." I just talked about "being." Since I'd learned that shouting wouldn't convince them, I whispered instead. I focused on different Scripture passages in this phase, like Micah 6:8, but in my teaching the commands to "love mercy" and "walk humbly with your God" seemed to somehow trump the command to "act justly."

> "The crisis of American church and theology becomes even more intensive when one reflects on two opposite patterns that can be witnessed in churches throughout the United States. The first pattern offers *a gospel without demands...* The second pattern lies at the other end of the spectrum: *demands without the gospel."*
>
> ORLANDO COSTAS, *CHRIST OUTSIDE THE GATE*

This quickly degenerated into what German theologian Dietrich Bonhoeffer called "cheap grace," or a form of "grace" that allows us to maintain the status quo without seeking God's justice for others. As Bonhoeffer describes, "Cheap grace is not the kind of forgiveness of sin which frees us from the toils of sin. Cheap grace is the grace we bestow on ourselves."[17]

Kids were comforted by the grace I talked about, but they got a little too comfortable. Truth be told, so did I. We were going to heaven, but we weren't taking anybody with us. And we did precious little to help others experience a taste of heaven's love and justice here on earth.

In talking with youth workers around the country, I've realized I'm not the only one who's dabbled in excessive guilt

---

[17] Dietrich Bonhoeffer, *Cost of Discipleship* (London: SCM Press, 1964), 47.

or cheap grace in the past. In fact, my hunch is that most youth workers have **Now** set up their justice teaching tents in one of those two camps.

In describing our theological shallowness, Dallas Willard in *The Divine Conspiracy* warns, "Should we not at least consider the possibility that this poor result is *not in spite of what we teach and how we teach, but precisely because of it?*"[18]

If Dallas is right (and I think he is), youth ministry as a whole needs to do more **Now** than simply fine-tune how we teach kids to right wrongs. As I realized myself ten years ago, youth ministry needs a major overhaul.

NEW? (REFLECTION)

STEP 2: NEW?

CYFM RESEARCH: LEARNING FROM THE EXPERTS

In order to understand the type of **New** overhaul that is needed, we at the Center for Youth and Family Ministry at Fuller Theological Seminary decided to ask the experts. In Fall 2005, we interviewed 70 youth workers, 30 of whom were recommended to us because of their effectiveness in engaging students in serving our broken world, and 40 of whom were local youth workers in Los Angeles.[19]

---

[18] Dallas Willard, *The Divine Conspiracy* (San Francisco: Harper Collins, 1998), 40 (emphasis added).

[19] To identify the 30 youth workers nationwide, we invited World Vision, Vision Youth, the Urban Youth Workers Institute, Compassion International, the National Network of Youth Ministries, the Center for Student Missions, Amor Ministries, and Presbyterians for Renewal to nominate a handful of urban, suburban, and rural youth workers in their circles who do exemplary social justice work with kids. Then we contacted these "exemplar" youth workers and carefully interviewed 30 of them.

Next we asked 40 urban and suburban youth workers who are part of our Los Angeles Youth Ministry Network to answer questions like: "When it comes to service, social justice, and missions, what do you wish was happening in your students overall that isn't?" "What types of tools and resources would help you engage your students in kingdom justice?"

For more information about the findings from these 70 interviews, please see the *Deep Justice* resources available for free at www.cyfm.net.

As we compiled the input of these 70 diverse youth workers, one **New** theme repeatedly emerged: As a whole, youth workers have failed to help students grasp the deep story of the Scriptures that invites all kingdom followers to play a part in the King's work in the world.

STORIES *IN* THE BIBLE OR THE STORY *OF* THE BIBLE

Our 70 youth worker interviews confirmed that a key difference between shallow service and deep justice is whether we teach stories *in* the Bible or the story *of* the Bible. The table below illustrates the difference.

Stories *in* the Bible	The Story *of* the Bible
The Bible is like a *newspaper*; each book of the Bible is like a different section of the newspaper with different articles that don't affect one another.	The Bible is like a *movie*; each book of the Bible contains a "scene" of God's unfolding story that sheds light on all others and builds toward the conclusion the Divine Director intends.
We teach individual passages of Scripture as *isolated* units.	We teach individual passages of Scripture as *interrelated* units.
Those who sought justice in the Bible are *examples* to learn from.	Those who sought justice in the Bible are *both examples* to learn from *and contributors* to God's unfolding kingdom.
We who obey the Bible today are part of *God's work in the here and now.*	We who obey the Bible today partake in the story of *God's work throughout time.*

THE STORY BEYOND THE STORY

I'm about to give my best description of the story of the kingdom. In all honesty, I'm a bit nervous. For one, it might feel too "linear" for some of you. While I present the story in a roughly chronological order, the reality is that God's story is far too grand and far too breathtaking for us to plot in an orderly time sequence. And yet, as Western humans, we normally tell stories in the order the

events occurred. ("First I showed up at our youth group meeting, next I grabbed a soft drink, and then a kid bumped into me and I spilled my drink on my shirt.") So take the movements of the kingdom story with a grain—make that a huge mountain—of salt, for as you'll see in a few pages, the story bounces around in the Bible and in our lives.

> "God's kingdom is what narrates the world for Christians."
>
> BOB WEBBER, AS QUOTED IN "TOGETHER IN THE JESUS STORY," *CHRISTIANITY TODAY*, SEPTEMBER 2006

Second, some of you might think my version of God's story is too truncated. Mine has four movements; maybe yours has six. Or seven.[20] Of course, no matter how many movements we might use to describe God's story, it's inherently impossible to describe the story in its fullness. It is, after all, *God's* story.

Third, while I believe the Bible is a wonderful photo album filled with snapshots of God's story, it doesn't provide us with *all* of God's story. God's story is so transcendent, and so alive and active from the beginning of time until its end, that while we can appreciate the Bible as the best version of God's story we have, there is an unfolding story that lies beyond even its texts.

BOTH GUILT *AND* GRACE AND SO MUCH MORE

Having said all that, let's work together to come up with a working definition of God's story. It definitely includes guilt and grace. In fact, it emphasizes them. It's just that they're only about half of the story—the middle half to be precise.[21] And just like in any good story, we'll gain a **New** appreciation of that middle half when we understand what comes before and after it.

---

[20] One of our colleagues at Fuller Seminary, Dr. John Goldingay, describes the plot of the Old Testament as: "God began. Humanity turned its back on God's instructions, and God started over. God promised, and a family grew. Israel cried out, and God delivered. God sealed, and Israel imperiled. God gave, and Israel took. Israel equivocated, and God accommodated. Israel turned away, and God wrestled. God preserved, and Israel turned back." John Goldingay, *Old Testament Theology: Volume 1 Israel's Gospel* (Downers Grove: InterVarsity, 2003), 32.

[21] Our version of God's story very closely resembles one common in Reformation theology that was derived from the *Heidelberg Catechism of 1563: Guilt, Grace, and Gratitude.*

Good

To find out more about what the image of God means for deep justice, flip to page 188.

Before we help students grasp their guilt before the King, we need to help them grasp that he originally created us as *good*. We didn't start out condemned; we were created in God's image (Genesis 1:26-27). Being created in the image of God (or in Latin, the *"imago dei,"* pronounced "ih-mah-go day") makes us able to receive his love and respond to his invitation to right wrongs around us.

Guilt

By "dialectic," we mean the bounce back and forth between two contradictory ideas until they are eventually resolved.

Now comes the bad news. The inherent goodness we derived from being created in the King's image was permanently marred in the Garden of Eden. Whether you believe that image was obliterated or merely obstructed, the end result is roughly the same: Our world and relationships are broken. Because of our universal sin, every single one of us—from the richest investor on Wall Street to the nameless child caught up in sex trafficking on the streets of Calcutta—is broken. We can no longer have relationship with the One who sits on the throne.

The well-known twentieth-century theologian Karl Barth introduces a theological dialectic that helps us understand the transition from good to guilt. Barth labels our original potential for relationship with God a divine YES. Human nature is still "good" in the sense of our being created by God. But as a result of Adam and Eve's rebellion, our relationship with the King has been broken. The YES has, in effect, become a NO.

GOOD   GUILT
God's creation   Our sin
YES   ➡️   NO

Grace

But the NO is not the final word in God's kingdom. The radical and pervasive brokenness created by our guilt is mirrored by the King's radical and pervasive solution through Christ. The NO is penultimate—or, second to last. Through Christ, God's YES is ultimate and final. Through Christ, the all-pervasive wrong of our sin has been righted. The mega-injustice has been taken care of. Barth teaches, "God is the one who with his NO says YES to us—a full, unrestricted YES with no question marks, a YES pregnant with God's will and power to save us, to carry us, to set us on our feet, to make us free and merry."[22]

> "God's relation to the world is characterized by the polarity of justice and mercy, providence and concealment, the promise of reward and the demand to serve him for his sake. Taken abstractly, all these terms seem to be mutually exclusive, yet in actual living they involve each other; the separation of the two is fatal to both...Tension, contrast, and contradiction characterize all of reality."
>
> ABRAHAM HESCHEL,
> *GOD IN SEARCH OF MAN*

GOOD	GUILT	GRACE
God's creation	Our sin	God's response
YES →	NO →	YES

Gratitude

The YES of the King's grace now allows humankind to respond with our own YES that accepts his invitation. When our own YES echoes God's YES, we join his kingdom and joyfully accept our role as the body of Christ in its kingdom mission. We live out this acceptance in both our individual and our corporate efforts to see kingdom justice brought to all.

> "The remarkable thing about fearing God is that when you fear God, you fear nothing else; whereas if you do not fear God, you fear everything else."
>
> OSWALD CHAMBERS, *THE HIGHEST GOOD*

GOOD	GUILT	GRACE	GRATITUDE
God's creation	Our sin	God's response	Our acceptance
YES →	NO →	YES →	YES

---

[22] From a sermon preached by Barth on October 7, 1956 in the Bruderholz chapel on Leviticus 26:15. See Geoffrey Bromiley, *Introduction to the Theology* of Karl Barth (Edinburgh: T&T Clark, 1994), 84 (capitalization added).

> "Be the change that you want to see in the world."
>
> MOHANDAS GANDHI

This final movement in God's story is my favorite to explain to teenagers. As we live in awe of the King's grace, we can't help but want to serve him. Because of who he is and what he's doing in us, our entire lives become *thank-you notes* back to God. As kingdom followers, we don't right wrongs out of duty, or out of our destined-to-fail attempts to earn our own salvation. We right wrongs because of all God has done for us.

HISTORY IS HIS-STORY

All that is happening today—and all that has ever happened throughout history—finds *New* meaning as it is viewed through the lenses of Good/Guilt/Grace/Gratitude. That means every time you teach about justice—or any other topic for that matter—you are robbing your students if you don't show them how the Scripture you're discussing contributes to, and is affected by, the unfolding plot. Let's look at some of the "oldie but goodie" texts you and I tend to use to motivate kids toward deeper justice through the perspective of kingdom Good/Guilt/Grace/Gratitude.

Passage	Good	Guilt	Grace	Gratitude
Micah 6:1-8		"For the Lord has a case against his people; he is lodging a charge against Israel." MICAH 6:2B	"I brought you up out of Egypt and redeemed you from the land of slavery." —MICAH 6:4	"He has shown all you people what is good. And what does the Lord require of you? To act justly and to love mercy and to walk humbly with your God." —MICAH 6:8
Matthew 25:31-46	"Then the King will say to those on his right, 'Come...take your inheritance, the kingdom prepared for you since the creation of the world.'" —MATTHEW 25:34	"Then he will say to those on his left, 'Depart from me, you who are cursed, into the eternal fire...For I was hungry and you gave me nothing to eat, I was thirsty and you gave me nothing to drink, I was a stranger and you did not invite me in, I needed clothes and you did not clothe me.'" —MATTHEW 25:41-42	"Then they will go away to eternal punishment, but the righteous to eternal life." —MATTHEW 25:46	"The King will reply, 'Truly I tell you, whatever you did for the least of these brothers and sisters of mine, you did for me.'" —MATTHEW 25:40
Matthew 28:18-20			"Then Jesus came to them and said, 'All authority in heaven and on earth has been given to me. Therefore...'" —MATTHEW 28:18-19A	"...go and make disciples of all nations, baptizing them in the name of the Father and of the Son and of the Holy Spirit, and teaching them to obey..." —MATTHEW 28:19-20A

A quick glance at the table above reveals that not all these passages contain all four movements in the kingdom story, and the Good/Guilt/Grace/Gratitude story isn't always presented in a linear order. Given the complexity of the story, it would be unrealistic to think that all four elements will appear in every slice of Scripture or in the same order. But the threads of this story weave their way through the Scriptures as a whole.[23]

[23] Some books of the Bible, especially the New Testament epistles, follow this Good/Guilt/Grace/Gratitude flow. They first discuss our creation and curse, next they describe our new life in Christ, and then they conclude their final chapters with commands about reflecting this new life in our attitudes and actions.

MOTIVATION FOR JUSTICE: FINDING OUR PLACE IN GOD'S STORY

I've alluded to this already, but I need to say it clearly: Our lives find meaning as we view ourselves as participants in God's unfolding story. Just as we need to discern how Scripture passages fit into the story of Good/Guilt/Grace/Gratitude, we also need to recognize how our own stories do.

In partnership with World Vision and Youth Specialties, CYFM has developed a free 100-page *One Life Curriculum*, specifically geared to help youth ministries find their place in God's story in the midst of the worldwide AIDS pandemic. To download this curriculum and use it in your youth ministry or small groups, please visit www.cyfm.net.

My last decade of teaching about justice, as well as the 70 youth worker interviews we've conducted, confirms that students' motivation to right wrongs is directly related to their view of themselves as participants in God's story. When kids shift from thinking of themselves as the audience of God's drama to seeing themselves as participants in a **New** community living out Good/Guilt/Grace/Gratitude together—and helping others live out the kingdom story also—their interest in serving our broken world skyrockets.

THE ROLE OF JUSTICE IN GOD'S STORY

As a youth worker, you're probably familiar with Micah 6:8 and its command to "act justly," but the threads of justice weave their way through the kingdom story far more than you might realize. The table below includes *less than half of the verses about justice in the Old Testament alone.*

Selected Old Testament Verses about Justice

Exodus 23:2	"Do not follow the crowd in doing wrong. When you give testimony in a lawsuit, do not pervert **justice** by siding with the crowd."
Exodus 23:6	"Do not deny **justice** to your poor people in their lawsuits."
Leviticus 19:15	"Do not pervert **justice**; do not show partiality to the poor or favoritism to the great, but judge your neighbor fairly."

Deuteronomy 16:20	"Follow **justice** and **justice** alone, so that you may live and possess the land the Lord your God is giving you."
Deuteronomy 24:17	"Do not deprive the foreigner or the fatherless of **justice**, or take the cloak of the widow as a pledge."
Deuteronomy 27:19a	"Cursed is anyone who withholds **justice** from the foreigner, the fatherless or the widow."
1 Kings 3:28	"When all Israel heard the verdict the king had given, they held the king in awe, because they saw that he had wisdom from God to administer **justice**."
1 Kings 10:9	"Praise be to the Lord your God, who has delighted in you and placed you on the throne of Israel. Because of the Lord's eternal love for Israel, he has made you king to maintain **justice** and righteousness."
Job 8:3	"Does God pervert **justice**? Does the Almighty pervert what is right?"
Psalm 7:6	"Arise, Lord, in your anger; rise up against the rage of my enemies. Awake, my God; decree **justice**."
Psalm 9:16	"The Lord is known by his acts of **justice**; the wicked are ensnared by the work of their hands."
Psalm 11:7	"For the Lord is righteous, he loves **justice**; the upright will see his face."
Psalm 36:6	"Your righteousness is like the highest mountains, your **justice** like the great deep."
Psalm 72:2	"May he judge your people in righteousness, your afflicted ones with **justice**."
Psalm 89:14	"Righteousness and **justice** are the foundation of your throne; love and faithfulness go before you."
Psalm 99:4a	"The King is mighty, he loves **justice**."
Psalm 101:1	"I will sing of your love and **justice**; to you, Lord, I will sing praise."
Psalm 103:6	"The Lord works righteousness and **justice** for all the oppressed."

Psalm 106:3	"Blessed are those who act **justly**, who always do what is right."
Proverbs 8:20	"I walk in the way of righteousness, along the paths of **justice**."
Proverbs 16:10	"The lips of a king speak as an oracle, and his mouth does not betray **justice**."
Proverbs 18:5	"It is not good to be partial to the wicked and so deprive the innocent of **justice**."
Proverbs 21:15	"When **justice** is done, it brings joy to the righteous but terror to evildoers."
Proverbs 29:7	"The righteous care about **justice** for the poor, but the wicked have no such concern."
Isaiah 1:17	"Learn to do right! Seek **justice**, encourage the oppressed. Defend the cause of the fatherless, plead the case of the widow."
Isaiah 1:27	"Zion will be delivered with **justice**, her penitent ones with righteousness."
Isaiah 5:16	"But the Lord Almighty will be exalted by his **justice**, and the holy God will be proved holy by his righteous acts."
Isaiah 10:1-2a	"Woe to those who make unjust laws, to those who issue oppressive decrees, to deprive the poor of their rights and withhold **justice** from the oppressed of my people."
Isaiah 28:17a	"I will make **justice** the measuring line and righteousness the plumb line."
Isaiah 30:18	"Yet the Lord longs to be gracious to you; therefore he will rise up to show you compassion. For the Lord is a God of **justice**. Blessed are all who wait for him!"
Isaiah 42:1	"Here is my servant, whom I uphold, my chosen one in whom I delight; I will put my Spirit on him, and he will bring **justice** to the nations."

Isaiah 51:4	"Listen to me, my people; hear me, my nation. Instruction will go out from me; my **justice** will become a light to the nations."
Isaiah 56:1	"This is what the Lord says, 'Maintain **justice** and do what is right, for my salvation is close at hand and my righteousness will soon be revealed.'"
Isaiah 61:8a	"For I, the Lord, love **justice**."
Jeremiah 9:24	"But let those who boast boast about this: that they understand and know me, that I am the Lord, who exercises kindness, **justice** and righteousness on earth, for in these I delight."
Ezekiel 22:29	"The people of the land practice extortion and commit robbery; they oppress the poor and needy and mistreat the foreigner, denying them **justice**."
Ezekiel 34:16	"I will search for the lost and bring back the strays. I will bind up the injured and strengthen the weak, but the sleek and the strong I will destroy. I will shepherd the flock with **justice**."
Hosea 12:6	"But you must return to your God; maintain love and **justice**, and wait for your God always."
Amos 5:24	"But let **justice** roll on like a river, righteousness like a never-failing stream!"
Micah 6:8	"He has shown all you people what is good. And what does the Lord require of you? To act **justly** and to love mercy and to walk humbly with your God."
Zephaniah 3:5a	"The Lord within her is righteous; he does no wrong. Morning by morning he dispenses his **justice**."
Zechariah 7:9-10a	"This is what the Lord Almighty says: 'Administer true **justice**; show mercy and compassion to one another. Do not oppress the widow or the fatherless, the foreigner or the poor."

TEACHING THE KINGDOM STORY HELPS US SIDESTEP TWO DANGEROUS JUSTICE TRAPS

The interviews we conducted revealed two traps that hinder the steps of youth ministries as they move toward God's intentions for deep justice. Teaching and ministering with a **New** sense of God's story helps us sidestep them both.

Trap 1: *"Those Poor People…"*

As you've helped your students right wrongs on behalf of the broken and the brokenhearted (both in their midst and around the world), you've undoubtedly heard students express pity by describing them as *"those poor people…"* While those three words might seem harmless, they actually pose a significant threat to your students' ability to offer deep hope in the midst of brokenness. When students feel pity for those who are "worse off" than they are, this can often rob those people of their God-given dignity, and hide the God-given part we all play in the King's story.

> "There is always the creeping danger that even our servanthood is a subtle form of manipulation. Are we really servants when we can become masters again once we think we have done our part or made our contribution? Are we really servants when we can say when, where, and how long we will give of our time and energy? Is service in a far country really an expression of servanthood when we keep enough money in the bank to fly home at any moment?"
>
> DONALD P. MCNEILL, DOUGLAS A. MORRISON, AND HENRI J. M. NOUWEN, *COMPASSION*

Following Hurricane Mitch in 1998, Kurt Ver Beek and his team conducted interviews with members of short-term mission teams and those in the Honduran communities they visited. They asked the 40 Hondurans who received homes from the short-termers if they would prefer to have the North Americans come and build the home or be given the $20,000 the short-term groups raised to cover the expense of their trip—an amount that would have enabled the Hondurans to build not just one home but ten. While the Hondurans appreciated the chance to build relationships with North Americans, they often said they would rather have the financial resources so they could help *more* families and employ *more* Hondurans.[24]

One Honduran, while very appreciative of the help she received, reported through tears, "It is better for them to send the money in order to help more people who are in need."

---

[24] Kurt Ver Beek, "The Impact of Short-Term Missions: A Case Study of House Construction in Honduras After Hurricane Mitch," *Missiology* Volume 34, no. 4, October 2006, 482-483.

Another local Honduran leader answered, "They gather money to come here to do work, work that we are capable of doing."

Of course, the Hondurans were also consistently appreciative of all the North Americans had provided for them. Yet their comments leave us wondering: How can we create an environment of mutual ministry and reciprocal learning so those who "receive" are also in a position to teach and give back?

Often, even subconsciously, we subtly view ourselves as the "great white (or black or Latino or Asian) saviors" who swoop in to "rescue" others, thereby minimizing the God-given gifts and resources of those we are "rescuing." Viewing all people as made in God's image and equally capable of participating in God's unfolding kingdom story not only eliminates this degrading position, but also invites us to ask: How can we better partner with the poor so that they live their own lives as thank-you notes to the King?

> The painful truth is that much of what we currently do in the name of service and justice is based on the assumption that we who have more power and resources play a more important role in the kingdom than others. This justice trap is alluded to in research on short-term missions recently conducted by Kurt Ver Beek, an assistant professor of sociology and third-world development at Calvin College. While his surveys weren't confined to youth ministry, his findings have **New** implications for us if we want students to grasp that "those poor people" have a role in the story that's as important as our own.

Trap 2: *"There's not much I can do..."*

The needs and injustices of the world are overwhelming, even downright paralyzing—especially if you're a 15-year-old still wrestling with issues of your own identity and significance in the world.

The kingdom story doesn't come with any age requirements. In a world in which our national and state laws require kids to cross certain age thresholds to drive, drink, and vote (not all at once, we hope!), the kingdom story invites all of us—whether we're five, fifteen, or eighty-five years old—to step into its pages and contribute a few sentences—or maybe even paragraphs—of our own.

> "Reading the Bible from the margins of society is not an exercise that reveals interesting perspectives on how other cultures read and interpret biblical texts. To read the Bible from the margins is to grasp God in the midst of struggle and oppression."
>
> MIGUEL A. DE LA TORRE, *READING THE BIBLE FROM THE MARGINS*

This brings **New** freedom to all kids, but our interviews with urban youth workers confirm that it brings a special sense of destiny and purpose to kids who come from under-resourced or high-risk backgrounds. Those kids are used to standing on the receiving end of governmental and social services. When youth leaders like us invite them to stand on the other side of the table and not only receive but give their skills, time, and dreams, we help them realize all they have to offer as children of the King.

We are seeing this now in our church as we invite kids from the poorer areas of Pasadena who are part of our ministry to serve others. As they help repair roofs, paint rooms for the church, and support our church's computer lab, they're relishing the chance to contribute their own text to God's story. As one of these kids summarized, "I haven't had it easy, but now it's my chance to give back."

One of these young people is Demetrice. He was a sophomore when his stepdad stopped paying the rent, forcing Demetrice to move in with his friend, Adam. Adam was a part of our youth ministry, so Demetrice started coming to our youth group because (in his words), "I heard there were pretty girls there."

But Demetrice met more than just cute girls; he also met Dave, one of our mentors, who looked beyond Demetrice's past and saw kingdom hope for his future. In a world in which Demetrice had experienced people making assumptions about him because he's black and lived in a "bad neighborhood," Demetrice says, "Dave saw me for who I really was, and helped me see the kingdom of God for what it really is."

Now Demetrice is a junior college student and a part-time middle school intern at our church. He focuses on reaching out to kids who act out in school and in youth group. Demetrice is one of a very few African-American male middle school leaders at our church, and most of the kids in Demetrice's small group are white. As a result, he often has to fight against people's stereotypes and assumptions about him. At our last winter camp, another small group leader asked Demetrice to teach him how to hold a gun. Why? Because that leader assumed all young black men know how to hold guns.

Yet in the midst of people assuming Demetrice plays drums (when he really plays piano), or guessing he only likes hip-hop (when he also likes rock and classical music), Demetrice is committed to helping the kids in his predominantly white small group understand all they have in common. His dream is that his small group becomes a place "where we can all be ourselves, where we can realize our similarities and our differences, and learn how we all fit together like a puzzle."

WHO? (OBSERVATION)

STEP 3: WHO?

GLEN STASSEN and JIM WALLIS are two justice leaders who have dedicated their lives to motivating both kids and adults to deeper justice through their teaching. As president and executive director of Sojourners/Call to Renewal and the author of *God's Politics: Why the Right Gets It Wrong and the Left Doesn't Get It,* Jim Wallis is a highly acclaimed speaker and teacher **Who** brings kingdom perspectives to faith, politics, and culture. Jim's long time friend, Glen, is Smedes Professor of Christian Ethics at Fuller Theological Seminary. Glen has written several books on justice and peacemaking, and was coauthor (with David Gushee) of *Kingdom Ethics: Following Jesus in Contemporary Context* (one of *Christianity Today's* 2003 Books of the Year).

Jim and Glen, as you have observed youth workers teaching about justice, how do they try to guilt kids into serving? When is that helpful and when is that not helpful?

Glen: Kids—and adults—who feel pressured by guilt practice evasion, including evasion of the way of Jesus.

Jim: Glen's right. Guilt can get you some standing ovations, but it doesn't sustain a justice movement long term.

Instead of guilt, other youth workers often rely on grace to motivate their kids toward deep justice. How do youth workers know if what they're teaching is authentic grace or what Dietrich Bonhoeffer would call "cheap grace"?

Jim: Authentic grace means we do everything in gratitude because of what God has done for us. We're all just hopeless sinners in need of God's grace, and we have nothing over anyone else—except that God has saved us. That's different from saying we somehow are blessed in our wealth, and there are those who haven't been blessed for whatever reason, and we want to now be a blessing to them. That's cheap grace.

Glen: Bonhoeffer got it right. Authentic grace overcomes our shame by entering into the midst of our lives with love and caring, and inviting us to participate in a new community that includes folks like us, and includes us as participants in a new way of living—not as isolated individuals, but—as the apostle Paul said— I, yet not I, but Christ in me" (1 Corinthians 15:10). "Participation in Christ," and Christ's participation in us, was a central theme for Bonhoeffer.

Many youth leaders are helping kids understand that God has a kingdom story, and that we as his creation find meaning within that story. How can youth workers help teenagers realize that justice for the least of these is part of what it means to find ourselves in God's story?

Jim: As I've been saying for the last two years on the road, when I find 2,000 verses in the Bible about poor people, I insist that fighting poverty is a moral issue. Somehow, most churches are skipping over all those verses. But the God of the Bible is a God of justice, not just charity.

What's the difference between charity and justice?

Jim: Charity is just dealing with the symptoms of problems—feeding people, housing people, and clothing the naked. But William Booth, the founder of the Salvation Army, used to say that we can't keep picking up bodies at the bottom of the mountain and not climb the hill and see who or what is throwing them off the edge. Justice climbs the hill and tries to stop folks from stepping off the cliff.

What else would you like to change about the way youth workers tend to teach about social justice?

Glen: Jesus confronted the authorities in Jerusalem, and the Pharisees and wealthy, 40 times in the Synoptic Gospels, for their injustice. Many Sunday school classes skip by that or don't realize it. As Dave Gushee and I show in chapter 17 of *Kingdom Ethics*, Jesus confronted the authorities for the same four dimensions of injustice that his favorite prophet, Isaiah, emphasized: injustice as domination and suppressing independence; injustice as exclusion of outsiders; injustice as greed oppressing the poor; and injustice as violence to victims. Different kids identify with different dimensions of injustice. I suggest including all four, and asking youth which of the four they have experienced. That is likely to hook their interest. Then connect all four so they identify with the causes and consequences of injustice more broadly.

> "Because the Scriptures spend so much time on the poor, we will too. This is the most important 'political' issue in the Bible, and it must be ours as well."
>
> JIM WALLIS, *GOD'S POLITICS*.

What would you say to a youth worker who feels like justice is a step beyond what a sixteen-year-old can do?

Glen: Kids care about injustice; they are struggling for some independence themselves, and struggling against being excluded, and they have a passion about injustice. Adolescence is a great time to teach about justice and injustice. The best group in a church to begin with in starting a program to mentor kids who have needs, or to help feed the hungry, or to do visits and engage in conversation with recipients of injustice, is youth. They're not set in their ways and their ideologies, and they care.

For more ideas on how to help students process and interpret their justice experiences, flip ahead to chapter 6.

But the key is not only to engage in some service project; it's crucial to ask an expert or two about the causes of poverty and what can be done to make a difference for justice to come, and help students process and interpret what they are experiencing.

Jim: I agree with Glen. We're finding that young people are not as narcissistic or apathetic as we might think. As I speak around the country, kids are responding in deep and profound ways. They're coming to me to tell me how they are changing the world already.

> "If the faith community is really ready to get to know those kids who would be sleeping in bunk beds that night, we won't just be providing them shelter. We'll start asking why the shelters are needed in the first place."
>
> JIM WALLIS,
> *FAITH WORKS*

I had a nine-year-old come up to me after I had spoken about the "Silent Tsunami" killing children. This nine-year-old girl told me, "You talked about a Silent Tsunami killing little children like me. I was sitting there and thinking to myself, 'If I'm a Christian, I better do something about that.'" So the next week I told the students in my class at Harvard University, "If you want to lead this movement, you'd better move fast, because there's a whole generation coming behind you, and they're going to push you out of the way." In 30 years of working for justice, I've never seen such a growing student movement.

How does the fact that every single person is made in God's image affect the movement that you're describing?

Jim: It's central. Because we're all made in God's image, a kid living in a garbage dump in Mexico is just as important as my own kid. I'm going to pick up my two kids from school this afternoon—and what has got to motivate me is that other people's kids are just as important to God and to me as my own kids.

Part of why I'm concerned about the religious right is that they care about the sacredness of life, but if I want their support and I'm an unborn child, I'd better stay unborn as long as possible. Once I'm born, I'm off their radar screen. The reality is that we are just as much made in God's image after we're born as before we're born.

What are your favorite scriptural texts to use when you teach about justice? Why do you like them so much?

Glen: My all-time favorite is Jesus' baptismal text, Isaiah 42:1-7, because it says God will bring justice to the nations, which means all people get included; and will not do violence, which means justice and healing for the victims of violence; and will bring healing to the blind, which means justice for the sick; and will deliver the prisoners from the dungeon, which means justice for the dominated and oppressed; and "He will not grow faint or be crushed until he has established justice in the earth," (42:4, NRSV) which means when we work for justice, we are participating in what God is doing through Christ.

The interviews we've conducted with youth workers have revealed two traps that prevent youth ministries from deep justice. The first is when kids look at those they serve and think, "Those poor people." How can we view those we serve as people who play just as big a part in the kingdom story as we do?

Glen: First, I'd encourage us all to engage in conversations with people we serve, and to ask questions that lead them to talk about their life stories. Second, I'd encourage youth also to engage in discussion with a couple of experts on injustices that cause or contribute to this suffering. Just serving isn't enough, because we come with ideologies that have infiltrated our ways of perceiving, and with shyness about asking questions that can reveal shame. We need help from people who have worked with the poor. Youth ministries would be wise to remember how often Jesus said, "You're not seeing what's happening."

The second trap is when kids look at the overwhelming needs of the world and think, "There's not much I can do." What would you say to a teenager who feels that way?

Glen: I wouldn't say anything. I'd help my youth group engage in projects with Bread for the World, World Vision International, my Baptist denomination's World Service, the Heifer Project, or in a local project like mentoring teenagers who could use some help with their studies and with setting their values for life.

Any last advice for youth workers trying to teach kids about deep social justice?

Jim: If you're a youth worker serving kids who are middle or upper class, please tell them flat-out that most people in the world don't live like they or their friends do. As

> "Integrity of character is shaped when we see ourselves, our lives, and our loyalties as *part of a larger drama* that shapes our community."
>
> GLEN H. STASSEN AND DAVID P. GUSHEE, *KINGDOM ETHICS*

> "If the church is functioning as it should, it will continually and very earnestly engage in a search for authoritative direction and insight concerning its character and its conduct. It will desire above all else to know and live out the answer to the prophet's question, 'What does the Lord require?' (Micah 6:8)."
>
> GLEN H. STASSEN AND DAVID P. GUSHEE, *KINGDOM ETHICS*

> "My neighborhood has constantly given me a perspective that I would not otherwise have had. Once, I returned from a meeting at the White House about youth violence only to find the infamous yellow police tape on the sidewalk right across from my house, indicating where another young man had just been shot and killed. I remember reflecting that most people who attend such meetings don't come home to places like this."
>
> JIM WALLIS, *FAITH WORKS*

long as they have a narrow view of reality, they'll never understand the world. We have an enormous opportunity to expose teenagers to the world as it really is, because young people like to go places. They like to get out of the house. So we have the chance to send them into the world so they see it as it really is.

HOW? (APPLICATION)

STEP 4: HOW?

DEEP JUSTICE APPLICATION QUESTIONS

1. Which are you more prone to over emphasize in teaching kids about deep justice: guilt or grace? How has that affected your youth ministry and your justice work?

2. How would describing God's kingdom story as Good/Guilt/Grace/Gratitude affect your teaching and justice work?

3. What impact would it have on your students to realize that participation in the kingdom story doesn't come with any age requirements? How could your teaching help them embrace that?

4. Glen points to four dimensions of injustice: domination, exclusion, greed, and violence. Which of these four dimensions would most resonate with your students? Why do you think that is?

5. Jim points out that "Because we're all made in God's image, a kid living in a garbage dump in Mexico is just as important as my own kid." How would the deep justice work of you and your students be different if that truth was imprinted on the minds and souls of those in your youth ministry?

6. Of the following list of Deep Justice Recommended Action Steps that flow from this chapter, which would best help you as a kingdom follower right wrongs? How about your youth ministry?

DEEP JUSTICE RECOMMENDED ACTION STEPS:

For Yourself

- Read through one, two, or all of Paul's New Testament letters, noting the good, guilt, grace, and gratitude he describes. See if you can observe any patterns in Paul's descriptions of these four movements of the kingdom story.

- Take 30 minutes and think about how you'd like your life to contribute to the ongoing and unfolding kingdom story. Jot down some notes and put them in a location where you'll see them regularly and be reminded of our privileges and responsibilities as kingdom followers.

- The next time you're out with friends, ask them how they would describe the kingdom story and the part they hope to play in it.

- Find another youth worker who is part of a different denomination or ethnicity and ask that person to share his or her version of the kingdom story with you, and share your own vision with that person. Discover ways your different contexts can enrich each other.

- In your own personal Scripture study, jot down passages of Scripture that reflect good, guilt, grace, and/or gratitude.

- Choose a few of the Old Testament verses about justice listed in the table on pages 48-51 and memorize them and/or use them as prompts for prayer.

- Go to www.biblegateway.com or use a Bible concordance to create a list of all Bible passages that use the word "justice." Reflect on a few of these verses every day during your own prayer time.

- Spend some time thinking about how you might recast the Good/Guilt/Grace/Gratitude story in terms or concepts that better fit your own theology and experiences.

For Your Youth Ministry

- Ask a few trusted adult volunteers to read this chapter and give you feedback on your talks to see if you lean too heavily on either guilt or cheap grace in motivating students toward justice work.

- For the next month, try structuring all your talks and small group discussions around three of the Deep Design steps followed in this book:

  1. **Now** what is happening?

  2. What **New** insights from Scripture can help us better respond to what is happening?

  3. **How** can we live out that Scripture? Frame the **New** insights around the Good/Guilt/Grace/Gratitude kingdom story. Even if a specific Scripture passage or topic leans toward one or more of the story movements, at least make sure that you mention the others.

- Working from the Old Testament verses about justice listed in the table on pages 48-51, design a four-to-six-week teaching or small group series about deep justice.

- Whenever you talk with students about a passage of Scripture, look for justice themes in the text by asking: What wrongs is God righting? What wrongs does he then want us to right?

- Before your next service opportunity, spend some time teaching students about God's story, and the fact that all people—including the broken and brokenhearted—are equally important in God's story. Brainstorm ways your ministry can better partner with the poor and marginalized so that both your students and those you are partnering with realize their own potential to live as thank-you notes to the King.

- Help your entire church see that participation in the kingdom story does not come with any age requirement by asking your senior pastor for opportunities during your church services for students to share ways they are righting wrongs around them.

- Identify the students in your ministry or community who are high-risk in various ways, and figure out creative ways they can serve others. Perhaps they have gifts in art or music that could be integrated into your church. Maybe they'd participate in your youth ministry's justice work—if you invited them.

- Follow Glen's advice and ask a few local leaders who understand poverty in your area to share with your kids about the causes of poverty as well as what your ministry can do to right wrongs in your community.

WHICH JESUS TAKES US TO DEEP JUSTICE?

BY CHAP CLARK

"Everything in Christ astonishes me."

—Napoleon Bonaparte (1769-1821)

NOW? (DISCERNMENT)

STEP 1: NOW?

The story of the kingdom has one center: God. As one part of the divine trinity, Jesus is a walking and talking "main character" in this kingdom story whose presence weaves from good and guilt all the way to grace and gratitude.

Regardless of geography or religion, around the globe and across the centuries, those who have heard about Jesus are consistently enamored with him. Our fascination goes far beyond his "moral teaching" or his poignant stories. The uniqueness and complexity of his teaching and life have always baffled scholars, confounded skeptics, and warmed the hearts of the multitudes—just as they still do today.

After all, Jesus' story is amazing. He was "only" a peasant from an obscure village who lived in a relatively poor agrarian religious community. He apparently had no more formal education than any other boy from his part of the world. When Jesus finally began his work, he started slowly, speaking to small crowds and inviting a handful of people to follow him. He led, journeyed, and preached for a mere three years.

ARE WE MISSING THE REAL JESUS?

As men and women who want to love young people in the name of Jesus and help them right wrongs in a world broken by sin, corruption, and oppression, there is no more important aspect of our ministry than what we believe about the King who was made the Lamb. In the busyness of responding to hurting kids, training leaders to change oppressive systems and structures, and teaching about our role in God's kingdom story, we tend to assume that what we communicate about Jesus is exactly what the Scriptures intend. Yet in light of the complexity of ministry in our postmodern world, is it possible that our youth ministries are **Now** missing the real Jesus, the Jesus who calls us to bind up the brokenhearted, proclaim freedom for the captives, and release the prisoners from darkness?[25]

In *Talladega Nights*, stock-car driver Ricky Bobby (played by Will Ferrell) offers a mealtime prayer thanking "Lord baby Jesus" and, later, "tiny infant Jesus." When reminded that Jesus didn't stay a baby, he responds, "I like the Christmas Jesus...I like the baby version the best." We may laugh, yet many of us find that the easiest way to deal with the unimaginable power of the Incarnate King is to grab onto one aspect of his character or teaching and make it the central theme of our lives and ministries. Even if we think we have a fairly well-rounded perspective on Jesus as described in Scripture, does the way we right wrongs **Now** emphasize a limited Jesus? Our youth ministries might not "like the baby version the best," but we probably lean heavily on our own Jesus-of-Choice.

---

[25] See Luke 4:16-21, in which Jesus begins his public ministry by reading Isaiah 61:1-2.

Jesus-of-Choice	Scriptural Support
Little Baby Jesus	"So they hurried off and found Mary and Joseph, and the baby, who was lying in the manger." (Luke 2:16)
Tender, Understanding Jesus	"'Then neither do I condemn you,' Jesus declared." (John 8:11)
Wild, Rebellious Prophet Jesus	"Jesus entered the temple courts and began driving out those who were buying and selling there." (Mark 11:15)
Great Moral Teacher Jesus	"Everyone who hears these words of mine and puts them into practice is like a wise man who built his house on the rock." (Matthew 7:24)
Santa Claus Jesus	"'I have come that they may have life, and have it to the full.'" (John 10:10)
"Mr. Fix-it" Mechanic Jesus	"'If you believe, you will receive whatever you ask for in prayer.'" (Matthew 21:22)
Contemplative Jesus	"But Jesus often withdrew to lonely places and prayed." (Luke 5:16)

When it comes to God's character as offered in the person of Jesus of Nazareth, we easily fall prey to grabbing hold of one or two caricatures of the Jesus we like the most. We might prefer Jesus as the tender savior who forgave the woman caught in adultery (John 8:2-11). Or maybe our Jesus-of-Choice is the "wild, rebellious" king, who in his anger tossed tables around like a martial arts hero. Or maybe we tend to focus on Jesus' model of solitude and early morning prayer as the most important aspect of his justice work. As a result of these narrow views, our youth ministries **Now** end up with a Jesus-of-Choice who is *either* firm *or* loving, *either* active *or* prayerful.

As with any caricature, each of these views of Jesus, and their numerous variations, is based on an aspect of the authentic person and character of the historical Jesus as described in the Bible. As you can see in the chart above, he does show mercy and forgiveness to us when we sin, he displays seemingly out-of-character flashes of rage toward the moneychangers in the Temple, and he does spend lots of time praying and talking about "turning our cheeks" when someone hits us.[26]

The problem **Now** is that once we allow ourselves to emphasize one characteristic of Jesus, by default we also *de-emphasize* the rest. When we lift up a gentle, merciful Jesus who wants to bring us peace and fulfillment, we have trouble hearing the Jesus who calls us to deny ourselves and sacrifice our happiness for the good of others. When we limit our kingdom faith to following Jesus in spiritual disciplines and personal piety, we discount the Jesus who, when his attempt to grab some rest was interrupted by the pursuing crowds, sacrificed his "quiet time" and served the needs of the multitudes. Albeit usually inadvertently, we **Now** both believe and communicate to kids that "our" Jesus-of-Choice is the *only* Jesus, thus hiding the complex and *biblical* Jesus from them.

> "The revolutionary image of Jesus didn't come to me in Sunday school as a boy; there, Jesus was a nice, quiet, gentle, perhaps somewhat fragile guy on whose lap children liked to sit, or he was a fellow in strange robes who held a small sheep in one arm and always seemed to have the other raised as if he were hailing a taxi."
>
> BRIAN MCLAREN, *THE SECRET MESSAGE OF JESUS*

---

[26] Matthew 18:19, Mark 11:14-16, and Matthew 5:39 respectively.

NEW? (REFLECTION)

STEP 2: NEW?

What does our Jesus-of-Choice have to do with righting wrongs?

Everything.

Jesus gives his followers, then and now, a simple and straightforward invitation: "Follow me." Yet in this simple and straightforward call, he provides our youth ministries with little wiggle room. We don't follow our favorite version of Jesus when it's comfortable and convenient. We follow all of him, all of the time, and to all people and places.

Following the marvelously complex and multifaceted Jesus will move our youth ministries into deeper justice. In fact, we who long for deep justice should not make calling students to the poor our starting point. Instead, we should first call students to Jesus, who then calls them—and us—to the poor. Because the "Tender Jesus" defied Jewish Law, societal guidelines, and common sense when he let the leper get close enough to touch him (Mark 1), we feel the pain of those who are excluded or in pain. Because the "Teacher Jesus" treated money as something to be dedicated to his kingdom instead of our own security and comfort (Mark 10), we make different choices about how we use our money and possessions. Because the "Radical Jesus" filled his calendar by hanging out and even eating with "unacceptable" people (John 4 and Luke 15), we spend time with those who are neglected and forgotten. As we embody all the marvelously diverse pictures of Jesus we glimpse in Scripture, we become more fully engaged in the overall Good/Guilt/Grace/Gratitude kingdom story.

THE KING OF SCRIPTURE

If our youth ministries are going to embrace the full Jesus, who unites all of these slices into a clearer whole, then we need to move toward a **New** and deeper understanding of Jesus in Scripture.

The Scriptures reveal to us the nature, character, and calling of both God the Father and Jesus the Son. In the Old Testament, the idea of God as King is only implicitly developed—but it is there. And God is portrayed not as *a* king, but *the King!* In the New Testament, we gain an up-close and personal look at our King in the person, work, and invitation of Jesus. Because of how we so easily degenerate into following our Jesus-of-Choice, it is important to take a comprehensive **New** look at the Scriptures so our youth ministries can right wrongs for the least, last, and lost in our midst.

> "Jesus' good news, then, was that the kingdom of God had come, and that he, Jesus, was its herald and expounder to men. More than that, in some special, mysterious way, he was the kingdom."
>
> MALCOLM MUGGERIDGE, *JESUS: THE MAN WHO LIVES*

The Hebrew word in the Old Testament for king is *melek*. While some believe the concept of God's plan to bring in his "kingdom" feels out of place and too militaristic in light of the love and mercy of God expressed in Christ, the Bible makes use of the metaphor for a reason—to emphasize that all of creation is ultimately subject to the God who reigns. The Old Testament consistently affirms that God, and God alone, is the King. In the Old Testament, although the actual phrase "kingdom of God" is not used, the notion that Yahweh is the preeminent ruler over all creation is constant—and consistent with Jesus' claim that the "kingdom of God is near" (Luke 10:11).

The Psalmist declares: "God reigns over the nations; God is seated on his holy throne." (Psalm 47:8) Daniel echoes this same theme when asked to interpret King Nebuchadnezzar's dream:

> In the time of those kings, the God of heaven will set up a kingdom that will never be destroyed, nor will it be left to another people. It will crush all those kingdoms and bring them to an end, but it will itself endure forever. (Daniel 2:44)

THE OLD TESTAMENT KING IS ACTIVE IN RIGHTING WRONGS

Throughout the Scriptures, God the King is never portrayed as "too busy" to care about the ordinary affairs of humanity. Nor is the Lord passive when it comes to the needs of those he loves. Yahweh is an active, passionate God who exhibits strong emotion over the plight of the oppressed, beaten down, and brokenhearted. "He defends the cause of the fatherless and the widow, and loves the foreigners residing among you, giving them food and clothing" (Deuteronomy 10:18). When we talk about his kingdom we are speaking of God's mission to bring healing and reconciliation to a world broken by human sin and devastated by human selfishness.

To learn more about how your youth ministry is teaching kids about God's character—whether you realize it or not—check out our free additional Deep Justice resources available at www.cyfm.net.

When Jesus entered history and initiated the arrival of the kingdom of God in his person, he chose to make his pronouncement in his hometown temple by reading from the Prophet Isaiah:

> "The Spirit of the Sovereign Lord is on me, because the Lord has anointed me to proclaim good news to the poor. He has sent me to bind up the brokenhearted, to proclaim freedom for the captives and release from darkness for the prisoners, to proclaim the year of the Lord's favor." (Isaiah 61:1-2)

Isaiah describes in detail God's kingdom purposes for the world he created and loves. In Isaiah 16:5, for example, we are told that the King who comes to reign will be one who "seeks justice" and "speeds the cause of righteousness." In Isaiah 42:3-4, we learn that this King will "bring forth justice" and "will not falter or be discouraged till he establishes justice on earth."

In Yahweh justice and kingship are indelibly linked. As he speaks through his prophet:

> Of the increase of his government and peace there will be no end. He will reign on David's throne and over his kingdom, establishing and upholding it with justice and righteousness from that time on and forever. The zeal of the Lord Almighty will accomplish this. (Isaiah 9:7)

GOD'S KINGDOM AFFIRMS A UNIQUE CONCERN FOR THOSE IN GREATEST NEED.

How our God is both faithful and gracious to all while also showing a focused care for those in need may be hard to fully comprehend, yet this is clearly the case in Scripture. Throughout the Old Testament, when the reign or rule of God is mentioned, there is often special mention of God's favor on the poor, the oppressed, and the brokenhearted. Psalm 146 is a prime example of this:

> He upholds the cause of the oppressed and gives food to the hungry. The Lord sets prisoners free, the Lord gives sight to the blind, the Lord lifts up those who are bowed down, the Lord loves the righteous. The Lord watches over the foreigner and sustains the fatherless and the widow, but he frustrates the ways of the wicked. The Lord reigns forever, your God, O Zion, for all generations. (Psalm 146:7-10)

Any biblically rooted understanding of the kingdom of God cannot be separated from God's commitment to uphold justice by providing for the needy, judging in favor of the oppressed, helping widows and orphans, and caring for strangers. God who reigns over all creation looks upon the brokenness of his children, and in his mercy takes special favor on behalf of those most affected by humanity's sin and rebellion.

In *Reading the Bible from the Margins,* Miguel De La Torre describes God's heart for the poor and oppressed in this way:

> "I have two children, a ten-year-old boy and a nine-year-old girl. I love both children deeply...My son is about a foot taller than my daughter, a year older, and a bit stronger. When their verbal fights become physical, my son has the clear advantage...When I see them physically fighting, I step in, pick him up by the nape of his neck, and defend my daughter...not because I love her more but because she is being oppressed."[27]

---

[27] Miguel A. De La Torre, *Reading the Bible from the Margins* (New York: Orbis Books, 2002), 133.

GOD'S KINGDOM REVEALED IN CHRIST

In Jesus, the kingdom arrives in this world, proclaiming the fulfillment of hope that God's reign has been personally delivered to this broken world. In the New Testament, the King enters human history through the second person of the Godhead, taking on human flesh in order to personally bring the kingdom into our broken world. The multifaceted Jesus Christ is not just "the image of the invisible God" (Colossians 1:15), and the "one mediator between God and human beings" (1 Timothy 2:5), he is also the long-anticipated king.[28] While first-century Jews were expecting a king who sought after worldwide political and military domination, Jesus as King instead embodied righteousness, grace, and peace.

> "By his passion Jesus fulfills what was written concerning the Son of Man and unfolds the mystery of the kingdom of God."
>
> F.F. BRUCE, *NEW TESTAMENT DEVELOPMENT OF OLD TESTAMENT THEMES*

When Jesus came to live among us, he not only *brought in* the kingdom, he *was* the kingdom. Theologians have wrestled for centuries to describe this adequately, but few argue the essence of this truth. In the person and work of Jesus Christ, the Bible makes no distinction between the kingdom of God and the King who has come. As E. Stanley Jones teaches, "Jesus is the kingdom of God taking sandals and walking. The kingdom and the person belong together."[29] Or as Lesslie Newbigin writes, "The kingdom of God now has a name and a face."[30]

How does this **New** understanding of Jesus as King translate to deeper justice? We'd like to suggest the following two ways that embracing the full Jesus makes a difference in the way we lead our students to right wrongs around them.

1. Jesus' kingdom justice is radical (but not *Braveheart*).

There is a fairly common and growing trend in youth ministry that passionately depicts Jesus as a wild-eyed "radical" who calls us to "radical faith." Surely there is something to be said about the radical nature of not only our faith but of the Lord himself. But what does "radical faith" look like? Does it give us permission to be arrogant or aggressive in living out our faith? Should we "stand up" and make sure others know we are Christians by, for example, wearing cer-

---

[28] Micah 5:2 tells of a "ruler" coming from Bethlehem, and this prophecy is applied to the birth of Jesus in Matthew 2:6.

[29] E. Stanley Jones, *The Unshakable Kingdom and the Unchanging Person* (Nashville: Abingdon, 1972), 34.

[30] Lesslie Newbigin, *Sign of the Kingdom* (Grand Rapids: Eerdmans, 1981), 18.

tain clothing or decorating our car? Or is the kind of kingdom living Jesus taught radical because of its firm but thoroughly loving commitment to God?

When we look carefully at the life, heart, ministry, and teaching of Jesus, it seems we are called to a "radical" lifestyle that is much more than simply being militant. For examples of this kind of witness, take a look at the radical Jesus-style social justice of Martin Luther King Jr. in his commitment to nonviolence in the face of unbelievable racial oppression and aggression or Mother Teresa in her unflagging compassion in confronting the ravages of human disease and suffering.

Our radical King is a defender of the weak, the poor, and the outcast. Our King is radical because, unlike most leaders in the world, he tells us we are to love those who hate us, to give our enemies double what they seek from us, and to be peacemakers. The message and justice work of Jesus, the King of Kings, is so radical that only those who are willing to become like little children can enter his kingdom. When his disciples were arguing over who would be the greatest in his kingdom, Jesus' response was radical:

> "With the person and ministry of God incarnated through Jesus of Nazareth, the culture of the kingdom became a living power and presence. Through the calling of the twelve disciples, Jesus reconstituted the kingdom community and culture. He delivered the ethical mandate of the kingdom as the Sermon on the Mount and invited everyone, without discrimination, to enter the kingdom."
>
> RAY S. ANDERSON, *THE SHAPE OF PRACTICAL THEOLOGY: EMPOWERING MINISTRY WITH THEOLOGICAL PRAXIS*

> Jesus called them together and said, "You know that the rulers of the Gentiles lord it over them, and their high officials exercise authority over them. Not so with you. Instead, whoever wants to become great among you must be your servant, and whoever wants to be first must be your slave—just as the Son of Man did not come to be served, but to serve, and to give his life as a ransom for many." (Matthew 20:25-28)

2. The King is on the move.

In youth ministry, it is easy to feel like God is not doing enough. Although few of us would openly admit it, we find ourselves wondering what Jesus the King is up to when we encounter devastating injustice, poverty, or hopelessness. Whether it is hearing a 15-year-old confide that she was sexually abused by a family member, or watching a 12-year-old bleed out on a dingy sidewalk after a drive-by shooting, there is pain and brokenness everywhere.

Sometimes such injustice is due to the obvious and overt sin of humankind. Other times it's a result of decades (or centuries) of economic and political oppression that keep millions from clean water, education, and any hope of a meaningful future. Where is our King in these and so many other devastating situations and circumstances?

It is vital we keep in mind that the kingdom of God is *not* an *either/or*, but instead *both* a "right now" reality (because Jesus reigns *now*) *and* a "not yet" (because God is in the process of reconciling "to himself all things"[31]). Since we live in a fallen, broken, distorted world with lots of circumstances and places that cause us to wonder what our King is up to, or even where our King is, we cannot help but cry out in despair.

Jesus has proven not only that he cares but that he is actively and passionately committed to bringing hope and healing into our broken world. When he saw a widow in Nain who had lost her only son, Jesus' "heart went out to her" and in response he healed the son (Luke 7:11-16). Another time, when the powerful synagogue leader Jairus was about to lose his 12-year-old daughter, Jesus wasted no time in going home with him. On the way, a lonely and desperate woman illegally crept through the crowd simply to touch his clothes in search of her own healing. When he felt his power being accessed, Jesus stopped, interrupted Jairus' emergency, and sought her out so as not only to physically heal her but to emotionally restore her sense of worth by listening to her story (Luke 8:41-48).

Jesus remains every bit as compassionate today as he was while walking the earth. Even when our youth ministries can't see his response to the brokenness, pain, or oppression we encounter, Jesus' character and mission has not changed since before time began. He remains on the move, bringing in his kingdom. And he invites us to become part of that movement. *That is precisely the point of this book: The church is called to follow the leading and ministry of the Holy Spirit by venturing into those circumstances and arenas where God is working to redeem our broken world.*

As we look at the fullness of Jesus as revealed in the Scriptures, we are compelled to follow him into those dark, lonely, disturbing, and depressing situations and places where his light is struggling to shine. That's the work of the in-breaking kingdom of God, and we therefore go where Jesus goes.

---

[31] Philippians 2:20.

WHO? (OBSERVATION)

STEP 3: WHO?

Dr. William Pannell is someone **Who** passionately helps kingdom followers understand and embrace the full Jesus. Bill was the first African American to serve on the Board of Trustees at Fuller Theological Seminary before he joining the seminary's faculty in 1974. Today, as senior professor of preaching and special assistant to Fuller's president, Bill has a lifetime of insights to share with youth ministries seeking after God's justice.

Bill, why are we so prone to accept a mere caricature of Jesus instead of the full Jesus?

Hard to say, but for both adults and teenagers, our view of Jesus is largely shaped by how and where we've been raised. In much of America, the reigning ideology about personhood is private and individualistic, so we tend to see Jesus through the same individualistic lenses. Jesus becomes "my personal Savior." Our way of imitating Christ becomes a personal pietistic discipleship. The tendency, then, is to shun the world, and focus on so-called "spiritual" matters.

Underlying much of this narrow view of Jesus is a misunderstanding of Jesus as both fully human and fully divine. Those who emphasize Jesus as "my personal Savior" tend to focus on his divinity and the way he offers us a path to heaven when we die. They tend to think of Jesus as standing against the world instead of actually working in it.

What about those who emphasize his humanity instead of his divinity?

That's the other end of the spectrum. Those who underemphasize Jesus' divinity and focus only on his humanity view him as a great moral example and a great teacher who wants radical social change, but they miss out on his offer of salvation. Either extreme is an exercise in negative self-definition—we define ourselves by what we're not instead of what we are; we are who we are because we are not what they are.

What effect do these caricatures have on the way we engage in social justice in our youth ministries?

In the first extreme, which is more "conservative," we don't get involved at all—or if we do, it is rather superficial. That's why evangelicals were conspicuously absent from the civil rights movement. This has changed in recent years as conservatives have begun to involve themselves in national politics. But this is still quite personal in its application, tending to fixate on abortion, prayer in schools, and a few other issues. But for the most part, we let history unravel at God's discretion. We assume God will do what he's going to do, and our job is to get people saved. Once we get people saved, we hope they are transformed into Christ-like-ness, which often means making them more like us.

On the "liberal" extreme, the preference is to quote from the Beatitudes and tell Jesus stories, but we don't take his salvation as exclusive. I just heard a talk by the recently elected bishop of a major U.S. denomination. She's a great communicator and as sharp as a tack. She outlined her denomination's agenda with a strong focus on poverty, homelessness, AIDS, and other diseases, which is great. The problem was that any good social agency or the United Nations regularly focuses on the same issues. But there was no mention of Jesus or evangelism as a crucial part of Christ's mission in the world.

Bill, how would you describe Jesus?

To start off with, Jesus is Emmanuel, God with us. To me, that's utterly astonishing. Jesus is sent from God as our Savior.

The next question then becomes: What does it mean to be saved? I can do no better than the Apostle Paul who said that Jesus died to deliver us from all iniquity and to purify a people who were passionate to do good works. Oftentimes, we who are evangelicals have made salvation narrow—too narrow. We have tended to view being saved as a personal private enterprise. But the reality is that Scripture teaches God's salvation of creation as well as individuals.

It teaches a grand sweeping salvation that delivers our world and its people from bondage. We as humans are not the authors of salvation, but we do bring the good news of God's salvation to the entire world.

> "The Cross stands for God's judgment of the world and all its systems, ideologies, stratagems, and processes that exalt themselves over Christ and his kingdom."
>
> WILLIAM PANNELL, *EVANGELISM FROM THE BOTTOM UP*

In the midst of Jesus as our saving Emmanuel, what about him makes him the ultimate justice worker?

God is holy, and his people are called to be like him. And God hates iniquity and all forms of injustice. He proclaims his intention to liberate the oppressed. Sometimes our understanding of liberation needs to be corrected. In the 1960s and 1970s, many folks claimed Jesus was in favor of their own brand of revolution, like the black revolution or the women's revolution. But Jesus has his own revolution, which is called the kingdom of God and is the in-breaking of a whole new social order. That new order is characterized by justice, and peace, and the joy that the Holy Spirit gives.

What's the relationship between the kingdom and the church?

The Christian community is a visible expression of Jesus' new order, and justice must reign in it if it is to be authentic. Anyone who asks what the kingdom of God looks like ought to be invited over to the church.

What keeps us who follow Jesus from being a mirror of the kingdom?

In the church today, we're always looking for comfort. People want to join a church where they're comfortable, or they want to hear preaching that makes them feel good. That's not what the kingdom is about. If that's what you want, go to the country club.

In contrast to this search for comfort, how is Jesus' justice work radical?

As humans we are fundamentally self-centered. Jesus comes into history and says that if we're going to follow him, we have to give up all rights to ourselves, take up our cross daily, and follow him. To an American society that is deeply committed to life, liberty, and the pursuit of happiness, Jesus says that true life and true liberty and true happiness is a result of allowing God to be God in our lives. If we want to live, we must die.

Given Jesus' interest in justice, do you think he favors the poor?

Well, I'm not so sure he favors the poor, but he is favorably disposed toward them because he knows that, for the most part, people are poor as a result of injustice heaped upon them by the powerful. And he also knows something about the poor that others don't know. The poor are often more responsive to the good news than those who are well-off. People with credit cards up to their navels are not as interested in being saved. Their salvation is in their left hip pocket.

What God really favors is justice. He is just as open to saving the wealthy and powerful as anybody else. It's just that they are often not as open to him.

What signs do you see that the kingdom is on the move?

I think of the kingdom as a visible manifestation of the presence of God. Given that, some of the areas in our world where we're seeing the most visible signs of God's presence are in China and in many African nations. In those countries, we're seeing the Holy Spirit align himself with the dispossessed, and we're seeing justice beginning to emerge, and thousands of people becoming believers.

How would you respond to someone who wonders where Jesus is in the midst of injustice and poverty?

First off, I'd say that much of the injustice and violence we see in the world isn't because of God, it's because of us as humans. Religious people—like the Palestinians and Jews in the Middle East or the Protestants and Catholics in Ireland—all have prayer meetings. Yet in the midst of seeking God there remains a self-centered grab for power.

Whether injustice is caused by human sin or other circumstances, the good news is that Jesus is still there. He is in the lives of those who are out there waging battle on behalf of the poor and oppressed. I think our final apologetic—our ultimate sign of God's work in the world—is the church acting on behalf of the poor and making sure they have the gospel preached unto them.

HOW? (APPLICATION)

STEP 4: HOW?

DEEP JUSTICE APPLICATION QUESTIONS

1. What are some of the more common caricatures of God and/or Jesus you have heard or witnessed? Describe them, especially in how they affect the way people you know, including your own students, live out their faith.

2. What are one or two aspects of the Jesus-of-Choice that you tend to lean toward yourself? How does this play out in the way you try to right wrongs around you?

3. How, if at all, do your preferred versions of the Jesus-of-Choice relate to Bill's description of the common misunderstanding of Jesus as both fully human and fully divine?

4. If you really lived as if Jesus were the King of your life and the world, what would be different? What would be different for your students if they really lived as if Jesus were the King of their lives and the world?

5. In what ways do you think Jesus is radical? What do you think of the idea that Jesus is radical but not in a *Braveheart* way? How does your definition of Jesus' radical-ness make a difference in the way you engage in deep justice?

6. Of the following list of Deep Justice Recommended Action Steps that flow from this chapter, which would best help you as a kingdom follower right wrongs? How about for your youth ministry?

DEEP JUSTICE RECOMMENDED ACTION STEPS:

For Yourself

- Set aside some time to read one of the Gospels in one sitting. Jot down your impressions of Jesus' character as you read about his life and ministry. What questions arise for you? Find some way to explore these questions either through reading, taking a class, or finding a mentor or conversation partner.

- Bill states, "Jesus comes into history and says that if we're going to follow him, we have to give up all rights to ourselves, take up our cross daily, and follow him. To an American society that is deeply committed to life, liberty, and the pursuit of happiness, Jesus says that true life and true liberty and true happiness is a result of allowing God to be God in our lives. If we want to live, we must die." Spend some time thinking about what you need to die to, and how that death would actually bring you life.

- Ask a trusted friend to write down aspects of your life and character that remind him or her of Jesus. As you read that list, think about what is missing, and what you can do to experience and embody more of those aspects of Jesus in your own life.

For Your Youth Ministry

- Instead of giving a talk at youth group, distribute paper and crayons to your students and ask them to draw their pictures of Jesus. When they're finished, tape the pictures to a wall and ask questions like: What themes do you see in these pictures? What aspects of Jesus are missing from our pictures? What does that tell us about ourselves? How does that affect our justice work?

- Chapter 3 described four kingdom story movements: Good/Guilt/Grace/Gratitude. Give each of your students four pieces of paper, and ask the students to draw their versions of one movement on each piece of paper, making sure that they put themselves, Jesus, and whatever and whoever else seems fitting on each piece of paper.

- Do some searching online to find a bunch of pictures of Jesus and show them to your students. Ask: Which one do you think is most accurate? What does that say about your view of Jesus? How do these views of Jesus impact the way we understand justice?

- At an adult or student leadership team meeting, read the following quote from Philip Yancey's *The Jesus I Never Knew:* "Two words one could never think of applying to the Jesus of the Gospels: boring and predictable." Ask your leaders to identify parts of your ministry that are somewhat boring and predictable, as well as elements that are not.

- After your next service opportunity, debrief the experience with students by asking: Where did you see Jesus at work in those we got to know? Where did you see Jesus at work in us?

IS THE GOSPEL ABOUT PERSONAL SALVATION OR SOCIAL REFORM?

BY CHAP CLARK

"We need to study and be formed into a profound relationship with God in order to know his character—and when we know his character, we will know that he grieves over the widow, the oppressed, the suffering."

Richard J. Mouw, "Educating for Justice," September 27, 2006, Opening Convocation address, Fuller Theological Seminary

NOW? (DISCERNMENT)

STEP 1: NOW?

As youth workers, we **Now** have a reputation for going to extraordinary lengths to help students in their faith journeys. One spring, following a powerful weekend camp experience during which lots of kids expressed a desire to follow Christ, I let out all the stops.

Although neither my wife nor my son had ever seen me without a mustache, I decided that during my message at our next group meeting, I was going to shave off my mustache as an illustration of committed faith.

As I talked about our great weekend together, I subtly began to prepare my shaving gear on a small table at the front of the room. As I described the emotions of that Sunday morning at camp, when so many made a public decision to live for Jesus Christ, I started dabbing shaving cream on one side of my mustache.

Kids finally caught on to what I was about to do. The girls started yelling, "No, no!" while the guys screamed, "Go for it!"

Just before I made that first cut, I told them, "Saying you want to belong to Christ but not actually following him is like walking around with only one half of a mustache..." And then I shaved off one half of my own mustache, and left it that way for the rest of my talk.

Yet I have to admit, for years I had been guilty of half-mustache youth ministry. I often told students God's main concern was our response to his love, and then I would focus all I said and most of what I did on that single message. Later, under the rubric of "discipleship," I would try to convince those same kids that following Christ also meant serving our broken world by addressing the needs and hardships of others. But in the way I prioritized my ministry emphases, I was in truth living, teaching, and leading with only half a theological mustache!

TWO *EITHER/OR* EXTREMES

Last summer I informally surveyed youth workers across denominations, asking them how they describe and present the call of the gospel in their ministries. Most of the youth workers I surveyed, especially when they were not prompted toward any viewpoint, tended to land squarely in one of two camps.

The majority of the youth workers I surveyed landed where I was in the early years of my ministry. Typically defining the gospel as the "invitation to accept Christ's sacrifice on the cross," their single-focused description was limited to an individual's internal response to this invitation.

The other group of youth workers, smaller but no less passionate about their perspective, was equally single-focused in describing the essence of the

> "Although evangelism may never simply be equated with labor for justice, it may also never be divorced from it. The relationship between the evangelistic and the societal dimensions of the Christian mission constitutes one of the thorniest areas in the theology and practice of mission."
>
> DAVID BOSCH, *TRANSFORMING MISSION*

gospel as serving others and righting wrongs in God's name. These are two important, even vital, aspects of the gospel's call. Yet when given an open-ended opportunity, just about every youth worker took one "side" that was explicitly opposed to the other. One group emphasized the finished work of Jesus on the cross, and the other the ongoing work of the risen Christ in bringing his kingdom to fulfillment.

While the responses themselves were not all that surprising, I was struck by the extreme polarity of the two viewpoints. I was especially intrigued by the way most people seemed to go out of their way to diminish the importance of the other perspective as they defended their own. Among those who felt a personal faith decision was primary (often citing for support a passage like John 3:16, "... *whoever believes in him shall not perish...*"), there seemed to be a general skepticism toward emphasizing the call to service and justice.

In the same way, youth workers who experienced the gospel as God's mandate to give our lives to serving and caring for others tended to discount those who stressed a "personal faith decision" as more concerned with self than with the kingdom of God. Typically emphasizing the teachings and example of Jesus, like in the parable of the sheep and goats ("whatever you did for the least of these...you did for me," Matthew 25) and Jesus' encounter with people like the Rich Young Ruler ("Go, sell all you have and give to the poor..." Mark 10:21), the call to fulfill the Great Commandment to love God, neighbor, and self (Matthew 22:34-40) took center stage.

Although *both* positions are solidly rooted not only in the Bible but in the instructions and life of Jesus himself, very few in my informal poll expressed any interest in trying to bring these two positions together. These results confirmed my own experience. Those youth workers who **Now** believe a vital personal faith in Jesus Christ is primary tend to fear that those who advocate for justice and service might "water down" the gospel. At the same time, those youth workers who are **Now** convinced of God's concern for the poor and oppressed fear that those who emphasize personal piety inevitably direct others toward a faith that is self-absorbed and narcissistic. This two-way suspicion causes both sides to dig in their heels and easily fall prey to wearing only half a theological mustache.

The Gospel as Personal Piety	The Gospel as Social Justice
Emphasis on the individual	Emphasis on the community
Focus on Jesus as Savior	Focus on Jesus as Lord
Internal response—"Decision"	External response—"Action"
Spiritual disciplines and purity as central spiritual activities	Social engagement and service as central spiritual activities
Devotion to Jesus is the end product of discipleship	Commitment to the poor, oppressed, and suffering is the end product of discipleship

The majority of contemporary evangelical churches and youth ministries (especially in white or middle-class contexts) **Now** stress a distinct personal "decision for Jesus" as the primary calling of the gospel. This focus supersedes or at least preempts an emphasis on God's concern for the poor, marginalized, and oppressed. In some cases it is assumed that once someone "becomes a Christian," then righting wrongs of poverty and oppression will happen as a matter of course. In other situations, because of the way political ideology has stuck its nose under the tent of the church, such social change efforts may even be viewed as something to be avoided. Critics of this emphasis observe that rarely does "personal relationship with Jesus" seem to actually translate into much (if any) commitment to the least, the last, and the lost.

In a similar way, churches and youth ministries who are driven by a commitment to address the needs of the poor and disenfranchised are **Now** viewed with suspicion as being disconnected from an individual alignment with the personal aspects of faith, especially in terms of lifestyle and ethics. The result is these extremes further separate the body of Christ into two camps that regularly find themselves distrustful of (and even disgusted with) each other.

NEW? (REFLECTION)

STEP 2: NEW?

> "We fall into 'sin management'—the right focuses on individual sins and the gospel as an eraser for our individual sins. The left focuses only on social sins. We need to do both."
>
> DALLAS WILLARD, *THE DIVINE CONSPIRACY*

As much as youth workers try to separate these two definitions of the gospel, the gospel itself does not allow such division. Personal piety that does not produce a life committed to peace, justice, and mercy for all struggling people is hollow and self-serving and, as such, is not actually pious at all. At the same time, a commitment to righting wrongs that ignores the call to abandon one's life to Jesus Christ and "fix our thoughts" on him may align itself with God's commitment to the poor and broken but vacillate in its submission to his authority and reign as King. **In other words, neither extreme taken alone represents the gospel at all.** Both are inseparable emphases of the same call—to proclaim a new way of life that is fully devoted to Jesus Christ and to express that devotion by seeking justice as he advances his kingdom toward all people.

GOD RESTORES SHALOM

From the very beginning, God's plan has been to establish his *shalom* (pronounced "sha-lome") over all creation. The word *shalom* is commonly translated as "peace"—but that often reduces it to one of two inadequate definitions: Either we think of it as the absence of war and conflict, or we tend to view it as a sense of personal, subjective peace for us as individuals. In reality, shalom has a much wider meaning that brings **New** depth to our justice. Biblical shalom is far more than just a lack of fighting or a warm and fuzzy feeling

In describing *shalom* and its relationship to justice, Nicholas Wolterstorff, professor of philosophical theology at Yale University, writes:

> The state of *shalom* is the state of flourishing in all dimensions of one's existence: in one's relation to God, in one's relation to one's fellow human beings, in one's relation to nature, and in one's relation to oneself. Evidently justice has something to do with the fact that God's love for each and every one of God's human creatures takes the form of God desiring the shalom of each and every one.[32]

God's shalom is an all-inclusive peace that encompasses our whole selves and all our relationships: with God, with self, with others, and with the world. When humanity fell, that sense of well-being was broken, leaving in its wake darkness, pain, and death. Yet despite our rebellion and the sin-filled consequences that leave the whole of creation "groaning" (Romans 8:22), God has not wavered in his commitment to restore his shalom. We know this from Jesus' own words in Luke 4:18-19:

> "The Spirit of the Lord is on me, because he has anointed me to proclaim good news to the poor. He has sent me to proclaim freedom for the prisoners and recovery of sight for the blind, to set the oppressed free, to proclaim the year of the Lord's favor."

Jesus wants all who are imprisoned and oppressed—physically, relationally, emotionally, or psychologically—to experience the freedom and release of his kingdom shalom. As the pinnacle of God's faithfulness in the face of our lack of faith, shalom was reestablished on the cross when Jesus proclaimed, "It is finished" (John 19:30). Yet those forces and powers that oppress and beat down individuals and societies rob the possibility of shalom. The kingdom of God brings shalom as the experiential reality of being touched by the power of grace, justice, and mercy; the battle is against any system, structure or institution that makes shalom unavailable. That is the call of the kingdom—to follow the call of the Holy Spirit and fight against anything that would stand in the way of shalom for those God loves.

---

[32] Nicholas Wolterstorff, "The contours of justice: An ancient call for shalom," in *God and the Victim: Theological Reflections on Evil, Victimization, Justice, and Forgiveness*, edited by Lisa Barnes Lampman and Michelle D. Shattuck (Grand Rapids: Eerdmans, 1999), 113.

Jesus told his disciples, "Let the little children come to me, and *do not hinder them*, for the kingdom of God belongs to such as these" (Mark 10:14, emphasis added). We must help our students realize that when we ignore or rationalize away the pain and needs in our families, our towns, and around the world, our inaction "hinders" the work of the Spirit in bringing shalom. The call is to do as Jesus did; to gather the children, the lonely, the sick, and the oppressed into our arms and bless them (Mark 10:16) with shalom.

RESTORING SHALOM IN OUR YOUTH MINISTRIES

The shalom that has been regained through Christ is best experienced within a community in which God's gracious commandments are honored and obeyed. When the poor and needy are deprived of their God-given right to flourish, it is both an opportunity and a responsibility for our youth ministries to try to restore divine peace and potential. Far more than just "stuff we do to help poor people," we can help students see justice as one of God's—and our—means to remove the obstacles that prevent others from flourishing.

> "From our covenant relationship with God to our social institutions, shalom is God putting back together a broken world...Precisely because shalom is about the world made right in holiness and truth, it cannot be detached from right relationships, but is preceded by and dependent upon justice."
>
> MARK R. GORNIK, *TO LIVE IN PEACE*

God invites the youth in our ministries to so much more than just an escape from hell, or even a sense of fulfillment now that our eternal status is settled. The in-breaking shalom of the kingdom is not just God rescuing us from our foibles and failures, or "allowing" us to make sure we are saved. *The wonder of the gospel is that the shalom we receive by faith in Christ compels and empowers us to give ourselves away for the sake of the kingdom of God.* E. Stanley Jones writes that the gospel "is not just the way of salvation from sin, but the Way written into our blood, tissues, relationships...We are structured for the kingdom. Jesus and the kingdom are the Way and the life and therefore the truth."[33]

Being true to the gospel means celebrating that God not only rescues us from sin but also creates in us a whole **New** kingdom-driven agenda for all of life. To come to Christ by faith means we accept not only our need for the forgiveness offered on the cross by the Incarnate Word of God, but also that we are lifted by the resurrection into a whole **New** purpose for life. Once we have

---

[33] E. Stanley Jones, *The Unshakable Kingdom and the Unchanging Person* (Nashville: Abingdon, 1972), 52.

tasted the shalom of God, we then find our calling in serving Jesus as he brings his shalom to the world. The gospel is about Jesus Christ and his kingdom—and we invite kids into the trajectory of kingdom service that comes as part of the package of salvation.

To get updated on more recent research about evangelism and justice, check out our free additional Deep Justice resources available at www.cyfm.net

A DEEP SENSE OF RIGHTEOUSNESS

Just as students' interest in kingdom justice will be increased by a deeper understanding of the power of *shalom*, the same is true with a deeper understanding of the word *dikaiosune* (pronounced "dih-ky-oh-sue-nay"). In general, this Greek word used in both the gospels and the epistles is translated "righteousness." While that is an accurate translation, it's not the full story. *Dikaiosune* also means God's just rule—or God's justice.

Let's look at a few of the more well-known verses that include the word *dikaiosune* in light of this expanded, or secondary, meaning. For instance, Jesus teaches, "Blessed are those who hunger and thirst for *dikaiosune*, for they will be filled" (Matthew 5:6) and "But seek first his kingdom and his *dikaiosune*, and all these things will be given to you as well" (Matthew 6:33).

When we insert the word *righteousness* for *dikaiosune* in these two passages, our North American minds often associate it with an individualistic form of "right living" that falls in line with those who equate the gospel with personal salvation. As long as our students do not "smoke, drink, chew, or go with those who do," they're honoring Jesus' intention.

What happens when we insert the word *justice* for *dikaiosune*? Suddenly, our minds jump to a **New** form of "right living" that is much more holistic. We seek to build youth ministries that hunger and thirst to extend God's kingdom to meet others' spiritual, emotional, social, and physical needs. Indeed, that type of New Testament *dikaiosune* echoes the Old Testament *shalom* that allows all to experience the kingdom in its fullness.

"Salvation must...be understood as *shalom* in the Old Testament sense. This does not mean merely salvation of the soul, individual rescue from the evil world, comfort for the troubled conscience, but also the realization of the eschatological *hope* of justice, *humanizing* of man, the *socializing* of humanity, *peace* for all creation."

JÜRGEN MOLTMANN,
THEOLOGY OF HOPE

APPROPRIATING THE NEW: MAKING CHRIST'S MISSION OUR MISSION

Certainly there are countless self-described "Christians" who are more interested in the warm and fuzzy *shalom* and the moralistic *dikaiosune* than God's call to be ambassadors of peace, justice, and mercy. The folly is that this kind of self-centered "faith" is really not faith at all.

> "A fascinating feature of Matthew's summary of Jesus' ministry is not only that it confirms that Jesus' evangelization was centered in 'the good news of the kingdom,' but that it describes Jesus' holistic method: teaching, preaching, and healing. The good news of the kingdom is for the whole person—physically (healing), intellectually (teaching), and spiritually (preaching)."
>
> MORTIMER ARIAS, *THE GOOD NEWS OF THE KINGDOM*

But what about those who *do* care, those who are sincere in their desire to follow Jesus Christ? How do they take seriously the compelling call of the gospel that reflects a **New** self-sacrificing commitment to take on poverty and oppression in our broken world? The answer lies in our ability and commitment to translate our devotion to God into service and justice. We must broaden our perspective and understanding of what it means to follow Jesus to include every aspect of our lives so we are transformed into living a kingdom agenda that is reflected in a sacrificial kingdom lifestyle.

In our youth ministries, it is our responsibility as leaders to present the entire gospel—both personal commitment and social reform—in everything we say, do, and teach. We must help people to follow Jesus as he brings the kingdom to fulfillment. As Ruth Padilla DeBorst writes:

"Why, we asked, need each of us grapple with such issues as injustice, poverty, and hunger? Because God does. Acts of justice spring out of his heart of love. It must be the same with anyone who calls himself or herself God's child. Acts of justice are expressions of true worship. They delight God."[34]

As men and women who have great influence in shaping the lives, faith, and theology of future generations, we must take care to let our kids know that the gospel is *both* repentance *and* social justice, not *either/or*. As our youth ministries live and proclaim God's shalom and *dikaiosune* to a world filled with

---

[34] Ruth Padilla DeBorst, "Scrabble, Injustice, and Me," Ibid., 13.

racism, poverty, oppression, economic injustice, selfishness, abuse, and war, we experience transformation—both as individuals and in our social systems.

WHO? (OBSERVATION)

STEP 3: WHO?

There are few leaders alive today **Who** have worked harder, longer, or more effectively to right wrongs in our broken world than DR. JOHN PERKINS. John is the founder of Mendenhall Ministries, Voice of Calvary Ministries, and Harambee Christian Family Center, and the co-founder and chair of the Christian Community Development Association. An internationally known civil rights leader who has experienced racism himself as a black man in America, John has written nine books, including *A Quiet Revolution, Let Justice Roll Down,* and *With Justice for All.* As someone **Who** watched his brother die in his arms after being shot by a white police officer and was beaten himself and left for dead by his white Mississippi neighbors, John is a national treasure of inspiration and insight into deep justice that reconciles us both to God and to one another.

"I've become convinced that if the *good news* of Jesus were carried in a newspaper today, it wouldn't be hidden in the religion section (although it would no doubt cause a ruckus there). It would be a major story in every section, from world news (What is the path to peace, and how are we responding to our neighbors in need?) to national and local news (How are we treating children, poor people, minorities, the last, the lost, the least? How are we treating our enemies?), the food section (Do our diets reflect concern for God's planet and our poor neighbors, and have we invited any of them over for dinner lately?), the entertainment and sports sections (What is the point of our entertainment, and what values are we strengthening in sports?), and even the business section (Are we serving the wrong master: money rather than God?)."

BRIAN MCLAREN, *THE SECRET MESSAGE OF JESUS*

John, so often as youth workers, we tend to take the complexity of the gospel and kingdom justice and oversimplify it. Given your decades of experience and reflection, do you think the gospel is more about individual salvation, or is it more about reforming abusive and oppressive systems, or is it equally about both?

The short answer to your question is that it's about both. Within the evangelical community, we have created this dichotomy. Yet Jesus wants us to love God with our whole heart and soul, and as we do that, we will love others who are absolutely different from us.

> The marvelous kingdom blend of commitment to both personal salvation and social reform is often easier to find in the church outside of the United States. Seek out opportunities for face-to-face or e-mail conversation with leaders from other countries to learn ways they are already embodying this **New** *both/and.*

What happens when youth ministries emphasize just one half of that dichotomy?

I think we are already seeing that lived out in fundamentalism on one side, and liberalism on the other. In reality, both of those two extremes—meeting spiritual needs and meeting physical needs—are two halves of the whole gospel. Jesus illustrated that whole gospel in Luke 10, the story of the Good Samaritan. When describing what love for God and neighbor looked like to the expert in the law who had questioned him, Jesus pointed to the sacrifice of the Samaritan as the model of God's intent for how we are to treat each other. The expert thought he knew what love for God looked like, but Jesus made it clear that true love for God is expressed through the Samaritan man's love for his neighbor.

Why are we so prone to do one half without the other?

It's our pride. If you listen closely, folks who are "liberal" pride themselves as being better than those "conservatives," and the "conservatives" see those "liberals" as not being quite all they need to be. Each side has this sort of imperialistic view to it, as if they are the only ones who know what's right. I find that same dislike of the "other side" in issues about women in leadership and homosexuality. It lacks the humility that ought to accompany the gospel.

What advice would you give a youth worker who's been emphasizing one half of the gospel but now wants to help his or her kids and ministry both love God and love others?

Fundamentally, we have to understand that all people are created in God's image. That gives us all equal dignity before God. I don't see how you can accept that other humans are created in God's image with inherent dignity and then exploit them. Once we view others as created in God's image, we won't want them to live without him, and we won't want them to live in unjust social structures. So we're going to want to embody both halves of the gospel.

> To download and hear the full audio interview with John, check out our free additional Deep Justice resources available at www.cyfm.net

What should a youth ministry that wants to embody both loving God and loving others do?

We can't do it apart from living with and interacting with people in different classes and races. Tribalism, and the sense that we are superior to one another, keeps us apart. Only people who have interactions with folks who are different from them can get rid of injustice.

Martin Luther King Jr. claimed that 11:00 on Sunday mornings was the most segregated hour of the week. Do you think that's still true 40 years later?

It's not as true now as it was then, but he still might be right. But I have hope for the church as I watch the students who come and visit our work in Jackson, Mississippi. They are generally middle- and upper-class students, but once they come and live among those who are oppressed, they usually find a creative way to express their sense of justice. And they are healed in the process.

When it comes to building relationships with folks who are different and understanding that we are all created in God's image, is it more incumbent on those who are white to reach out, or equally incumbent on both whites and people of color?

On a practical level, since justice is an issue about not just race but economics, it's more incumbent upon whites to take the first steps. But whites cannot heal themselves. They need blacks and Latinos and Asians. It would be unjust of those of us who are people of color to remove ourselves and expect whites to heal themselves. They can't do it. So we all end up being equally responsible.

Can youth workers help their kids experience the fullness of the kingdom and its invitation to love both God and others if they aren't doing it themselves?

That question is a lot like the question about the chicken and the egg. In an ideal world, it would be the adult leader who would be really leading. But sometimes it's in the midst of serving with kids among the poor that adults really get transformed. When we have students and youth workers come down to Mississippi, it's often the youth worker who's most impacted.

John, as a black man who has been physically beaten by whites just because of your skin color, how have your personal experiences with injustice deepened your commitment to eliminate the dichotomy between loving God and loving others?

I think I've been blessed because, even as I began to confront racism, and racists began to confront me, I never felt inferior. The theology that lies behind the song, "Jesus loves the little children, all the children of the world. Red and yellow, black and white, all are precious in his sight" has always been a part of me. I think that's why I do what I do.

HOW? (APPLICATION)

STEP 4: HOW?

DEEP JUSTICE APPLICATION QUESTIONS

1. Do you agree that most Christians tend to view the gospel as *either* about personal salvation *or* about social reform? Why or why not?

2. When have you seen, felt, or experienced God's shalom? In general, what keeps us from experiencing shalom? What does God want our youth ministries to be like and do in order to help restore shalom?

3. If you understand Matthew 5:6 as "Blessed are those who hunger and thirst for *justice*, for they will be filled," how would that change your own life and your ministry?

4. Chap writes, "We must broaden our perspective and understanding of what it means to follow Jesus to include every aspect of our lives so we are transformed into living a kingdom agenda that is reflected in a sacrificial kingdom lifestyle." As you think about the other youth workers you know, how well do they live out a kingdom agenda in every aspect of their lives? How successful are you in living out such an all-encompassing lifestyle of sacrifice?

5. Given the gap between our broken world and God's shalom, restoring wholeness to all people around the world is not something any one youth ministry can accomplish. What other churches, ministries, and social service organizations can you partner with to seek God's justice in your town, in our country, and around the world?

6. Of the following list of Deep Justice Recommended Action Steps that flow from this chapter, which would best help you as a kingdom follower right wrongs? How about for your youth ministry?

DEEP JUSTICE RECOMMENDED ACTION STEPS:

For Yourself

- Think back to your first experiences in Christian community and the mentors and leaders who shaped your view of what it means to be a kingdom follower. Consider whether they leaned toward either personal salvation or social reform, and how that still influences you today.

- How does the tension of the *both/and* gospel play out in your theology and actions? Make a two-column list of your beliefs and behaviors that lean one way or the other. How do you feel about the balance of the list? How does it fit with your understanding of the gospel?

- Spend some time thinking about how your preferred version of the Jesus-of-Choice from chapter 4 affects your ability to view the full *both/and* gospel. How, if at all, are the two related? How can you gain a broader view of Jesus that would similarly broaden your view of the gospel?

For Your Youth Ministry

- Ask your senior pastor to answer the question that drives this chapter: Is the gospel more about personal salvation or social reform? Think about how your pastor's answer influences both your church and your youth ministry.

- Ask your students the same question, possibly even by devoting one youth group meeting to a debate over the question. Even if students are inclined to say that it's "both," don't let them take that position initially. Force them to choose either personal salvation or social reform, and let them feel the frustration that comes from such a dichotomy, before you let them assume the position that it's both.

- Look back on the last three to six months of your ministry's calendar through the lenses of personal salvation and social reform. If you have emphasized one more than the other, identify ways you could embody a more healthy *both/and* kingdom balance in the next three to six months.

- Bring several newspapers to one of your group's meetings. Read the quote from Brian McLaren in the sidebar on page 91 to your students and then have them scan the newspapers, looking for ways that personal salvation and social reform are relevant to many types of newspaper stories (such as corruption in sports, shady financial decisions in business, the materialism that compels us to want expensive cars shown in newspaper ads). Brainstorm ways students can help others in the church (including their own parents) view daily living through the lenses of kingdom justice.

- Send an e-mail to your students' parents with a few paragraphs from this chapter. Encourage families to talk about how they tend to view the gospel: Is it salvation or social reform or both? Ask each family to consider making a justice covenant together, specifying the choices they are making together to right wrongs around them. You might want to give them tangible ideas ranging from baby steps of recycling glass and paper to major steps of contacting a local private school and offering an annual scholarship for a kid in need.

- The next time there's an election or political issue causing controversy in your city, talk with your students about how the gospel does (or some might say does not) relate to politics. Since the kingdom is about both evangelism and social action, encourage your students to call or write letters (perhaps along with their parents) to the relevant government officials to help change systems that perpetuate poverty.

- Read about the ministry of reconciliation Paul describes in 2 Corinthians 5 and design a talk or small-group discussion about a holistic understanding of what reconciling the world to God through Christ looks like in your city. You may even want to have students talk about what their school campuses would look like if students were reconciled both to God and to one another. Brainstorm the obstacles and systems that currently prevent this type of deep reconciliation, as well as key city or school leaders who might be interested in righting the wrongs that perpetuate injustice and divisions at your students' schools.

HOW DO WE HELP STUDENTS MOVE FROM DOING KINGDOM THINGS TO BEING KINGDOM PEOPLE?

BY KARA POWELL

NOW? (DISCERNMENT)

STEP 1: NOW?

Have you ever wondered why your kids seem fired up for deep justice after spending a day feeding the homeless, but the next week they ditch the chance to right wrongs on the street and instead go to Magic Mountain?

Maybe you've found that even though your kids say they "want to make a difference," the majority want to make a trip to the mall first.

Kids today are known to draw their significance from helping others, but most of yours seem drawn first to video games.

Portions of this chapter are derived from an article by Kara Powell, Terry Linhart, Dave Livermore, and Brad Griffin in the March/April 2007 issue of *The Journal of Student Ministries*.

The evidence **Now** points to two conflicting trends: *either* kids are selfish *or* they are selfless. As youth workers who want to help students dig into deeper kingdom justice, we're left wondering: Which one is it?

The truth is: They are *both*. No kid is 100 percent selfish or 100 percent selfless. As they navigate issues of identity, autonomy, and belonging, adolescents **Now** swing between self-denial and self-gratification—sometimes within the same five minutes.[35]

The fact that adolescents can think about others is partly why it's not all that hard **Now** to get them to take some baby steps in righting wrongs – to give some money to sponsor a kid overseas, or to choose coffee that is fair trade. The fact that they're still self-focused partly explains why they trip and fall and never race toward kingdom justice as a lifestyle.

MOVING THE NEEDLE

This tension between kids' ability to care about others and their ability to care about themselves can be pictured like a gauge with a needle that wavers between selfishness and selflessness.

Kids Waver Between Selfishness and Selflessness

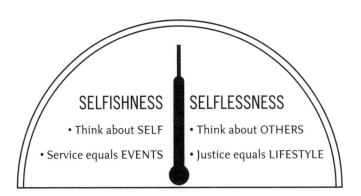

SELFISHNESS | SELFLESSNESS

• Think about SELF   • Think about OTHERS

• Service equals EVENTS   • Justice equals LIFESTYLE

---

[35] According to Chap, identity, autonomy, and belonging are the main issues adolescents work through during the process of "individuation."

As Tony Campolo describes later in this chapter, it's ultimately the Holy Spirit who moves the needle for kids. Yet the Holy Spirit often works in and through (and though we hate to admit it, sometimes despite) us as kingdom people. When we as youth workers **Now** try to create an environment in which the Holy Spirit is more able to move students from doing kingdom things to being kingdom people, we tend to resort to a few typical strategies.

Typical Strategy 1: Learn More Scripture

I love Scripture. As you know from chapter 3, I love the way the story of Scripture prods us to right wrongs.

But learning more Scripture **Now** is not enough to catapult average kids—or average adults—from doing kingdom work to being kingdom people. We know that from an experiment showing how rarely people stop to help someone in need who crosses their path. Literally.

In the experiment, students at a New Jersey graduate school were asked to give spontaneous, unplanned speeches in another building on campus. Students were told to head to the new building quickly, since they only had a few minutes before delivering their "pop" speeches.

The two researchers had "planted" a man along the path to the new building. Not only was he lying on the ground and wearing disheveled clothing, but he also appeared to be semi-comatose. Every student who walked that path had a decision to make: With the deadline of a spontaneous speech on their minds, would they stop or would they keep walking?

The majority did not stop. Those students who were told they had only a few minutes to get to the new building were especially unlikely to stop and help.

That might not be all that startling. But I've left out a few important details that might surprise you. First, the study didn't take place at just any graduate school. It was conducted at Princeton Theological Seminary, meaning the students—both those who stopped and those who didn't—were likely preparing for ministry.

Second, the researchers had given the soon-to-be-ministers a topic for their spontaneous speeches: the Good Samaritan. So those students were probably mulling over the Good Samaritan narrative *even as they walked past the man lying on the ground.*[36]

---

[36] H. Newton Malony, *The Psychology of Religion for Ministry* (Mahwah, New Jersey: Paulist Press, 1995), 60-62.

It's not that the seminary students weren't committed to God. And it's not that they didn't know what the Bible says about helping others in need. They were just about to stand up and preach about it. In the midst of studying Scripture, there was still a deep disconnect between what they knew in their heads and what they showed with their lives.

Jesus ran into this gap between knowledge and action constantly, especially when he dealt with religious leaders. He reserved his harshest words for those who claimed to *know about God* while their lives showed they didn't really *know God*.

If you want proof that simply studying Scripture isn't enough to move your students toward becoming kingdom people, check out Matthew 23, a passage commonly known as the "Seven Woes." Jesus starts his speech to the crowds and his disciples with some relatively positive words: "The teachers of the law and the Pharisees sit in Moses' seat. So you must be careful to do everything they tell you" (Matthew 23:2-3a).

If I were one of the teachers in the crowd, hearing those words would cause my shoulders to relax a bit. Finally, this Jesus of Nazareth wasn't condemning me! Instead, he was acknowledging my authority as a successor of Moses to teach the law. He was even commanding his followers to obey me.

But then Jesus lets loose.

"But do not do what they do, for they do not practice what they preach" (Matthew 23:3b).

So much for relaxing.

In the rest of the chapter, Jesus gives seven examples of the gap between what the Pharisees teach and how they live. When it comes to helping kids right wrongs, I am fascinated by Matthew 23:27 when Jesus says these teachers are "hypocrites" who are "like whitewashed tombs, which look beautiful on the outside but on the inside are full of the bones of the dead and everything unclean."

> "Anyone out in the open who...touches a human bone or a grave, will be unclean for seven days."
>
> NUMBERS 19:16

In Jesus' day, anyone who stepped on a grave became ceremonially unclean for seven days. In order to prevent the accidental tromping of graves, graves were whitewashed (painted white) every year before Passover to make them more visible, especially at night. On the outside these graves appeared clean and pristine. On the inside they were full of rotting corpses and filthy earthworms.

When it comes to righting wrongs 2000 years later, we often try teaching more Scripture to move kids' needles toward justice as a lifestyle. But if the Holy Spirit hasn't really permeated who they are and changed them into kingdom people, no matter how pretty they may look when they serve, there's decay down deep inside.

Typical Strategy 2: More Chances to Serve

If more Bible isn't enough to move kids toward deep justice, maybe giving them more chances to serve will do the trick. Unfortunately, as with the first strategy, research tells us otherwise.

As we saw in chapter 3, the way we sometimes devalue the contributions of those with whom we partner can make them feel dehumanized and separated from God's kingdom story as it unfolds on earth. But if we are really honest, some of us **Now** care more about the transformation that occurs in our own students than what happens among those who are supposed to benefit most immediately from our justice ministries. At least we can be sure that short-term mission (STM) trips are effective in moving the needle for the 13- and 17-year-olds we load onto buses and airplanes for a week of service and social justice.

Maybe, maybe not. When Kurt Ver Beek and his team from Calvin College studied more than 100 North American STMers, they examined 11 factors, including their levels of giving and the time spent volunteering, reading about missions, and praying for missions. In the case of financial giving to the organization that sponsored their trip, 16 percent reported that their giving significantly increased after the trip; 44 percent reported a slight increase in giving; 40 percent reported no increase.[37]

Ver Beek then compared the STMers' impressions of their own giving with the financial records of the mission organizations. According to the records, only 25 percent of the participants gave at all to the mission organization that sponsored their trip. Financial giving to the STMers' own churches increased an average of 1 percent, with six churches experiencing an increase in giving and eleven churches actually receiving less money.[38]

---

[37] Of course, financial giving is not the only indicator of whether the needle's tilted toward justice as a lifestyle.

[38] Kurt Ver Beek, "The Impact of Short-Term Missions: A Case Study of House Construction in Honduras After Hurricane Mitch," *Missiology* Volume 34, no. 4, October 2006, 490.

Ver Beek's findings run counter to several previous studies that cite the life-transformation created by STM. Yet critics of previous studies point out that such studies often rely on small sample sizes and are generally done right after the STM trip while participants are still on a "missions high." In addition, previous studies typically have asked participants to rate how their own lives have changed without checking their perceptions against other empirical measures of change. Such self-report data may be biased, as was possibly the case with the 127 STMers who described their increased giving to Ver Beek.

Further studies about short-term mission trips should leave us questioning whether the "If we send them, they will grow" mantra is really true. Consider the following:

- The explosive growth in the number of STM trips among both kids and adults has not been accompanied by similar explosive growth in the number of career missionaries.

- It's not clear whether or not participation in STM trips causes participants to give more money to alleviate poverty once life returns to "normal."

- Participating in a STM trip does not seem to reduce participants' tendencies toward materialism.[39]

These provocative findings make us wonder: What **New** approaches can we take to create space for the Holy Spirit to transform kids into kingdom people long after that "social justice high" wears off?

> Implications of these research findings are discussed in two articles that originally appeared in the "CYFM E-Journal" titled "Tough Questions to Ask Before Your Next Missions Trip" and "If We Send Them, They Will Grow...Maybe." These articles are available for free as part of our Deep Justice resources at www.cyfm.net.

NEW? (REFLECTION)

STEP 2: NEW?

[39] Robert J. Priest, Terry Dischinger, Steve Rasmussen, C.M. Brown, "Researching the Short-Term Mission Movement," *Missiology* Volume 34, number 4, October 2006, 431-450.

KIDS AND JUSTICE: WHAT MTV HAS TO SAY

It's not just those of us in the church who have something to say about moving youth from doing kingdom things to being kingdom people. MTV has a voice too.

In 2006, MTV conducted a nationwide survey in order to understand how and why youth in America are already active in social causes.[40] Here's what that study found:

- Of the kids they surveyed, 70 percent say it's important to help others in need. Only 19 percent are "very involved" in doing so.

- The Top Five reasons kids are not involved are:

    1. It's just not for me (18 percent).

    2. I like to hang out with friends (15 percent).

    3. I don't have enough time (14 percent).

    4. I don't know how to get started (14 percent).

    5. I want to see concrete results (8 percent).

- 62 percent say the issues that matter most to them are those that have touched them or someone they know.

- 70 percent of kids involved in activism report that their parents' encouragement played a major factor in their choice to get involved.

- The top two factors that would motivate kids to be more involved are:

    1. If they could do the activity with their friends.

    2. If they had more time to volunteer, or more convenient volunteer activities.[41]

As we think about our roles in creating space for the Holy Spirit to transform self-centered kids into kingdom people, one **New** theme emerges from the MTV findings: Justice needs to hit kids close to home. It needs to be in their

---

[40] MTV's national survey was comprised of 1,308 12-24-year-olds who completed online surveys and 98 students who were interviewed personally.

[41] This research can be accessed for free at http://www.mtv.com/thinkmtv/research/.

home *literally*—as we invite parents both to exemplify and to encourage their own kids to right wrongs around them. It needs to hit close to home *thematically*—as we help kids understand how particular injustices relate to their lives. It needs to hit home *logistically*—as we offer opportunities that can be done at various times and at various levels of intensity. It needs to hit home *personally*—as we expose our kids to people who have been oppressed, thereby giving injustice a face and a name. And justice ministry needs to hit home *relationally*—as we help kids right wrongs in partnership with their friends.

> Many of us have found that the parents of our kids are one of the chief obstacles to deep justice. Whether it is parents' fear of the unknown, or their hesitation to have their family's status quo shaken, often justice isn't all that close to our kids' homes. To find out more about how to help parents catch a vision for deep justice, check out the free resources available at www.cyfm.net.

CONVERSATIONS THAT HIT HOME

To help engage in **New** conversations that both hit home and provide opportunities for the Holy Spirit toward kingdom justice, we recommend an experiential education framework originally proposed by Laura Joplin[42], and later modified and used by Terry Linhart[43] on youth STM trips.

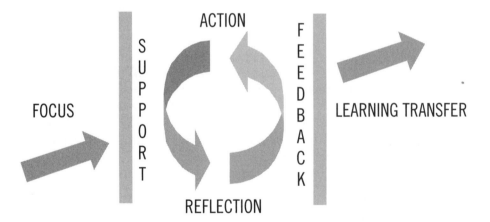

Figure 1: The Joplin (1995) model, modified by Linhart (2005).

> To learn more about this model and how to apply it to deep justice with your own students, check out the Deep Justice resources available for free at www.cyfm.net.

[42] Joplin, L. (1995). "On defining experiential education." In K. Warren & M. Sakofs & J. S. Hunt Jr. (Eds.), *The theory of experiential education* (pp. 15-22). Dubuque, IA: Kendall/Hunt Publishing Company.

[43] Linhart, T. D. (2005). "Planting seeds: The curricular hope of short-term mission experiences in youth ministry." *Christian Education Journal*, Series 3, 256-272.

Component 1: FOCUS

As students start doing justice work, we need to help them FOCUS and prepare for both the victories and challenges they will experience. Some key topics that could be included in this **New** FOCUS time are:

- Identifying our motivations for serving (both the shared motivation we have as a youth ministry and the honest reasons individuals have for doing justice work).

- Honestly exploring some of our fears and anxieties about what it means to seek God's justice for the broken and brokenhearted.

- Seeking to understand what God is already doing in those we will be meeting and serving.

- Identifying ways to ensure that we don't objectify or exploit those we serve, while also being intentional about our own growth.

If we're entering a different ethnic culture or economic class, efforts to increase cross-cultural understanding as part of our FOCUS can deepen our kingdom impact. According to David A. Livermore in *Serving with Eyes Wide Open*, youth ministries often lack "cultural intelligence," or "CQ." As a result we may underestimate the differences between our own culture and the culture of those we are serving—causing us to offend or unintentionally insult those in the other culture. Or we overestimate the differences between the cultures, causing an artificial distance to develop between "us" and "them." As youth workers we can help students FOCUS on cross-cultural understanding by learning how our own culture shapes us, understanding some basic differences among cultures as a whole, and identifying key differences between our culture and the other culture.[44]

During this FOCUS time, we may also want to encourage our students to keep written journals of their thoughts and feelings as they think about what lies ahead. Or we might want our group to study certain chunks of Scripture or even memorize passages that seem especially relevant to our justice work.

---

[44] For extensive insights on how to develop cultural intelligence in your youth ministry, see David A. Livermore, *Serving With Eyes wide Open* (Grand Rapids: Baker Books, 2006)

Component 2: ACTION-REFLECTION

A main component in creating space for the Holy Spirit to move students toward deep justice is the ACTION-REFLECTION process. In this ongoing cycle, students are placed in a situation or activity in which they are purposefully stretched by using a new set of skills or by exposure to **New** injustices.

Whether it's flirting with a new girl at school or talking with a homeless person over sack lunches, students are constantly making meaning out of their experiences. Though they are usually unconscious of this process, students are continually engaged in a highly personal, ongoing internal "conversation" about who they are in relation to God and others. Since these thoughts often go unspoken, students may draw conclusions from their experiences that do not reflect reality. As adult youth workers walking alongside students in the midst of **New** justice experiences, we can help the Holy Spirit move the needle by asking questions that help them decipher the meaning behind what they've experienced.

One way to help students more accurately interpret their justice experiences is to ask three **New** questions:

1. What?

2. So what?

3. Now what?[45]

> According to Dr. Duane Elmer of Trinity Evangelical Divinity School, we who seek deep justice should remember a few principles:
>
> 1. All of us are products of our unique cultural heritages, which dictate how we see and interact with the world.
>
> 2. We tend to think everyone else sees and interacts with the world the same way we do.
>
> 3. Withholding judgment can be the best gift we give to another person.
>
> 4. Asking why another person behaves in a certain way helps us suspend judgment and learn more about that person's cultural heritage.
>
> DUANE ELMER, *CROSS-CULTURAL CONNECTIONS*

By asking "What?" students have a chance to talk about what they actually saw, heard, smelled, and felt. In asking "So what?" students have an opportunity to think about the difference this experience can make in their lives. By reflecting upon "Now what?" students can consider how they want to live, act, or be kingdom people in the weeks and months to come.

---

[45] This 3-question reflection exercise has been popularized by the Campus Outreach Opportunity League.

> "I'm often at national conventions where short-term missions organizations are exhibiting. When I walk up to talk to ministry reps from these organizations, I ask them how the national church is engaged in what they're doing. Consistently I hear, 'Oh yes, we're very committed to working with the national churches there. We ask them if they want to be involved.' Did you catch that? We ask them if *they* want to be involved. Maybe we should start by asking if *we* should be involved at all, and if so, how?"
>
> DAVID A. LIVERMORE,
> *SERVING WITH EYES WIDE OPEN*

> "The ethics of Jesus are the ethics of the kingdom; and Jesus expected his followers to take them seriously, not only in his generation but in all generations."
>
> JOHN BRIGHT,
> *THE KINGDOM OF GOD*

Component 3: SUPPORT-FEEDBACK

To facilitate the ACTION-REFLECTION cycle, Joplin recommends surrounding the discussions and experiences with walls of SUPPORT and FEEDBACK. The support usually comes from other people involved in the experience, such as other students, adult leaders, and community members.

Unfortunately, many youth workers who long to move students' needles toward deeper justice overlook the importance of high quality, ongoing feedback. As the ACTION-REFLECTION cycle continues throughout the learning process, we must jump in with the students and help them talk about their reflections. Good feedback offered in the context of supportive conversations can help students see the systemic injustices that contribute to the wrongs they've tried to right through the ACTION of Component 2.

Component 4: DEBRIEF

When the action component is completed, the students begin the process of DEBRIEF. Different from the reflection time (which many of us call "debriefing"), the DEBRIEF used in the Joplin model is an organized process of identifying what learning has happened, discussing it with others, and evaluating it. This process can be done individually but is most effectively done in community.

Component 5: LEARNING TRANSFER

Part of the reason we so often fail to move kids toward deeper justice is we ignore the final component that makes justice work meaningful: LEARNING TRANS-FER. Since most of the significant learning during justice work takes place in a context different from students' normal day-to-day environments, the students often don't know how to transfer the learning to their own lives. If we're going to help create space for the Holy Spirit to transform kids into kingdom people, we need to gather with them regularly to translate what they have seen, heard, and felt into deeper justice every day. Whether we do this with one student at a time or with large groups, LEARNING TRANSFER is time consuming. But we'll never help kids embrace justice as a **New** lifestyle without it.

WHO? (OBSERVATION)

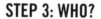

Who has done more to help move kids from doing kingdom work to becoming kingdom people—the church or MTV?

You might be surprised by TONY CAMPOLO'S answer. (On second thought, if you know much about Tony, you might not be so surprised after all.) As a nationally renowned speaker, longtime professor of sociology at Eastern University, and founder of the Evangelical Association for the Promotion of Education, Dr. Anthony Campolo has spent the last forty years motivating the church to care about those outside its walls. During that time, Tony has encountered plenty of youth ministries that create space for the Holy Spirit to move kids' needles from doing kingdom work to being kingdom people. But as you'll read below, he's also bumped into youth workers and kids who seem to prefer splashing around in shallow justice waters.

To download and hear the full audio interview with Tony, check out our free additional Deep Justice resources available at www.cyfm.net.

Tony, the media sends mixed messages about kids today. Some reports label them selfish and self-focused while others call them selfless. What do you think about kids today—are they selfish, selfless, or both?

It's all across the spectrum. I think to generalize about young people is a serious mistake. I find that the studies collecting empirical data show that in general there is an egocentricity to young people. However, the same studies indicate that young people with deep religious convictions have moved in a very altruistic direction. So, you can say one thing about young people in general, but another thing about young people who have deep religious orientations.

In the midst of relationship with Jesus making a difference in kids' levels of altruism, why do many youth workers find that their kids would rather go to Disneyland for a weekend than feed the homeless for a weekend?

I think a lot depends on where you live. I've observed regional differences in terms of how young people look at life. I think the Eastern seaboard has nurtured in young people a more serious orientation to social problems. In some parts of the country, like California, the segregation of the affluent in the suburbs and the poor is very dramatic. In cities in the Northeast, the interaction is much, much more prevalent, and this of course leads to young people becoming more conscious about the needs of the poor because they see the poor. It's very hard to get excited about doing something for the poor and the oppressed if you don't see them on a constant basis. But when you have to ride with them on the subway trains and see the homeless on the streets—when you are confronting poverty constantly—you will be more inclined to respond to those needs.

I find that in certain newer sections of the country, the segregation between the middle class and the underclass is much more pronounced. And that of course disengages young people from where the needs really are.

In thinking about the kingdom of God, what's the difference between simply doing kingdom tasks and being kingdom people?

The difference is that those who are into good works often do not have an overarching view of what the kingdom is all about. To be kingdom people is to be committed to the transformation of the world that *is* into the world that *ought to be*. It's to be involved in recognizing that when Jesus came into the world, he came not to get people into some kingdom in the sky somewhere. He came to transform people into agents of change who will work toward the realization of the social justice dimensions of Scripture.

> "God's kingdom is a new society that Jesus wants to create in *this* world—within human history, not after the Second Coming or a future apocalypse or anything else. But right now."
>
> BRIAN D. MCLAREN AND TONY CAMPOLO, *ADVENTURES IN MISSING THE POINT*

There are people who are trying to actualize what many of us call the "Isaiah covenant" outlined in Isaiah 65:17-25 where there's a call to change the world into a society in which children do not die in infancy, old people live out their lives in health, people have decent housing and good jobs, environmentalism is a reality, and people live with hope for the future. We don't do good works in order to get people to listen to the gospel. Instead, the gospel is the good news that God is at work in the world through people to transform this world into a society that actualizes what the Hebrew prophets were all about.

Anyone who reads Scripture seriously can't help but notice the themes of justice and care for the poor. Some youth workers tend to think that if we just teach more Scripture, then kids will become people who transform the world from what it is to what God wants it to be. What would you say to someone who thinks the key to helping kids become kingdom people is to teach them more Scripture?

> "See, I will create new heavens and a new earth..."
>
> ISAIAH 65:17A

Well, my answer is that the concept of praxis must be at work. By praxis, I mean the combination of Scriptural reflection in the context of social action. Reading Scripture divorced from actual experience will not do it. Nor will involvement with justice work without biblical reflection.

Real change happens when people are put to work, and in the context of working, look over passages of Scripture and are asked to discuss, "In light of what you've seen and what you've done as you've worked among the poor, what do you think this passage of Scripture has to say about what you have just seen, what you have just experienced, and what you have just done?" It's reflection in the context of action, rather than reflection without action, that is the core of transformational Bible study on this issue.

Do you think that can be done ahead of time as kids are thinking about serving? Can we as youth workers prepare them even before they are hands-on with the poor to do some of that praxis?

Yes, I think that praxis always presupposes what we call in sociology—and what Robert Merton, one of the deans of American sociology once called—the "serendipity pattern" of investigation. That serendipity pattern works like this: You read Scripture, you discuss it and say, "This is what I think it says." And then you go into the existential situation, and you begin to recast your understanding of the Scripture in light of that setting. Then you come back and ask, "What did we think about this Scripture prior to our involvement, and how has our perspective on the Scripture changed?" So that it's think first, then act, then reflect, then come back and recast your thinking, then act again. That process goes on endlessly.

What do we do in youth ministry that hinders this feedback loop in which Scripture informs our justice work, and our justice work informs our understanding of Scripture?

I think youth pastors are sometimes afraid and unable to recognize that there needs to be structural change in order for there to be social justice. It's not enough to work on the micro level. When youth ministers go to a third-world country, it is important for them to see the ways the political, social, and economic structures on the macro level create and maintain poverty. If all they do is see things on the micro level, they will fail to grasp the real causes of poverty. Doing micro projects is very good, and gives people an opportunity to see the pain and suffering of people. But to understand and see the social forces that create such poverty is very, very important. In most cases, young people very seldom grasp the macro situation.

For instance, a situation they are not likely to grasp is the relationship between the poverty in a place like Zimbabwe and the free-trade policies advocated by the U.S. government. Free trade, of course, says we do not want any barriers or any protective tariffs. The reality is that the U.S. subsidizes wheat farmers to the tune of $18 billion a year, which makes it possible for them to sell wheat in places like Zimbabwe at a much lower rate than the wheat and rice produced indigenously. This drives local farmers out of business, creating poverty. It's great for American farmers, and creates great markets for them because they can sell their products so cheaply, because their products are subsidized. But it's hell for farmers in Zimbabwe.

> "What can be done to eliminate poverty, rather than to merely relieve it for a season? Can we, like the adage says, not merely give starving families fish to eat now and then, but actually teach them how to fish so that they can feed themselves?"
>
> BRIAN D. MCLAREN AND TONY CAMPOLO, *ADVENTURES IN MISSING THE POINT*

I find that most youth workers haven't a clue as to what macro economics are all about, and how macro economic factors create the poverty in third-world countries. They don't understand why third-world peoples are angry with Americans. They listen to the President of the United States who says people out there hate us because they hate democracy. Well, it's deeper than that. They hate a powerful country that is able to control international trade in such a way as to increase poverty in the third world while it aggrandizes itself.

The ways that macro factors controlled by politics and economics in third-world countries and in our country foster poverty are rarely understood by most youth workers. As a result, what is generated is pity instead of anger. We should be angry at what is being done to these people by forces beyond their control. And we should be coming back to this country and not simply saying, "We're going to do more to raise money for the poor church in Haiti, or the Dominican Republic, or wherever." Instead, we should be saying, "We are going to sit down with our congressman or congresswoman and ask some very serious questions as to why the United States maintains certain economic arrangements with these countries that cause so much poverty."

Can you give a couple of tangible examples that get beyond what students *should* be doing to what they *actually are* doing?

There was a group of students at Eastern University who, through a stockholders' action, were able to bring about massive changes in the way a certain corporation functioned in the Dominican Republic. They were so effective that the company ended up spending over $100 million a year over a ten-year period investing in health programs, education programs, and the restructuring of the entire economy of the eastern half of the country. As a result, the country was totally transformed.

Right now a group of students in a Christian student organization called SPEAK has been very active in the peace process in Northern Ireland. They have arranged for representatives from the conflicting parties to come share their positions, and then will help organize peace talks between the two parties in that country, held at Eastern University. This is an example of what students are able to do.

What is the role of the Holy Spirit in moving kids from doing kingdom work to being kingdom people?

I am fascinated by the ways that mystical experiences with Christ transform young people into ardent social activists and evangelists. We have to recognize that we need more than just a socially conscious youth worker who has a good program. We need young people to be invaded by the Holy Spirit, and inwardly motivated. I really believe the Holy Spirit is a transforming force in people's lives and, when the Spirit of Christ is alive in people, they become very aware of injustices. They become very sensitive to the needs of the poor and oppressed.

I don't want the church to simply become just another social activist group. I want it to be packed with people who are filled with the Spirit that has sensitized them to injustices in the system and to the sufferings of the poor. Increasingly we're finding that as we nurture intimate spirituality, one of the consequences is not this "me and Jesus" faith where Jesus becomes my best friend, but a process whereby Christ becomes a motivating force within people that drives them into ministry with needy people.

What else do youth workers need to know about deep social justice with their kids and communities?

I think they need to know that their young people don't know what's going on in the world. They don't read newspapers. They don't ever discuss the crucial events of the day. As a case in point, most young people haven't a clue that, of the 22 industrialized nations, the United States is dead last in the proportion of its national budget that it assigns to helping the poor in the third world. The average young person in the United States thinks America is the most generous nation on the face of the earth, but in terms of our national budget, we are the least generous of all the industrialized nations. They aren't aware of these things, they don't get angry at these things.

Point blank, I'm not impressed with youth workers. I find that just like teenagers, they don't know what's going on in the world. Youth ministry is far too often a matter of fun and games. When I go to youth ministry conferences, I sometimes get depressed because I find that youth workers are primarily interested in techniques. They seldom want to deal with the issues. They often evade the hard-nosed facts of what's going on in the world.

As a matter of fact, I think MTV may do more to help kids become sensitive to the needs of the world than youth workers. If you're asking me who is more likely turning young people on to poverty issues, I'll have to say it's Bono of U2 rather than youth workers. Youth workers are pressured into maximizing big turn outs at the youth gatherings at their churches, and that doesn't usually come by making kids sensitive to the needs of the poor and the oppressed. That's a very sad thing, indeed.

HOW? (APPLICATION)

STEP 4: HOW?

DEEP JUSTICE APPLICATION QUESTIONS

1. When have you glimpsed the tension between selfishness and self-lessness in your kids in the last month?

2. Of the two strategies we tend to use to move kids toward kingdom living (more service or more Scripture), which one do you tend to lean toward?

3. In what ways is your youth group similar to whitewashed tombs Jesus speaks of Matthew 23:27?

4. Of the findings in the MTV study, which two or three statistics are most provocative to you? Why do you find them interesting?

5. A theme in this chapter is that we as youth workers create space for the Holy Spirit to move kids' needles from doing kingdom work to being kingdom people. How would you describe your role in the midst of the Holy Spirit being the ultimate force that transforms your kids?

6. According to Tony Campolo, "Youth pastors are afraid and unable to recognize that there needs to be structural change in order for there to be social justice." Would he say the same about you specifically?

7. Of the following list of Deep Justice Recommended Action Steps that flow from this chapter, which would best help you as a kingdom follower right wrongs? How about for your youth ministry?

DEEP JUSTICE RECOMMENDED ACTION STEPS:

For Yourself

- As mentioned on page 104, the 2006 MTV survey indicates that the top five reasons that kids are not involved in pro-social causes are that "it's just not for me," "I like to hang out with friends," "I don't have enough time," "I don't know how to get started," and "I want to see concrete results." Odds are good that your own hesitations to get involved personally with deep justice echo these students' obstacles. Think about the top two or three reasons you are not doing more to right wrongs around you, and imagine how the King might respond to those.

- Tony comments that kingdom people are "committed to the trans-formation of the world that *is* into the world that *ought to be*." Watch the local or national news one day to be reminded of what the world is, then turn off the TV and spend 15 minutes writing down phrases or drawing pictures of what the world *ought to be* according to your understanding of God's vision for the world.

- Spend 10 minutes per day reading—either online or in print—about world news and international events. Do it for a month and see if it makes any difference in your views about justice and poverty.

- Tony contrasts the "micro level" of justice, in which we alleviate the pain and suffering of others, with the "macro level" of justice in which we understand and counter the social forces that create that pain and suffering. As you think about your own city, identify some of the social forces that create pain and suffering, perhaps with a focus on one particular justice issue (i.e., public education, employment, or housing/homelessness). Meet together with other key leaders in your church to consider how your church and youth ministry could serve as advocates for policies and structural changes that would bring about deep justice.

For Your Youth Ministry

- Above we recommended that you spend time watching the news to see what the world *is*, and then later reflect on what it *ought to be*. At your next small group meeting, do the same two steps with your students, and have them share their feelings and impressions as they contrast the two. Conclude by reading the passage Tony recommended in Isaiah 65:17-25, making sure you reference the Good/Guilt/Grace/Gratitude kingdom story we discussed in chapter 3—so kids don't end up feeling like their actions are driven by guilt.

- Given the findings of the 2006 MTV survey that indicate that justice needs to hit close to home, invite a handful of your kids out for pizza and ask them the following questions: When does our justice work hit closest to home? How can we offer service opportunities that would hit closer to home for more students? How can our justice work help us develop deeper friendships?

- Before your next justice experience, review the Joplin model with your adult leaders. Assess which of the components your ministry already does well, and which could use some help. Brainstorm with them how you can effectively help students walk through all five of its components so that the final learning transfer is maximized.

- As you FOCUS with students before your next service or justice experience, invite them to keep their eyes open for the ways God is already at work in the people they are serving. During your AC-TION/REFLECTION times, discuss what they observed.

- As you FOCUS with students before your next service or justice experience, ask them to identify an adult mentor who can meet with them afterward to maximize their learning transfer.

- Tony believes "the Holy Spirit is a transforming force in people's lives, and that when the Spirit of Christ is alive in people, they become very aware of injustices." Spend some time with the adults and students who help lead worship in your ministry to identify ways you can create more space for the Holy Spirit to transform students into dedicated kingdom followers.

WELCOME TO BOTH/AND KINGDOM LIVING

Hopefully by now you're convinced that the depth and breadth of kingdom justice transcends the narrow *either/or* categories into which we slice and dice it. You're probably wondering how to apply the full Jesus and the full kingdom story to what you do with kids every day. And we hope you're also ready to do all you can to move kids' needles toward being kingdom people.

Enter Section 2.

Section 2, *Both/And Kingdom Living*, holds up the magnifying glass to three areas to which youth ministries have often turned a blind eye: race, money, and class.

This is where deep justice rubber meets the day-to-day road.

We've invited three highly respected leaders who have devoted their lives to righting wrongs—Noel Castellanos, Larry Acosta, and Jeremy Del Rio—to share their own experiences and insights about race, money, and class.

> "The Sermon [on the Mount]—to take it for the moment as a whole—is not a mere miscellany of ethical instruction. It cannot be generalized into a set of suggestions, or even commands, on how to be 'good.' Nor can it be turned into a guidemap for how to go to 'heaven' after death. It is rather, as it stands, a challenge to Israel to be Israel."
>
> N.T. WRIGHT, JESUS AND THE VICTORY OF GOD

So please link arms with us as we read and dream together about youth ministries that seek deep justice for our oh-so-broken-but-still-redeemable world.

SECTION TWO
BOTH/AND KINGDOM LIVING

WHEN IT COMES TO RACE, WHY CAN'T WE ALL GET ALONG? KINGDOM LOVE THAT BUSTS RACIAL BARRIERS

BY NOEL CASTELLANOS

Noel Castellanos, the associate executive director of the Christian Community Development Association, has worked in full-time ministry in urban communities since 1982, serving in youth ministry, church planting, and community development in San Francisco, San Jose, and Chicago. Noel is a highly sought after speaker, motivator, and mentor to young leaders throughout the United States, and has a deep passion to serve and invest in the lives of emerging leaders. He and his wife, Marianne, have three children, Noel Luis, Stefan, and Anna, and make their home in the barrio of La Villita in Chicago.

NOW? (DISCERNMENT)

STEP 1: NOW?

A few years ago at a Christian Community Development Association Conference, I was given the responsibility of introducing Rodney King, the central figure of the 1992 race riots in Los Angeles. I said, "I want to introduce you to a man who you'll recognize by his now famous words 'People...can we all get along?'"

Rodney King came to the microphone and said, "I don't have anything else to say. You just took my only line with your introduction." To my surprise, Rodney really didn't seem to want to say much more—so I prayed for him, and the two of us sat down.

I felt terrible that I had stolen his thunder. But I assumed he'd have more to say about race relations than simply urging everyone to get along despite our differences.

Yet in a similar way, when we as youth ministries **Now** enter into discussions about race, we often have very little of substance to offer. The best we can do is ask, like Rodney King, "Can we all get along?"

EITHER COLOR-BLIND OR COLOR-FULL

When I have conversations **Now** with youth workers about how we should right racial wrongs, it's common for someone to suggest we should all be "color-blind" when it comes to race. Instead of seeing black people or Asian people or white people or Latino people, we should just see people. Period.

To be honest, whenever someone tells me, "When I see you, I don't see a Mexican person, I just see a person," I don't believe him. That's a little bit like someone looking at me and saying, "When I see you, I don't see a male." You can't help but notice that I'm male, and you can't help but notice that my skin, my eyes, and my hair reflect that I'm Mexican.

The irony is that **Now** I also hear the opposite. Just as some youth workers claim to be "color-blind," others seem to be "color-full." All they see is my color, my race. When they look at me, they attribute everything about me to the fact that I'm Mexican.

Why do I think the way I do? In their eyes, it's because I'm Mexican.

Why do I treat people the way I do? Because I'm Mexican.

Why do I view the world that way I do? You guessed it—because I'm Mexican.

As a result, instead of denying that I am Mexican like the color-blind folks do, the color-full folks deny that I am anything *but* Mexican.

Maybe part of the reason we as youth workers are often left muttering nothing more than "Can we all get along?" is that we have **Now** bought into these *either/or* views about race. While I believe our youth ministries can and should relate to people of all races with respect and kindness, we don't have to deny people's ethnic or racial reality to accept who they are. Nor do we have to focus solely on their ethnicity, thereby denying the rest of who they are as human beings. Instead, kingdom justice makes our racial differences opportunities to experience intimate community with others who all express and bear the image of God in unique ways.

NEW? (REFLECTION)

STEP 2: NEW?

THE MO' COLOR THE MO' BETTER

To read more about the pressure that kids of color feel to act "white," check out our free additional Deep Justice resources available at www.cyfm.net.

I am convinced that well-known movie director and Knicks fan Spike Lee understands God's **New** vision for racial unity and reconciliation better than most youth leaders. A number of years ago, Lee filmed a commercial for Nike in which a bunch of guys were playing a heated game of very competitive basketball. As you watched the two teams involved more closely, it became clear that all the players on one team were white, the other team's players were all black, and there was a whole lot of trash talking going on.

The trash talk escalated to the point where the guys stopped playing ball and ended up at center court, looking like they were ready to throw down. Just as the scene was about to get ugly, Spike Lee's big head filled the TV screen, and he yelled, "Yo!" After everybody stopped in their tracks, the commercial ended with him saying, "If we're going to live together, we have to play together. The mo' color the mo' better!"

The apostle Paul says basically the same thing in a letter he wrote to kingdom followers in a city named Galatia:

> So in Christ Jesus you are all children of God through faith, for all of you who were baptized into Christ have clothed yourselves with Christ. There is neither Jew nor Gentile, neither slave nor free, neither male nor female, for you are all one in Christ Jesus. If you belong to Christ, then you are Abraham's seed, and heirs according to the promise. (Galatians 3:26-29)

That passage is probably familiar to you. Maybe you've even heard a portion of Galatians 3:28—"you are one in Christ Jesus"—used as a slogan reminiscent of Rodney King's "Can we all get along?" But righting racial wrongs in and through our youth ministries means taking a deeper look at what was happening in first-century Galatia when Paul wrote the letter.

In Paul's day, a growing number of non-Jewish people (known as Gentiles) were responding to the **New** kingdom message of God's love. This might seem like something the early church would welcome, but the animosity between Gentiles and Jews made it both controversial and complicated. During the early Old Testament era, the Gentiles generally received hospitality and favor from the Israelites (see Deuteronomy 10:19, Exodus 23:9, Judges 1:16). But while the Jews were in exile during the later Old Testament era, their Gentile captors often mistreated them. As a result, during the New Testament era, many Jews viewed Gentiles with scorn and hatred. Gentiles were regarded as unclean, and it was unlawful to befriend them. Gentiles were seen as enemies of God and his people, and if they asked questions about divine matters, Jews were expected to curse them.

As people who had been excluded from Jewish culture, the Gentiles were blown away by the way Jesus—a Jewish Jesus no less—loved everyone regardless of class, gender, or race. When the Gentiles heard that they too could become a part of God's family, they must have flipped, realizing it would mean

> So in Christ Jesus you are all children of God through faith, for all of you who were baptized into Christ have clothed yourselves with Christ. There is neither Jew nor Gentile, neither slave nor free, neither male nor female, for you are all one in Christ Jesus. If you belong to Christ, then you are Abraham's seed, and heirs according to the promise
>
> GALATIANS 3:26-29

becoming brothers and sisters with Jews. They must have wondered how this was going to work, since they had always been shunned by these Jewish people and considered their enemies.

Take some time to reread Galatians 3:26-29 (printed in the sidebar to the left) through the **New** backdrop of the Gentile/Jewish division.

In essence, Paul does what Spike Lee did by helping these first-century believers—and the believers of our day—see that, in Christ, we are all part of the same family. If the Jews and Gentiles of the early church were going to be part of the same family, they would have to learn to play together. Instead of helplessly wondering why we can't "get along" without offering any kingdom hope, Paul reminds them (and us) that the mo' color, the mo' better!

WE NEED DEEP RACIAL JUSTICE
BECAUSE THE ROOTS OF INJUSTICE ARE SO DEEP

One reason Paul's **New** message is hard to implement in our youth ministries today is because so many ethnicities and races have been wronged throughout our country's history. Take a look at a few historical examples of how racism has birthed oppression and suffering for people of color:

> According to Joni Hersch, a Vanderbilt University professor who analyzed data from 2,084 male and female immigrants, those with the lightest skin color earned, on average, 8-15 percent more than immigrants with the darkest skin tone. The effect of skin color persisted even among workers with the same ethnicity, race, and country of origin.

• Native Americans have been killed by the millions, had their land stolen from them, and have experienced extreme discrimination. Today, only 1 percent of the U.S. population is Native American, and the majority of us have virtually no knowledge of any public figures or governmental leaders who are Native American.

• Much of the wealth of our nation was built on the brutality of slavery, with African men, women, and children forced to come to this country for the benefit of whites. Even after the abolition of slavery, African Americans have struggled to be seen as fully human, have been denied numerous human rights, and have struggled with the slavery aftermath and the continuing burdens of discrimination, racism, and segregation.

- Latino immigrants have been valued by our country's economy when we have needed cheap labor, and then have been kicked out, asked to leave, or criminalized as "illegal aliens."

- Japanese residents and citizens have been detained by our government; many Asians struggle to be seen as fully American because of their different cultures and languages.

KINGDOM LOVE THAT BUSTS BARRIERS

Unfortunately, **New** research indicates that racial injustice still continues in our country, and even in our churches. Through a nationwide telephone survey of 2,000 adults as well as 200 face-to-face interviews, Michael O. Emerson and Christian Smith found that U.S. churches reflect our "racialized society." According to Emerson and Smith, a "racialized society" is a society in which race creates profound differences in life experiences, life opportunities, and social relationships. Even if we believers don't intend to perpetuate racial inequality and division, research indicates that even though formal segregation by race ended in the United States in 1964, informal segregation still exists in our housing developments, our schools, and perhaps most tragically, in our churches.[46]

Given our nation's past and present, what **New** insights must pervade our youth ministries if we would try to right wrongs in a racially divided world? Simply put, our youth ministries are called to be filled with radical love in a broken world torn apart by racism, discrimination, and oppression. Our youth ministries need to overflow with the same love Jesus and Paul had, a love for every kind of person —especially those who are different from us, and whom we might even consider to be our enemies. As we

> "Whites can move to most any neighborhood, eat at most any restaurant, walk down most any street, or shop at most any store without having to worry or find out that they are not wanted, whereas African Americans often cannot...Whites are assumed to be middle class unless proven otherwise, are not expected to speak for their race, can remain ignorant of other cultures without penalty, and do not have to ask every time something goes wrong if it is due to race, whereas African Americans cannot."
>
> MICHAEL O. EMERSON AND CHRISTIAN SMITH, *DIVIDED BY FAITH*

---

[46] Michael O. Emerson and Christian Smith, *Divided by Faith* (New York: Oxford University Press, 2000), 7-9, 48.

right wrongs through barrier-busting love, the world can see that God's plan and design for his kingdom people and for the church is different from anything found on this broken and divided planet.

I had an unforgettable taste of the power of a barrier-busting love when I met Pat Williams, a well-known and successful general manager of professional basketball teams. Besides his high-profile job, there's something else unusual about Pat Williams. He and his wife have 19 children; 14 of them are adopted children from 14 different countries.

Imagine the amazing diversity that exists in that family! That's the kind of diversity our heavenly Father has always envisioned for his church: Men, women, and children from every nation loving one another, caring for one another's needs, and absolutely committed to one another as sisters and brothers of the same family—the family of God.

In a broken world filled with racial strife and hatred, we as kingdom followers have a **New** message: We can go beyond just getting along. We can actually learn to appreciate and love one another as members of God's family.

NEW WAYS TO SHOW BARRIER-BUSTING LOVE

We youth workers can play a primary role in helping our kids live as God's family in a number of **New** ways:

- *We can teach kids to be **intentional** in reaching out to friends who are different from them.* Encourage your students to be like Lydia, a girl in our mostly Latino youth group, who was always inviting her African-American friends to our ministry because she cared about them.

- *We can challenge kids to be **intense** in confronting misconceptions about race.* Once I invited a Latino young man to camp who couldn't wait to get into a fight with a black kid—because he hated all black people. Once he got to know a few of the guys in his cabin that week, he not only asked Christ to come into his life, but admitted to others that he was wrong in his attitudes toward blacks, and asked for forgiveness.

Interestingly, many of our kids need to confront not only their misconceptions about other races, but also false ideas about themselves and those of their *own* race or class. I've personally seen Latino and African-American kids from our youth group transformed when they've traveled to another country with great poverty and realized they aren't just "poor minority kids." As people created in God's image, they have talents, passions, and resources to give.

- *We can help our kids be **informed** about the racial injustice that goes on around us.* When news events with racial themes erupt in your city or in our nation (which happens regularly), invite your students to share their responses with you. When possible, push them to think about the underlying causes of these racial tensions, as well as how Jesus would respond.

> The Christian Community Development Association revolves around eight philosophical components crucial to deep justice: relocation, reconciliation, redistribution, leadership development, listening to community, church-based, holistic approach, and empowerment. (see www. ccda.org for more)

- *Finally, we can help our kids push toward all forms of **integration**.* These days, as some churches are priding themselves on making progress toward racial integration, we must recognize how racial and class barriers overlap. Just yesterday, I heard from a youth pastor who was celebrating that his formerly mostly white church was becoming more racially diverse, thanks to the example of the youth ministry. While this is encouraging, the problem is that even though the church is more racially diverse, it's still basically an upper-middle- class congregation. The only non whites are people of color who fit the socioeconomic level of the vast majority of the congregation, so everyone still feels pretty safe. (Jeremy will cover class divisions in more detail in chapters 11 and 12.)

A SNAPSHOT OF BARRIER-BUSTING LOVE

For ten years, I pastored a church in a Mexican neighborhood in southwest Chicago called La Villita. The barrio has about 100,000 residents who are almost all of Mexican descent. From the time my family arrived here, we worked hard to establish a church where everyone felt welcome, regardless of their race.

We had many Spanish-speaking families and kids in our church as well as a good number of white families who had a deep burden to live and work with Mexican people. We also had families like mine that were mixed. I am a fourth-generation Mexican-American and my wife is Italian, so we brought biracial kids into our church, as did a few other families. Together, we all had to compromise and sacrifice and work at celebrating our diversity. When conflicts arose, many of us felt like it would be much easier to worship with others who were all alike.

I was always surprised at how little misunderstandings between our white members and our Mexican members became the seeds for huge blow-ups and conflicts. Once a white sister in our church decided to have a party for one of her Mexican friends, but didn't invite all of the women in our small church. While she didn't intend to leave anyone out, the women who were not invited felt rejected and hurt. Instead of talking openly about the expectations of different cultures regarding party invitations, some of these mothers stopped bringing their kids to our after-school program. It wasn't until months later that the truth about their feelings came out.

As a Mexican pastor I had to wrestle with questions about race when a group of white leaders seemed resistant to my leadership. Instead of taking their concerns at face value, it was easy for me to play the race card and assume their problems with me were racially motivated. I assumed they did not want to follow a Latino leader, instead of accepting that they might have been right about certain issues. It was only after I took the time to listen—really listen—that we were able to work through conflicts that were fueled by our racial backgrounds.

> "The commitment to submit to Jesus and follow him into displacement all our days is a lordship commitment. It means a lifetime of allowing Jesus to call us out of comfort and ease and into places and communities where we are awkward and weak. Those of us who have made this commitment know that displacement will always be a part of what we do. Our worldview leads us to regularly ask, 'Where in my life am I the minority, the learner, the one who is displaced?'"
>
> PAULA HARRIS AND DOUG SCHAUPP,
> *BEING WHITE*

In spite of the many challenges we faced, we knew we were experiencing something in our diversity that was pleasing to God. One of the most committed youth workers in our church was an African-American young woman who learned Spanish and became immersed in the Mexican culture so she could minister better to the kids in our youth group. Because of her willingness to be an agent of reconciliation, she has had a huge impact on the people of our church and community.

Imagine the impact our generation could make if we truly committed ourselves to realizing God's desire that his church would be one big diverse family. Imagine if you and your students decided to learn Spanish or Chinese so you could reach out to the other kids in your neighborhood. Imagine if urban and suburban youth ministries began **New** partnerships to address the racial injustices in their communities. Imagine if it became normal to see black and white and Asian and Latino kids and adults all celebrating and worshiping God together on Sunday mornings. Do you think this type of kingdom love might help us get along in cities all across America?

WHO? (OBSERVATION)

STEP 3: WHO?

EFREM SMITH thinks this kind of kingdom love can make a difference in our world. As senior pastor of Sanctuary Covenant Church in Minneapolis, coauthor of *The Hip-Hop Church*, and author of *Raising Up Young Heroes*, Efrem is one of our country's leading voices in helping youth ministries bring deep justice to our racially divided world. Regardless of whether your group is of one ethnicity or already full of diversity, Efrem is someone **Who** is full of practical ideas for you and your kids to bust racial barriers through kingdom love.

How do you feel when someone says to you, "When I look at you, I don't see your skin color?"

I don't feel like I'm in an authentic dialogue. We live in a racialized society, and if someone has the natural ability to see, they see I'm an African American. But I know what people are trying to say when they say that. They're trying to say, "I'm attempting to live a life where skin color is not a barrier for me," and I respect that desire.

> To read much more about hip-hop and what it means for your youth ministry, check out our free additional Deep Justice resources available at www.cyfm.net.

What about when you face the other extreme and people seem to attribute everything about you to your race or ethnicity?

To say you don't see skin color is unhealthy, but to attribute everything to skin color is just as unhealthy. I think multiple ethnicities, cultures, and languages are opportunities to see the creative power of our loving God. At the same time, if everything is attributed to race or ethnicity, then we build stereotypes by believing, "All white people think like this," or "All black people are like this." Those stereotypes begin to fuel prejudice.

Why is it tough for us as youth workers to bridge the racial divide that exists in this country?

Because youth ministry is part of the broader church, and the broader church in America struggles with the issue of race.

When you say the broader church is struggling with race, what do you mean?

We can't talk about race, slavery, Jim Crow segregation laws, or the Civil Rights movement without talking about the church, because for good and bad, the church has been at the center of justice issues, particularly race, throughout our country's history. We have various ethnic churches because people of color were not historically welcomed in the white church. The black church in our country was forced into existence because African Americans were not welcome in the all-white church.

At the same time, we can celebrate the ways the church has historically spoken out against slavery, inequality, and racism. So we as the church have to wrestle with the part we've played in racism as well as the part we've played in fighting against racism.

What are you doing at Sanctuary Covenant Church to be a reconciling racial community?

The Sanctuary Covenant Church began in 2003, so we're fairly young, but we've grown into a multicultural church by being very intentional from the beginning about building a multi-ethnic community. Our staff, our elder board, and our core groups are all multi ethnic. We've tried to be very intentional about being multi ethnic in our preaching, teaching, and ministry models. As a result, our congregation is 55 percent white, 32 percent black, 8 percent Latino, 2 percent Asian, and 3 percent Jamaican or bi racial.

In your 12 years of hands-on youth ministry and your time now as a senior pastor spending time with students and young adults, what have you learned about effective racial reconciliation in youth ministries?

As a teenager here in Minneapolis I was greatly impacted by the ministry of Park Avenue United Methodist Church. Later I became Park Avenue's youth pastor, and I still have the privilege of observing its justice work, since it's located near our church. One reason that church is effective at racial reconciliation is because in the late 1960s and early 1970s, as the racial dynamics of our city began to change, the youth ministry embraced that change. Through its youth ministry, this affluent, all-white church began to integrate intentionally. As the youth ministry experienced deep racial reconciliation, the entire church was influenced. Just recently the church called an African-American senior pastor for the first time in its history. And for the first time in the history of Park Avenue, white folks are not the majority of the staff. I think it's amazing that this intentionality began with the heart of one youth worker, Art Erickson.

What did Art and the youth ministry do to right the racial wrongs around them?

Art was a Young Life leader before he came to Park Avenue. I think that parachurch background made him more of a pioneer in developing a reconciling youth ministry model. Art and the team of volunteers he developed went out to schools to get to know all types of kids. They'd invite them not just to church but also on rafting trips and other fun events. As a result, churched and non-churched kids got to know one another, and kids of all skin colors realized what they had in common. They all needed Jesus, and they all needed one another.

What other recommendations do you have for youth workers who want to engage in racial justice?

Well, first we have to preach it and teach it. I think we need to teach the Bible as the most multicultural piece of literature that exists. When we read the genealogy of Jesus in Matthew 1, we can't help but conclude that Jesus walked the earth as a multicultural human being. When we read of Jesus' travels, we have to ask ourselves why Jesus went through Samaria in John 4 and what that means for us today. When we read of the Day of Pentecost in the second chapter of Acts, or Revelation 7 and its vision of a multitude of every tribe and language in heaven, we have to wrestle with its implications for us as kingdom followers.

> "God yearns to interact with young people, and he is in the business of using them to do incredible things in the world."
>
> EFREM SMITH, *RAISING UP YOUNG HEROES*

In addition to teaching about it, we have to make it a priority to ask, "How can we begin to have monthly or quarterly services with churches different from our own? What would it look like to go on a service or missions trip together?" Whether our ministry is urban, suburban, or rural, we all need to network with other diverse groups. You can do it through an official youth worker network in your city that coordinates joint training seminars or youth events, or by connecting with another church for your next winter retreat. Or maybe the next time you're planning an event for your church, you make sure to invite a speaker of a different ethnicity so you model diversity before your kids.

What should we do when our kids resist building relationships with folks of other ethnicities?

I don't see many kids resisting racial reconciliation these days. I think young people in the United States, whether we realize it or not, are becoming more and more multicultural. Kids today want something more than the racialized labels they live with.

> The church ought to be engaging hip-hop culture but should be seeking to create Holy Hip-Hop culture as well."
>
> EFREM SMITH AND PHIL JACKSON, *THE HIP-HOP CHURCH*

In our own country, especially in places like California, New York, and Texas, European Americans are no longer the majority. If that is true, and our job is to proclaim Christ in such a culture, then we can't live in all-white or all-black worlds anymore. Through the Internet, kids are tapping into a multicultural world on a regular basis, and we as youth workers must help them realize it's also a multicultural *kingdom* world.

What are the differences between urban youth ministries and suburban youth ministries when it comes to racial justice?

I think urban churches have unique opportunities, because they tend to be located in communities with greater racial diversity. For example, we have people who drive to our urban church from suburban areas because they want a multiethnic experience. They want to be in a worship experience that looks like heaven.

Even suburbs are getting more racially diverse. Many first-ring suburbs are starting to look like the city. Also, because of gentrification, many urban people, poor people, and people of color are being relocated to first-ring suburbs and beyond.

What message would it send to our broken world if we as kingdom youth ministries were leaders of racial reconciliation?

I think it would send a tremendous message to our world. Usually the American church wears one of two faces. The first is the politicized church that tends to focus on two issues: abortion and gay marriage. The second face of the American church is all about consumerism and materialism, believing God wants to bless you, make you rich, and make your life easy.

Efrem defines *gentrification* as the revitalization of a city as housing projects and abandoned buildings are torn down and replaced with new housing and businesses. While that improves the conditions of a neighborhood, it doesn't necessarily result in justice. Often poor people who live in these neighborhoods are not prepared to take advantage of or well integrated into these developments or they can't afford the higher rents, so they remain not only poor but also displaced from their homes and community.

Neither of those faces of the U.S. church is the church I read about when I read about Jesus. Being the church in this culture is complex and difficult. Being a Christian today is not an easy road. But I think if we work toward justice and righteousness together, we will see some phenomenal kingdom-building in our country.

HOW? (APPLICATION)

STEP 4: HOW?

DEEP JUSTICE APPLICATION QUESTIONS

1. How would your kids answer the question of why we can't, in Rodney King's words, "all get along"? If your kids fully understood the kingdom story of Good/Guilt/Grace/Gratitude presented in chapter 3, what would their answer be?

2. Paul dealt with the division between Jews and Gentiles. What are the primary racial or cultural divisions in your community? What would it look like if Galatians 3:26-29 started to change your community?

3. In MTV's 2006 youth survey on page 104, in chapter 6, it was clear that issues that hit close to home are more likely to move the justice needle toward our becoming kingdom people. How does the issue of race hit close to home with your students?

4. In chapter 5, John Perkins stated that when we view others as made in God's image that will make us want to help them be reconciled

both to God and to one another. Similarly, how will viewing others as made in God's image affect the way we respond to racial injustice?

5. Which of the ways to show barrier-busting love described on page 126 is most relevant to your youth ministry? What could you do in the next few months to experiment with that type of barrier-busting love?

6. Do you agree with Efrem that kids today don't resist racial reconciliation? Why or why not?

7. Of the following list of Deep Justice Recommended Action Steps that flow from this chapter, which would best help you right wrongs as a kingdom follower? Which would most help your youth ministry?

DEEP JUSTICE RECOMMENDED ACTION STEPS:

For Yourself

- If you are of the dominant ethnicity in your town or state, take a few minutes to consider how you might receive preferential treatment because of that. Take a few additional minutes to consider how it might feel to be a different skin color and perhaps be judged, stereotyped, or marginalized because of it.

- If you are of the dominant ethnicity in your area, think about potential challenges faced by those who aren't.

- In the next few months, attend a church service or Bible study in which you are in the racial minority. Pay attention to how you felt when you walked into the room, and your perceptions of how others viewed you.

- Think about the various ethnicities represented in your town and honestly assess whether you hold any prejudiced or stereotypical views toward any of these ethnicities. If possible, identify the root of that bias (i.e., one isolated experience, the media, prejudice that existed in your family), confess that to the Lord, and ask God to help you wholeheartedly love and embrace the diversity that surrounds you.

For Your Youth Ministry

- Gather demographic information about the racial and ethnic composition of your town and share that information with your students. Together as a group, compare those demographics with the ethnicities represented by the students in your youth ministry. Invite students to suggest ways your ministry could better reflect the diversity of your city.

- One current justice dilemma affecting many communities is immigration. Invite your students to discuss the tough questions about undocumented immigrants using Galatians 3:26-29 as a springboard for your discussion. Specific questions you might want to include are: Why is this issue so heated? Why do you think immigrants want to come to the United States? Given that some people have crossed the border in ways that violate U.S. immigration laws, how should that affect our kingdom response? What do you think Jesus would say to a family of undocumented immigrants living in our neighborhood? What would happen if all kingdom followers made these words of Jesus the crux of their response to immigrants?

- Identify ways in which your ministry's adult leaders do not reflect your community's racial diversity and prayerfully recruit leaders who better mirror your local context.

- Distribute paper and pencils to students and ask them to journal their responses to two questions: How has race affected our country? And, how has my race affected me? Collect their responses and use them as a springboard for a teaching series on deep racial justice.

- Schedule a retreat—ideally with a church or another race or ethnicity—that focuses on barrier-busting love, with a special emphasis on racial reconciliation. Consider including a time for students to repent, either in silence or aloud, for ways they have judged others because of their race.

- Challenge your students to bust racial barriers by developing one new friendship in the next year with someone of a different skin color.

- Meet with students from one particular school to discuss how racial divisions permeate their campus. Ask students to explain why they think those divisions exist. Brainstorm steps students could take to share barrier-busting love and the good news of the kingdom at their school.

- Schedule an "Eating Around the World" event and invite students to bring in food that reflects their ethnicities. (You may want to include additional food from restaurants that specialize in food from particular nations). Invite students to share about family traditions that emerge from their ethnic background and identity.

- Efrem recommends planning monthly or quarterly services with churches different from your own or scheduling service or missions trips together. Gather with youth workers from a few other churches with different ethnic backgrounds and consider these possibilities together. If you are a suburban church that wants to connect with an urban church, try www.urbanyouthworkers.com.

- In the sidebar on page 130, we included this quote from Being White by Paula Harris and Doug Schaupp: "The commitment to submit to Jesus and follow him into displacement all our days is a lordship commitment. It means a lifetime of allowing Jesus to call us out of comfort and ease and into places and communities where we are awkward and weak. Those of us who have made this commitment know that displacement will always be a part of what we do. Our worldview leads us to regularly ask, 'Where in my life am I the minority, the learner, the one who is displaced?'" With your students, answer the question: Where in my life am I the minority, the learner, the one who is displaced? Follow up by asking: What is tough about that experience? What am I learning from that experience?

WHAT ELSE IS THERE BESIDES SILENCE AND SCREAMING AS WE TALK ABOUT RACE?

BY NOEL CASTELLANOS

"We must face the sad fact that at eleven o'clock on Sunday morning when we stand to sing 'In Christ There is No East or West,' we stand in the most segregated hour of America."

Martin Luther King Jr.

NOW? (DISCERNMENT)

STEP 1: NOW?

As I sit in a 24-hour Starbucks on the north side of Chicago at 10:30 p.m., I'm starting to wonder if this Starbucks has **Now** found the secret to creating diverse and multicultural community.

The place is filled with young people from every ethnic group imaginable. There are no open seats, and the place is humming with music of every variety at just the right volume. Folks are busy typing away on laptops, talking to friends, reading books—all while nursing lattes or espressos in hopes of being able to stay awake to complete their work or conversations.

The vibe is welcoming, and even though most of the people crammed together don't know one another, we are bound by the fellowship of the green mermaid and her brew. Sadly, many people find more acceptance, more camaraderie, and more loyalty at this coffee house (as evidenced by their willingness to shell out $4.00 for a cup of coffee) than they'd find in many of our youth ministries.

STRANGERS WHO ARE SILENT

But let's put the community at Starbucks **Now** under a microscope.

While people of all skin colors and languages are sitting at the same location, we aren't looking one another in the eyes. And while we exchange polite smiles and pleasantries ("Looks like you've got a lot of work there," "Yup, sure do..."), we remain strangers.

If I'm lucky, the Starbucks baristas I see a few times each week will memorize my first name and my preferred drink order (if you're curious, it's a grande, extra-hot, three-quarters Misto with foam). They know a bit *about* me, but they don't *really know* me.

We converse, but we don't really talk.

In spite of the diversity gathered inside, my local Starbucks, like many of our youth ministries, is stuck **Now** in comfortable silence instead of really dealing with racial injustices. At first glance, we may think we see community. But the deeper we look, the more we realize this community is about as deep as the lid on our café mocha.

Our youth ministries may be filled with kids of different skin colors, just like this Starbucks. But when it comes to honest conversations about race

Now, our lips are sealed. Whether our kids are all the same color or as varied as the rainbow, whether we don't know how to talk about race or we simply don't want to, the end result is the same: We stay silent.

ENEMIES WHO MAKE US SCREAM

Equally toxic to deep kingdom youth ministry is a second approach to racial injustice: Screaming at those whom we view as enemies. If silence doesn't right wrongs **Now**, then maybe yelling until we are hoarse will.

Sometimes it's actual yelling. It's blacks condemning whites for being "The Man" who keeps them oppressed. Or white parents blaming Asians because their kid wasn't accepted into their college of choice.

But probably more often in youth ministry circles, it's the way we keep others at arm's length by using language that alienates them. We might not be yelling externally, but our internal anger and frustration spews out in belittling sarcasm and stereotypes.

I'll never forget the struggle we had in our primarily Latino youth ministry when a few African-American kids from across the way began attending Friday night youth group. These kids wanted to come because our church was right down the street, but too often they did not feel welcome. The Mexican kids spoke in Spanish to hide their conversations from these youth who did not speak Spanish. Even the Latino parents voiced their doubts about the wisdom of "mixing" blacks and Latinos in the same youth group.

> "Strangely enough, the havoc wreaked by indifference may be even 'greater than that brought by felt, lived, practiced hatred.'"[47]
>
> MIROSLAV VOLF, *EXCLUSION AND EMBRACE*

I have one friend in youth ministry who's white and does all he can to help his students right wrongs around them. But he's been in countless discussions with folks of color who, in describing how their minority status has hindered them, have made him feel like the oppressor. He's been told repeatedly, "You're white. You just can't get what it feels like to be a minority." True, he can't. But every time he's been told that—whether it's been yelled at him or merely whispered—he's felt like the enemy with no friend in sight.

---

[47] The phrase "greater than that brought by felt, lived, practiced hatred" comes from Arne Johan Vetlesen, *Perception, Empathy and Judgment: An Inquiry into the Preconditions of Moral Performance* (University Park: The Pennsylvania State University, 1994), 252.

Now, at a time when people are looking for solutions to our race problems, our youth ministries must offer them the type of kingdom conversations that transcend the fears that keep us silent.

At a time when almost every war and major conflict in our world today has a racial element to it, we have to offer kingdom dialogue that rises above the anger that makes us want to scream.

As followers of the King, our youth ministries have to show others a **New** way.

NEW? (REFLECTION)

STEP 2: NEW?

"WATCH OUT FOR THOSE WHITE PEOPLE"

New approaches to racial justice that move beyond either silence or screaming will not be easy. I know from my own experience that the distrust and hateful language among the races runs deep.

When I was six years old, my grandfather used to take me on walks from our Texas border town into Mexico to buy beans and rice. It was only a few miles from our home, so it was not a very long walk, and we didn't have to worry about getting back and forth across the border as we would today.

During these trips across the border, he would warn me about the "Bolillos," or the white people (a *bolillo* is literally a white roll of bread). He would say in Spanish, "Those Anglos cannot be trusted, and they will always look to take advantage of you." As you can imagine, this made a huge impact on me as a youngster.

When I was seven, I moved to California, where I learned firsthand what it is like to be an ethnic minority in our dominant culture. I learned English in a special class and had to endure daily harassment from a group of blonde boys who got their kicks chasing me home as they made fun of the color of my skin and my thick accent. I can still hear their insults in my mind: "Go back to Mexico where you belong, you dirty wetback." I remember trying to defend myself by telling them I was born here in the United States. I hated going to school, and I hated these light-skinned, blonde guys for how they treated me.

Even more damaging than the fights and insults were the deep scars these experiences left on my heart and in my mind, which would make it nearly impossible to trust my white classmates for years to come. I often wonder how different my childhood could have been if I'd made one good white friend who spoke kindly to me and was willing to accept me even though I was different from him. Maybe I would not have had to fight so much.

JESUS-STYLE RACIAL COMMUNITY: UP CLOSE AND PERSONAL

I love the story of Jesus healing a man infected with leprosy in Luke 5:12-16. In Jesus' day, people with leprosy were viewed as repulsive, and were isolated physically, socially, and psychologically. When the leper saw Jesus, Luke reports that he fell to the ground, as if full of shame at his uncleanness. Luke also adds that the leper was so desperate for kingdom healing that he *begged* Jesus to make him clean.

To me, what's most amazing about this story is the way Jesus heals the man. In the first century, lepers were *always* kept at a distance. If you touched someone with leprosy, you were rendered unclean. Yet in Luke 5:13, Jesus reaches out his hand and touches the man with leprosy, at which point, the man is made well. In the midst of disease and brokenness, Jesus' **New** healing was up close and personal.

In our broken world, racial healing requires Jesus-style racial community, which means getting up close and personal. We cannot do "drive by" racial reconciliation, nor can we be satisfied with Starbucks-style false intimacy. We have to roll up our sleeves, look each other in the eye, and do the hard work of kingdom conversations about race and ethnicity.

I started learning this after I graduated from college and joined the staff of Young Life in San Francisco's Mission District, a community filled with Latino families from Central America. I was excited about getting to know some of the kids in my neighborhood and inviting them to a week of Young Life camp. But instead I was asked by our ministry director to take a group of students from Chinatown to camp instead.

I tried to hide my disappointment about having to take a group of Chinese guys—whom I didn't know—to camp. I felt called to work with Latino kids, and this assignment was not in my plans. I felt nervous about working with kids from a different culture, and I had no idea how to even begin relating to these young guys. Not only were they not Mexican and not into soccer, but they were all into the martial arts. Honestly, I was not looking forward to taking this group of guys to camp for a whole week—even if it was to hear about Jesus.

> While Jesus was in one of the towns, a man came along who was covered with leprosy. When he saw Jesus, he fell with his face to the ground and begged him, "Lord, if you are willing, you can make me clean." Jesus reached out his hand and touched the man. 'I am willing,' he said. 'Be clean!' And immediately the leprosy left him.
>
> Luke 5:12-13

By the end of the week, I felt so ashamed at my initial negative reaction toward working with these kids. During my many hours of conversations with them about their families, their experiences in Chinatown, and their feelings of rejection growing up in America, I realized I had treated them like many of my white peers had treated me in my childhood. (I wish I'd known martial arts when I was growing up and those other kids were kicking my behind.)

My time at camp that week not only served to reveal my own need for deeper racial sensitivity, but in actuality, helped prepare me for three years of working with many African-American, Samoan, and Filipino kids, along with the Latino kids I was used to relating to. It wasn't until I had to reach beyond what was safe and get up close and personal with young people from other cultures that I became aware of some of my own prejudices and fears when it came to race. I was beginning to discover that racial healing was not going to happen from a distance, but by mixing it up with others—getting close, risking conversation, making mistakes, and eating lots of great ethnic food.

UP CLOSE AND PERSONAL CONVERSATION

I know it will be risky, but our youth groups need to be places where we can talk openly and honestly about race, and about the barriers that keep us from being the kingdom community that God intends. When we don't talk honestly with one another, we live with untested assumptions. Black, Asian, and Latino folks think white folks don't care about them or the injustices they face. White people react with fear and defensiveness to the anger minorities often express over the way they feel wronged.

As I've worked with students, I've made a point of bringing up the topic of race. Some **New** questions I like to ask are:

- What are the stereotypes our culture holds toward different races?

- How have we learned these stereotypes? Family? Friends? The media? Jokes?

- Do you think there is truth in any of these stereotypes? Why or why not?

- What's it like to be a person of your race?

- How do you think it would feel to be someone of a different skin color?

- How do you think others view you when they first see your skin color?

- What do you wish others knew about what it's like to be of your ethnicity?

- What benefits do you enjoy because of your race?

- What does being of your ethnicity cost you?

- What's your favorite part about being of your race?

- What's your least favorite part?

- Have you ever wished you were another skin color? Why or why not?

- Why is it so tough for us to discuss questions like these about race?

I'll never forget a youth rally I helped plan with a number of youth workers from various churches and youth ministries. In all, about 200 kids gathered together for a night of games and music, with a gospel message at the end. Our goal was to get our kids from different cities across the Bay Area to mix and get to know one another.

Over the course of the night, I was pleased to see kids from different churches getting to know one another. But at one point, I suddenly realized that, while we were all in one room, we were still all divided by race. The Latino kids had found other Latinos to meet and hang out with; the whites had found other whites; the African-American and Asian kids had done likewise. We'd all gathered in the same room, yet we were still divided by race. I could not believe it. It was not intentional, but all of the young people *and the adult leaders* had clustered together in their racial comfort zones.

As I got up to speak that night, I shared my observation with the group and asked them to think about why we'd segregated ourselves by race. By the end of the night, we gave students an opportunity to share their thoughts and feelings about why it's hard to get up close and personal with others the way Jesus did. We actually saw the dynamics of the group change before our eyes, as all of us were intentional about going out of our way to talk to one another across racial lines.

It was a **New** lesson about the toxicity of racial segregation that those students and I will never forget.

"All who follow Christ are called to be bearers of God's good news to the poor. Ignorance of the underclass or immigrants and their world(s) leads to simplistic labeling of people as 'poor,' 'ex-cons,' 'illegals,' 'homeless,' 'underprivileged,' 'disabled,' 'poor white trash,' 'street workers,' 'runaways,' 'Mexicans,' 'disenfranchised,' and endless other designations. The church, then, becomes guilty of racial and social-class profiling."

BOB EKBLAD, *READING THE BIBLE WITH THE DAMNED*

For more practical suggestions for helping your kids talk about race, check out our free additional Deep Justice resources available at www.cyfm.net.

SPECIFIC QUESTIONS TO ASK IN YOUR YOUTH MINISTRY

Once you have made some progress in your kingdom conversations about race, you might want to try asking **New** questions about specific ethnicities. Either by using a panel of students or adults or simply through a large group discussion with your kids, consider asking the following:

For Whites	• Do you believe you are treated more favorably in this country because of the color of your skin? • When we talk about race, do you feel like you can share your honest opinions, or do you think people will judge everything you say because you're white? • Do you think it's fair that colleges and employers looking for racial diversity might hire or accept someone other than you because of your skin color? How would your answer be different if you were of a different ethnicity?
For Blacks	• Have you ever been accused of selling out for relating to a white friend? How did that make you feel? • Have you ever felt "passed over" for an opportunity because of the color of your skin? • How does it make you feel that most of the black kids (especially guys) on TV or in the movies are portrayed as thugs? • Is racial profiling ever okay? Why or why not?
For Latinos	• Has anyone ever accused you of being an "illegal immigrant"? How has this made you feel? • How do you respond when others say everyone who lives in the U.S. should speak only English? Do you agree or disagree? • Have you ever felt inferior around a person of a different color? Why?
For Asians	• How does it make you feel when people assume you're a "brain" because of your skin color? • Have you ever felt invisible in a group of kids from a different race? How did you overcome that feeling? • What pressures do you feel at home that others may not understand?

UP CLOSE AND PERSONAL CONVERSATIONS AS WE SERVE TOGETHER

Shortly after I established La Villita Community Church, a youth worker called on the phone with a very interesting story. Lou was a Mexican American who had lived in the La Villita community as a young man. He was later adopted by a white family in another state and left Chicago for good—or so he thought.

After becoming a follower of Christ and completing his studies, he moved to a city in southern Indiana where he became a junior high pastor. Lou saw something about our church in a magazine and called to investigate the possibility of bringing his kids to Chicago on a weeklong mission trip.

When Lou first told me he wanted to bring a mostly white group of 70 squirrelly junior high students to our inner-city barrio, I almost told him, "No thanks." First of all, how much help could they be to us? What kind of work or activities could they engage in that would be safe and positive for them and also a good experience for our own young people?

The week they spent with us that summer was so positive, I was blown away. These kids had really been prepared for this trip. They'd learned about Chicago and about the Mexican culture—even learning some essential words in Spanish.

They came to listen, learn, and serve, understanding that they were the outsiders coming into our hood. Together, we debriefed as many experiences as possible, allowing kids and leaders to ask questions about what they'd seen or experienced but did not really understand. One boy asked me, "What is the difference between a Mexican and a Hispanic?" I told him the terms *Hispanic* and *Latino* are used to identify all ethnic groups that come from Spanish-speaking countries, and that Mexicans were people from the country of Mexico. (In some communities there is

> I'll never forget an African-American friend of mine instructing his boys on what to do if they got stopped by the police—stay in the car, keep your hands in plain view, keep your mouth shut, and pray! I was shocked, because these were good kids. They were not gang-bangers or troublemakers, yet their father knew the dangers of being an African-American young person in our society. The same kind of fear is present in the Latino community and among most immigrant groups.

For more on the value of preparing students for short-term missions experiences, see page 105.

even disagreement about whether to use the term *Latino* or *Hispanic*.) Another young lady wanted to know the proper way to address the adults in the community, and began to call me Don Noel or Mr. Noel.

They joined in our activities without trying to change the way we did things, and they constantly communicated their gratitude to us for allowing them to come. Recognizing that attitudes about time vary across cultures, Lou and his kids learned to be more relaxed about schedules, instead of striving to finish each program in an hour and move on to the next activity. Although activities would often feel "unplanned" or less sophisticated than what they were used to, by the end of their stay they learned a **New** appreciation of our cultural differences.

Finally, they brought some funds they'd raised to help us establish a youth center in our building. Instead of dictating to us what they wanted to do for us, they worked hard to ask our kids and leaders what we needed, and then they tried to do their best to come alongside our dreams and desires.

We had such a good experience serving with this group that they've continued to return to La Villita to be with their Mexican brothers and sisters in Christ. Every time they come, not only do we serve together, but we have deeper kingdom conversations about righting racial wrongs. They are so committed to kingdom conversation that they have also established a relationship with an African-American church down the street, as well as with a church in Chinatown a few miles away.

I'll never forget the day I learned that a young Latina from our church had been invited to move to Indiana to live with one of these white families while her family was going through some struggles. That's deep racial community just like Jesus would want it: up close and personal.

WHO? (OBSERVATION)

STEP 3: WHO?

Up close and personal relationships and conversations lie at the heart of LINA THOMPSON's commitment to righting wrongs for the broken and brokenhearted. As the national director for training and capacity for World Vision's programs in the United States and an adjunct faculty member in Fuller Seminary's Urban Youth Ministry Certificate program, Lina is respected nationally as a thoughtful and passionate justice thinker, teacher, and leader.

For more information about the two-year, fully accredited Fuller Seminary Urban Youth Ministry Certificate offered through the Center for Youth and Family Ministry, visit www.cyfm.net.

Lina, why are youth ministries so hesitant to have honest conversations about race?

No matter what our skin color, anytime we talk about race, there is pain involved. So we often choose to ignore or deny deep reflection and conversations about race because we don't want to feel uncomfortable. And there aren't many places where youth workers can practice how to talk about race in a way that's safe and meaningful.

To download the full audio interview with Lina, visit the Deep Justice resource section of our Website at www.cyfm.net.

How do we get over these fears about race?

I think the degree to which we have meaningful relationships with people who are different ethnically and culturally is the degree to which meaningful conversations about race can take place. As a person of color and a Samoan woman, deep justice means I need to engage with people who are African American, Caucasian, and Asian—not just to talk about race but to actually have meaningful relationships. I cannot limit myself to people just like me.

Once youth workers have those types of relationships, how can they then start having conversations with kids about racial justice?

I've had people invite me to come and speak to their ministries or their leadership teams about race. Those conversations are really hard, because there is no context for those conversations outside of that meeting. You need to have an experience that brings up questions about race and justice before you can really talk about it. That experience becomes a catalyst for deep discussions about race.

What types of experiences are you talking about?

I am talking about creating a relational context for real transformation. It doesn't make any sense to try to talk about race relations if no real relationship or desire for relationships exists. It doesn't work when there isn't a commitment on both sides to pursue authentic relationships. You can't do it from a distance.

The experiences I am talking about are not necessarily creating *programs* either—unless those programs are intentionally designed to create relationships.

We all know relationships take time, especially for natural "enemies." I think time is the biggest barrier. We have to be willing to invest the time and resources over *years* to see relationships transformed. It only happens when people are intentional about their own development and growth related to breaking down racial, social, and ethnic barriers.

Can you give us an example of what you mean?

I serve as a commissioned lay pastor in a small, urban, multiethnic neighborhood. Over the last 10 years, we have forged a relationship with a very large, powerful, predominantly Caucasian congregation in our city.

This relationship has expressed itself in a variety of ways over the years.

Currently, this relationship is expressing itself in a building renovation project for our church.

To the uninformed outsider, it looks like the rich church helping the poor church. But to all of us insiders, it is far, far more. It is a commitment to walk together on this journey toward answering the missional question, "What does it mean to be and act like the church?" This question is the backdrop for the relationship between our two churches. While the "agenda" for our relationship is not overtly "reconciliation" or "justice" or "power," those conversations invariably happen because we are transparent about our commitment to authentic relationship.

So when you have experiences like these, what types of questions normally come up?

Questions about power almost always come up, especially with kids from urban or distressed communities. Kids who are on the margins have such an intuitive sense about justice, and it's always related to issues of power.

They start to wonder what God does when there's such an un-level playing field. Why does he allow it? What does God want his kingdom followers to do about it? And, why isn't the church doing more?

Do you think white, privileged kids have the same type of intuitive sense about justice?

I do. I think young people in general have a strong justice radar about what's right and what's not.

If that's true, then why aren't more conversations about justice and race happening in our ministries?

I think youth workers are often the ones who struggle with letting those questions surface. God uses young people to be his prophetic voice, and often that prophetic voice makes us very uncomfortable. So when you have youth workers who haven't struggled with these issues themselves or they're in a setting or church context that doesn't allow these questions to surface, they aren't able to frame these conversations.

So how can youth workers start working through issues about race?

Go find somebody who is different from you and be mentored. When I was leaving Young Life staff, they asked me a phenomenal question as part of my exit interview: "Talk about a relationship you have with a person who is different from you culturally and how that person has mentored you." We all need relationships like that.

What advice would you give to youth workers who live in communities where there's not a lot of racial diversity?

That's where the Internet is great. Even if you live in a monocultural place, you can go to a conference or a gathering in another city that draws diverse leaders and then keep in touch with them afterward online or by phone.

So if Jesus were to walk into a youth ministry meeting here in America and launch a discussion about race, what kinds of questions do you think he would ask?

That's a question we all need to ask ourselves. I think Jesus would ask, "What is the good news?" and, "What does the good news look like here?" Every youth ministry needs to ask these questions about their own communities.

What kinds of questions about race are taboo?

If you have a real relationship with someone, then I don't think any questions are taboo. If you have a friendship, then there's grace toward questions that might otherwise be offensive.

What should we do when our kids are making subtle but still derogatory jokes or comments about people of other skin colors or ethnicities?

When that happens to me, I ask the kids, "What's up with that? What's behind that comment? Does what you're saying bring dignity to others?" Even if kids say, "We were just kidding. It was just a joke," I think there's almost always something real behind the so-called joking.

What mistakes do youth workers tend to make in talking about race?

I think we're often not very well informed. We're not taking the time to do our own personal theological reflection. If you haven't spent time dealing with your own racism, then you can't pretend to be able to walk with kids through it.

HOW? (APPLICATION)

STEP 4: HOW?

DEEP JUSTICE APPLICATION QUESTIONS

1. When it comes to conversations about race, does your youth ministry lean toward silence or screaming? Instead of either silence or screaming, how do you think Jesus would engage in conversations about race?

2. Which of the suggested questions to ask about race on page 148 would spark the most provocative conversations with your students? When do you think you could ask them those questions?

3. Lina talks about a number of obstacles that prevent us from having deep conversations about race, including pain, fear, a shortage of time, and lack of practice. Which obstacle best explains your hesitations? Which best explains the hesitations of your students?

4. What is the deepest relationship you now have with a person of another skin color? Are you satisfied that this is enough? Why or why not?

5.   In chapter 4, we looked at the full Jesus who transcends our narrow *either/or* categories. When you picture Jesus, what color is his skin? How do you think that mental image affects your up close and personal relationships with people of other races?

6.   The Joplin framework in chapter 6 is designed to help you debrief justice experiences like the ones Lina suggests. In the midst of potentially awkward and heated discussions about race, how can you and the other adult leaders in your youth ministry provide the type of support and feedback that is pivotal to the Joplin model?

7.   Of the following list of Deep Justice Recommended Action Steps that flow from this chapter, which would best help you as a kingdom follower right wrongs? How about your youth ministry?

DEEP JUSTICE RECOMMENDED ACTION STEPS:

For Yourself

- Ask a close friend of another ethnicity to lunch, explaining ahead of time that you'd like to have an honest conversation about race. Use a handful of the questions on page 148 as a framework for your conversation, making sure you not only share yourself but also listen closely to your friend's insights and stories.

- Noel shares a story about his grandfather teaching him to "watch out for those white people." Spend some time identifying why and how others' words—in the forms of warnings, racial jokes, slang, or just plain old prejudiced statements—have shaped your views about race.

- Noel describes how it's been easy for him in the past to "play the race card" and assume others' criticisms of him are racially motivated. Spend some time thinking about past conflicts you've had with others and decide whether you tend to either play the race card and attribute too much to race or, inversely, to remain to racial dynamics that are present in conflict.

For Your Youth Ministry

- Start your youth group meeting a few minutes late, giving your students extra time to hang out. If possible, shoot some video footage of students standing, sitting, and talking together. Begin your meeting by playing the video footage. Ask them to share anything they noticed on the footage. Then show the footage again, this time asking them to pay special attention to racial dynamics that appear. When the video ends, lead your students into an up close and personal discussion about how race affects them even in youth group.

- Using the questions provided on page 148, schedule a panel of students and/or adults in which you ask participants to discuss how their ethnicity has influenced their lives and experiences.

- Invite members from your church or community who have vivid memories of the Civil Rights movement in the 1960s to come and share what has changed, as well as what is still mostly the same, since then.

- Brainstorm with your students the types of questions Jesus would ask about race. Then encourage them to gather with a few friends, especially friends of different races, and try to answer those questions together.

- Explain to students the three levels of justice we presented in chapter 1. Brainstorm ways they can move beyond relational responses and begin changing the systems that perpetuate racial conflict and injustice. Encourage them to take "baby steps" on their own campuses by joining a club or sports team in which they will interact with students of other races and ethnicities, writing an article or paper about racial justice, or shooting a video about race on campus and distributing it to teachers and school administrators.

HOW CAN OUR CHECKBOOKS BE TOOLS FOR JUSTICE?

BY LARRY ACOSTA

Larry Acosta is the president and founder of the Hispanic Ministry Center, Urban Youth Workers Institute, & KIDWORKS. Larry's passion is to envision and shape the emerging generation of urban leadership for transformational ministry. Larry is a graduate of both Biola University and Talbot School of Theology and completed his doctorate in leadership development at Fuller Theological Seminary. However, his claim to fame is that he is married to his lovely wife of 13 years, Jayme, and they have four wonderful children: Brock (9), Karis (8), Malia (3) and Diego (2).

NOW? (DISCERNMENT)

STEP 1: NOW?

Matt Ford and Craig Blodgett are heroes of mine, although I've never met either of them personally.

Matt and Craig are youth pastors from two different churches in suburban Fresno, California. Each of them had a nice, comfortable home in the suburbs—that is, until they realized that 40 percent of Fresno's families were living below the poverty line.[48] Compelled by their kingdom values and their desire to live incarnationally among the poor, they sold their homes in the burbs and bought two jacked-up fixer-uppers next door to each other in one of Fresno's poorest neighborhoods.

Every day these two youth workers face the complexities of being white while living in a predominantly Latino community.

Every day these two youth workers face the threat of gang warfare and violence.

Every day these youth workers are making sacrificial choices with their own checkbooks that make them my deep justice heroes.

Matt's and Craig's families are not alone in their bold justice move. Twenty-three other Christian families have also moved into various Fresno neighborhoods of intense pockets of poverty. One such family, Phil and Reese Skei, believe that, "If we want to see transformation in our city, we must go where the light is needed most. We are *choosing* to be here...to move in, to become an insider and care for our neighbors, to serve our schools, and to live out the gospel through relationships."

Not only am I amazed by the courage of these Micah 6:8 kingdom revolutionaries, I am also challenged by their rejection of our materialistic worldviews. In a world that **Now** tempts us to follow the "American Dream," where all that matters is the stuff we accumulate, their kingdom choice to be downwardly mobile both socially and financially as a way of righting wrongs is inspiring. Most people who have the educational or financial wherewithal to live in self-focused comfort do. Most folks—even Christians—spend their lifetimes trying to climb socially prescribed ladders of success to prove they've made it.

> "He has shown all you people what is good. And what does the Lord require of you? To act justly and to love mercy and to walk humbly with your God."
>
> MICAH 6:8

---

[48] The Brookings Institution Metropolitan Policy Program, "Katrina's Window: Confronting Concentrated Poverty across America," October 2005.

As youth workers, most of us are no different.

In the midst of an entire book focusing on deep justice within youth ministry, we are dedicating this chapter to your own *personal* justice choices with your own *personal* bank accounts. More than any youth ministry talk or sermon you give about money, the choices you **Now** make with your own checkbook are leaving a lasting impression on your students.

EITHER COMFORT OR RESENTMENT

Whether we live in an urban, rural, or suburban context, we are **Now** making *either/or* choices with our checkbooks and finances every day. Many of us are doing okay financially; we pay our bills every month, and we can even find a way to absorb the unexpected cost of a car repair here or a plane ticket there.

Yet we who have enough money to do what God is calling us to **Now** often take that for granted. We can easily slip into the cultural trap of feeling like we're entitled to keep buying bigger and better. It's natural for us to think of ourselves, especially when our ministries are successful and our job is secure, as *deserving* what others have. In the end, we spend more time thinking about what we want to do with "our money" than we spend considering how God wants us to use what we have for peace, reconciliation, and justice. We fixate on how we're going to spend what we have, and our money consumes us.

On the flip side, others of us in youth ministry are barely making it financially. Each month we wonder if we'll be able to pay all of our bills. Those of us in that category face different temptations. First, we may try to buy the right cars, wear the right clothes, and live in the right houses to give the impression we have money when, in reality, we're barely scraping by. Second, we may look at those around us (in our churches or on the other side of town) who have money and feel growing resentment that they seem immune to our financial stress. Either way, when we feel like we're not making it financially, we can easily find ourselves in a perpetual state of depression and fear.

UCLA's annual study of college freshman found that three-quarters of its first-year students in 2006 thought it was essential or very important to be "very well-off financially." That compares with 62.5 percent who said the same in 1980 and 42 percent in 1966. A similar recent poll from the Pew Research Center found that approximately 80 percent of 18-25 year-olds name getting rich as a top life goal for their generation.

"Most fundamentally for us, the kingdom of God is not just about us. It is not about justifying a lifestyle that we want to live at the expense of the rest of the world."

Kevin Blue, *Practical Justice*

Either entitlement *or* resentment.

Either self-focused comfort *or* propping up a life-style beyond our means.

For too many youth workers, money is **Now** a barrier to living justly.

HI, MY NAME IS LARRY, AND I'VE STRUGGLED TOO...

I am speaking from experience. I grew up poor and, as a Latino, felt the pressure to prove myself by the dominant culture's standards. Like so many who grow up feeling marginalized socially, economically, or otherwise, I compensated for feeling "less than" by excelling educationally. This eventually gave me access to a job as a youth worker in a thriving suburban church. Once I had enough degrees and the right youth ministry title on my business card, I felt like I—the son of a janitor—had finally made it.

After ten years of youth ministry at that church, my wife, Jayme, and I sensed God was calling us to leave the comfort of the church and reengage my Latino roots by launching KIDWORKS, a community-development corporation that seeks to holistically transform at-risk neighborhoods, and the Hispanic Ministry Center, an urban leadership-development organization in Santa Ana, California. It was here that my theological beliefs about justice, my commitment to God's kingdom, and my willingness to give up my selfish ambitions were rigorously tested.

While we youth workers don't make the big bucks, we would be wise to remember how our salaries compare with salaries around the world. Based on figures from the World Bank Development Research Group, the Global Rich List has calculated that the average annual income worldwide is $5,000. To see where your salary falls compared to others around the world, visit http://www.globalrichlist.com/how.html.

Now Larry leads the Urban Youth Workers Institute, which seeks to strengthen a new generation of global urban leaders for transformational ministry. The vision of UYWI is to build transformational relationships with 20,000 urban leaders by 2010 (www.uywi.org).

ARE YOU A "HAVE" OR A "HAVE NOT"?

What about you? When it comes to money, do you think of yourself as a "have" or a "have not"? Either way, for you and the students and families you serve, how you theologically reflect on money and its hold on you is a central question in the quest for a lifestyle of deep mercy and kingdom justice.

What are the kids in your ministry learning about money from the way you talk, what you drive, the clothes you wear, and the house you live in? In your own financial decisions, can you say along with Paul, "Follow me as I follow Christ" (1 Corinthians 11:1, NIV), or are you imprisoned by guilt and greed? Are you financing an image and lifestyle beyond your means, or are you living below your means and making sacrifices so wrongs can be righted? Are you trying to live missionally in terms of your finances, or have you settled for status quo comparisons with the Joneses and Rodriguezes?

When Fuller Seminary's Center for Youth and Family Ministry surveyed high school seniors entering college for our College Transition Project, these students seemed far more committed to make Jesus the Lord of their dating lives than of their checkbooks. Perhaps part of the problem is that many of us youth workers struggle ourselves with how to make our checkbooks tools of deep justice. For more information and free resources related to the CYFM College Transition Project, go to www.cyfm.net.

In an age when credit card debt is at an all-time high...

In an era when VH1 sets up *The Fabulous Life of Jay-Z* as the cultural standard...

At a time when youth workers are prone to project an image of success through serving at the right church, wearing the right gear, and driving the right car...

In the midst of God calling some of us to sell all we have and relocate to the inner city...

In a season in which God is inviting others of us to live a radical kingdom life in the midst of Starbucks-laden, minivan-driving, Saturday-soccer suburbia...

...It's time to launch a **New** justice revolution that not only impacts our own lives but will equip, enable, and empower our students to make their checkbooks tools of deep justice.

NEW? (REFLECTION)

STEP 2: NEW?

The justice revolution that moves beyond either comfort or resentment is a personal journey each of us must take individually. It begins with a **New** willingness to carefully examine our attitudes and actions in light of the gospel. In Luke 9:23-25, for example, Jesus challenges the view that life is about our comfort by proclaiming that his followers must be more concerned with the welfare and shalom of others than our own dreams of entitlement:

> "Whoever wants to be my disciple must deny themselves and take up their cross daily and follow me. For whoever wants to save their life will lose it, but whoever loses their life for me will save it. What good is it for you to gain the whole world, and yet lose or forfeit your very self?"

Three chapters later in Luke 12:15, Jesus talks specifically about money:

> "Watch out! Be on your guard against all kinds of greed; life does not consist in the abundance of his possessions."

And he continues in verses 16-21 with this parable, describing the consequence of hoarding resources for ourselves:

> "The ground of a certain rich man yielded an abundant crop. He thought to himself, 'What shall I do? I have no place to store my

crops.' Then he said, 'This is what I'll do. I will tear down my barns and build bigger ones, and there I will store my surplus grain.' And I'll say to myself, 'You have plenty of grain laid up for many years. Take life easy; eat, drink and be merry.' But God said to him, 'You fool! This very night your life will be demanded from you. Then who will get what you have prepared for yourself?' This is how it will be with those who store up things for themselves but are not rich toward God."

In these and many other passages, Jesus calls us to a **New** awareness of the allure of money that can lead us into a life of self-centered privilege. Interestingly, Jesus never says there's anything specifically wrong with money. It is when we allow ourselves to focus our allegiance and longings toward its superficial and destructive power that we deny not only our faith but the Lord himself.

In 1 Timothy 6:9-10, Paul writes about the destruction—both present and eternal—that awaits those who love money:

> Those who want to get rich fall into temptation and a trap and into many foolish and harmful desires that plunge people into ruin and destruction. For the love of money is a root of all kinds of evil.

NEW FREEDOM THAT HELPS US LIVE JUSTLY

Years ago, I was asked to speak at our home church on the topic of "materialism." Initially, I tried to delegate the task of speaking on this subject to another member of our team, but I knew all along the Lord was trying to deepen my commitment to kingdom stewardship through the experience. And in the process of developing this talk, I came up with some **New** "Better Practices" that have helped our family view money as a tool to right wrongs ever since.

The message was titled "Beyond Materialism...Living Financially F.R.E.E." and was based on 2 Kings 4:1-7:

> The wife of a man from the company of the prophets cried out to Elisha, "Your servant my husband is dead, and you know that

he revered the Lord. But now his creditor is coming to take my two boys as his slaves."

Elisha replied to her, "How can I help you? Tell me, what do you have in your house?"

"Your servant has nothing there at all," she said, "except a little olive oil."

Elisha said, "Go around and ask all your neighbors for empty jars. Don't ask for just a few. Then go inside and shut the door behind you and your sons. Pour oil into all the jars, and as each is filled, put it to one side."

She left him and shut the door behind her and her sons. They brought the jars to her and she kept pouring. When all the jars were full, she said to her son, "Bring me another one."

But he replied, "There is not a jar left." Then the oil stopped flowing.

She went and told the man of God, and he said, "Go, sell the oil and pay your debts. You and your sons can live on what is left."

The **New** practices for us that emerge from this text are captured in the acrostic for the word F.R.E.E.

In his book, *Rich Christians in an Age of Hunger,* Ron Sider offers some guidelines that can help us live and spend in **New** ways:

1. Move toward a personal lifestyle that is sustainable over time.

2. Distinguish between necessities and luxuries.

3. Remember that expenditures for the purpose of status or pride are wrong.

4. Distinguish between expenditures to develop hobbies and to have status.

5. Distinguish between expenses for occasional celebrations and making them part of your normal day-to-day routines.

6. Resist buying things just because you can afford them. The amount you earn has nothing to do with what you need.

FIGURE OUT...

1. The source of the crisis.

In 2 Kings 4:1-7, the widow's crisis was that her family's income had diminished after her husband's passing, and creditors were coming to take her two sons as payment. While this would be inhumane by our standards, Mosaic Law allowed creditors to enslave debtors and their children until the Year of Jubilee to work off a debt (Exodus 21:2-4, Leviticus 25:39). (For more on the Year of Jubilee, see chapter 11.)

Our family was in a similar place ten years ago when our income dropped significantly after my wife, Jayme, left her job to be home after our children were born. With the births of our first and second child, we could still manage on our one youth ministry income. But when we tried to stretch our finances further with the arrivals of kids three and four, like so many youth workers, we began financing our "shortfall" on our credit cards. After a while, we grew far too accustomed to accepting these incremental expenses as a manageable way of life. The **New** truth was that we'd gotten trapped in a lifestyle our salary didn't support. We needed to step back and create a realistic budget that would enable us to live within our means.

What's the source of your "crisis"? School loans, peer pressure, insecurity, credit-card debt, the inability to postpone immediate gratification? In today's economy, where banks target their credit card offers at those who have the worst chance of paying them off (and youth workers tend to fall into that category!), the issue of debt is a seldom-discussed hot topic in the church.

Or could it be in the other direction, where you have more than enough to live but get excited thinking about how you'll spend the excess on yourself? For a follower of Christ, financial crisis is *not* limited to when you don't have enough. In a world of great need, our having *more* than enough is a call to examine ourselves and our willingness to give to others.

> "This generation of twenty-somethings is straining under the weight of college loans and other debt, a crushing load that separates it from every previous generation. Nearly two-thirds carry some debt, and those with debt have taken on more in the past five years. Additionally, they're being urged to save early for their retirement, yet many can't and most aren't."
>
> MINDY FETTERMAN AND BARBARA HANSEN, "YOUNG PEOPLE STRUGGLE TO DEAL WITH KISS OF DEBT," *USA TODAY,* NOVEMBER 20, 2006

2. The assets you already have.

The good news from this passage is that, in most cases, whether you have a lot or a little, you still have something. In 2 Kings 4:2, Elisha asks the widow, "How can I help you? Tell me, what do you have in your house?" "Your servant has nothing there at all," she said, "except a little olive oil." The widow didn't have much, but she did have a little oil.

If you are struggling, ask yourself: What do you already have, and where do you need to be thankful and creative to make ends meet? Do you have your education and your family? Is your car older, but paid off? Someone once defined thankfulness as "wanting what you have." When I see someone's newer car, my mantra has become, "I *love* my car, it couldn't be better!" And I celebrate the fact that I don't have a car payment because we drive older cars.

REACH OUT FOR HELP

Here's more good news: We don't have to figure out how to turn our checkbooks into tools of deep justice alone. We can seek wise counsel from others. In 2 Kings 4:3, Elisha instructs, "Go around and ask all your neighbors for empty jars. Don't ask for just a few."

One of the best things I ever did in my twenties was to trust the counsel of our church's business administrator to contribute 10 percent of my salary to our 403(b) retirement account set up by the church. The church matched up to 3 percent of my contributions, and these pre tax dollars began to multiply. Throughout the years, this money has grown through the power of compounding interest and our continuing discipline to contribute through an automatic deduction program. If it were not for the wisdom of this financially savvy mentor, I would have missed the **New** opportunity to start young.

By "best practices," we mean tried and true wise steps.

Secondly, read books on stewardship and financial "best practices." Let's face it, few of us in youth ministry really understand money, and we need to decrease our ignorance through financially sound mentors who can resource us with the tools for fiscal responsibility. One such mentor for my wife and me is Randy Alcorn. His books, *Money, Possessions, and Eternity*, and *The Treasure Principle*, have reformatted our thinking about stewardship and put us on track biblically so our money can be a better tool of justice.

Here are two of Alcorn's "Treasure Principle Keys" that can help youth workers bring justice to a broken world:[49]

1. God owns everything. I'm his money manager.

We are managers of assets God has given to us, or some would say "entrusted" to us. But with these assets comes a responsibility to put this wealth into service for his kingdom's sake. He is the ultimate owner of all we have, and we get to be the dispensers of his shalom, grace, and justice. Money, when considered as a tool for good, compels us to be outrageously generous for his kingdom's sake. After all, it all belongs to him.

2. My heart always goes where I put God's money.

Watch what happens when you reallocate your money from temporal things to eternal things. One of the greatest freedoms we can know is when we take control over those things that formerly controlled us, and money is one of the most powerful controllers of all. When we release our suffocating hold on "our money," and freely give what we've been given, our hearts are softened, and we are able to see God's kingdom work in **New** and different ways—both in us and around us.

EXPECT GOD'S HELP!

Though she began with only "a little bit of olive oil," the widow in our story from 2 Kings was able to continue pouring that oil until every jar in the house was full. Only then, the Bible tells us, did the oil stop flowing (2 Kings 4:5-6).

In the same way, God will honor your **New** effort to be a wise and responsible steward. He will meet you at your point of need and help you move to a healthier place. When my wife and I got serious about wanting to be better stewards of our resources, we knew we had to focus first and foremost on paying off our credit card debt. With God's help, we began to courageously reconsider some of the expenses that we had previously thought were "non-negotiable"—like cable TV, dry cleaning, entertainment, eating out, and new clothes. It was during these cutbacks that God met us. We were pleasantly surprised at how easy it really was to live without some of these creature comforts. Our disciplined spending enabled us to pay off our credit card debt in five months. This led to a wonderful place of financial freedom and a continuing disciplined lifestyle, which empowers us to continue to use our checkbook as a tool of responsible living and kingdom giving.

---

[49] Adapted from *The Treasure Principle* by Randy Alcorn (Sisiters, OR: Multinomah Publishers, 2005).

EXECUTE THE PLAN

The story concludes with Elijah telling the widow: "Go, sell the oil and pay your debts. You and your sons can live on what is left" (2 Kings 4:7). Elijah offered the woman a plan that would help her steward her resources effectively. In the same way we need a plan to help us manage our resources in ways that promote deep justice. Here are four key principles you'd be wise to keep in mind as part of your plan:

1. Trust God by giving him the "first fruits."

In 2 Corinthians 8:7, Paul teaches:

> But since you excel in everything—in faith, in speech, in knowledge, in complete earnestness and in the love we have kindled in you—see that you also excel in this grace of giving.

Unfortunately, there has been a gradual decline in overall giving in the United States during the last 30 years.[50] While the New Testament does not specify a particular amount kingdom followers are to give, the Old Testament teaches tithing—or giving 10 percent (see Leviticus 27:30-33, Deuteronomy 14:22-23). Interestingly, even those who received that tithe from the Israelites—the Levites—were commanded to give a tenth of what they received as their own tithe (Numbers 18:25). The importance of tithing is echoed in Malachi 3:6-10 when God pronounces those who withhold their tithe as "under a curse" because they are "robbing" him.

> "You are under a curse—your whole nation—because you are robbing me."
>
> MALACHI 3:9

Since both Old and New Testaments affirm that giving is a central expression of trusting God, it would follow that Christians would exponentially surpass the generosity of the culture. But the facts show otherwise. According to the Gallup organization, those who attend church weekly give roughly the same amount to charity as their neighbors who do not attend.[51]

In the midst of the spirit of grace and freedom embodied by Jesus and the New Testament, our requirement to tithe is not eliminated. Even those contemporary leaders and pastors who encourage the giving of our "time" and "talents," still stress the importance of simultaneously giving our "treasure." As youth workers trying to make our checkbooks **New** tools of deep justice, if we don't tithe as God intends, we might slip into the Malachi 3 trap of "robbing God"—and that's not a trap we want to get stuck in!

---

[50] Since 1975, total charitable giving by Americans has averaged between 1.6 percent and 2.16 percent of income. (Figures from the Internal Revenue Service, the Gallup Organization, and Giving USA, a publication of the American Association of Fundraising Council.)

[51] Randy Alcorn, *Money, Possessions, and Eternity* (Wheaton, Illinois: Tyndale House Publishers, 2003) 180.

2. Save.

Proverbs 6:6-8 tells us:

> Go to the ant, you sluggard; consider its ways and be wise! It has no commander, no overseer or ruler, yet it stores its provisions in summer and gathers its food at harvest.

It is normal to treat saving as optional in order to increase our current standard of living. We grow accustomed to living at a level beyond our current means and never seem to have enough money to get around to saving.

There are some who look at saving—whether for retirement, our kids' college tuition, or other reasons— as a symptom of "not trusting God," or somehow choosing the American Dream over God's kingdom dream. While each youth worker needs to make his or her own personal decision about spending, giving, and saving, I believe giving and saving represent two halves of yet another kingdom *both/and.* In our family, we *both* give and save, *and* we constantly try to discern the kingdom balance between the two.

3. Create and live within a written budget.

A well-planned budget for anticipated expenses and an emergency fund for the truly unexpected can end dependence on credit cards. Set up a budget and review it every month. Don't try to create your budget based on the perfect month, because we never have those. Account for where every dollar will go before the month begins.[52]

Creative strategies that allow us to share resources with others can also help us live within our budget. Maybe you can join with other families by pooling your various tools and equipment instead of each family buying its own. Perhaps you could invite someone who's experiencing either temporary or long-term homelessness to share your spare bedroom, either for free or for a fraction of the cost of typical rent. If we youth workers applied the same creativity we use every day with kids toward our budgeting, we'd have much more to save and give for kingdom justice.

---

[52] Dave Ramsey, *The Total Money Makeover* (Nashville: Thomas Nelson, 2003), 99.

4. Carve out kingdom giving that is sacrificial.

Deep justice for us as youth workers, and for our students, means understanding that on the one hand, God cares about our lives and has promised to meet our needs. On the other hand, however, God's faithfulness assumes that, because he has promised to take care of us, we are therefore compelled to use our wealth, regardless of how ample or feeble it is, to relieve the financial pressure on others *before* we pursue our own self-centered comfort.

I think Randy Alcorn says it well when he writes, "Where we choose to store our treasures depends largely on where we think our home is."[53] As kingdom people, we know our home on this earth is only temporary, so we have to constantly ask ourselves: How can we radically and generously give of our finances so every dollar we earn is a kingdom tool?

That was a question eighteenth-century minister John Wesley wrestled with throughout his lifetime. At one point, John felt called to teach at Oxford University, a position that provided a far greater income than he required. As a single man, John spent the bulk of his 30-pound annual salary on playing cards, tobacco, and brandy.

In 1731, all that changed. On a cold winter day at Oxford, John noticed a chambermaid cleaning his room who was wearing nothing more than a thin linen gown to protect her from the bleak weather. He reached into his pocket to give her some money for a coat but didn't have enough. He immediately realized that the Lord was not pleased with the way he was spending and stewarding his money.

> "Some interpreters of Jesus' teachings...have concluded that Christians cannot support the concept of a right to private property...They find nothing in Jesus' witness on this issue to undergird the concept and much that points in the direction of economic disinvestment. Others are so committed to liberal capitalism as to find the issue unworthy of debate. We reject both poles and argue here for a qualified right to private property subordinate to the primary norm of economic justice as an aspect of God's reign."
>
> GLEN H. STASSEN AND DAVID P. GUSHEE, *KINGDOM ETHICS*

That year, John Wesley's living expenses were 28 pounds, so he gave the 2 pounds leftover to the poor and needy. The next year his income doubled, but he still chose to live on 28 pounds, so he had 32 pounds to give to others. The third year, his income rose to 90 pounds, but instead of raising his standard of living, he continued to live on 28 pounds and gave away 62 pounds. In the fourth year, he received 120 pounds but his expenses remained 28 pounds so

---

[53] Randy Alcorn, *The Treasure Principle* (Oregon: Multnomah, 2001), 45.

he was able to give 92 pounds to the broken and brokenhearted. Eventually, his yearly income rose to over 1400 pounds, but he continued to live on just 30 pounds, and gave away the rest.

At one point in his life, John's diet consisted primarily of potatoes for four years—partly for his health but mainly so he could give sacrificially to the needy. John explained, "What I save from my own meat will feed another that else would have none."

While John Wesley's willingness to identify with the needy is inspirational, we should remember that his background and education made him permanently privileged. In his book *Not All of Us Are Saints* (New York: Hill and Wang, 1994), David Hilfiker, a medical doctor who has lived among America's poor, reflected on that same dynamic: "There are privileges of birth and upbringing I could never renounce, even if I wanted to. I could give away all of my money, but none of my education. No matter how poor I became, I would always have the possibility of returning to the mainstream and beginning again. I could renounce the trappings of privilege...but were I ever in desperate need, my parents or my mother-in-law or my siblings or my church community or my friends...would be present to bail me out. No matter how poor I became, I would always have the connections that promise me a security unknown to those in the ghetto."

ALL OUR FINANCIAL DECISIONS ARE ETHICAL DECISIONS

As youth workers, I hope we follow John Wesley's example and move toward sacrificial giving and living so our money becomes a tool of kingdom justice. When you stop to think about it, every financial decision we make is an ethical decision—from saving to attend college or buy a car to spending change on a caramel macchiato. Every decision we make about money impacts the poor in some way. Let it be said that on our watch, we faithfully spent and gave our own money to right wrongs around us.

WHO? (OBSERVATION)

STEP 3: WHO?

ANTHONY FLYNN, Senior Vice President of Operations at the Urban Youth Workers Institute, is a kingdom justice leader **Who** makes major and minor decisions that convert his checkbook into a tool of deep justice. The majority of Anthony's ministry experience has occurred in Memphis, Tennessee, smack dab in a neighborhood with the city's highest rates of crime, HIV/AIDS, and gang activity. Anthony's growing commitment to community development has been furthered by his radical choice to right wrongs in a broken world—even at great personal cost.

Anthony, tell us a bit about your journey in turning your checkbook over for kingdom purposes.

Although I was raised in an urban community for a significant portion of my life, when I turned 12, my family moved into a suburban community. As a result of living among our culture's "haves," I quickly started equating success with material acquisitions. As someone who had been initially raised in an impoverished family, I was determined never to go back.

> To download and hear the entire audio interview with Anthony, please visit our free Deep Justice resources available at www.cyfm.net

When I graduated from the University of Memphis, I was recruited by several Fortune 500 companies. I had job offers from Coca-Cola, Kraft Foods, Philip Morris, R.J. Reynolds, and Saks Incorporated. I spent a season of my life working for R.J. Reynolds and later for 3M, another Fortune 500 giant, as a cardio-pulmonary representative in their pharmaceutical division. I must be honest and admit I was a young man of 23 who was ravenously chasing after money.

One day while sitting in a cardiology office, a mother and child entered the waiting room who reminded me of my old life—and I had somewhat of an epiphanous flashback. As I sat in that office, waiting minute by minute in hopes of seeing my "upper echelon" client, all I could think about was how I would much rather have been in an assignment that provided me the intrinsic value of knowing I could devote all my time to partnering with others in overcoming the very struggle my family managed to overcome. It was at that moment that I realized I'd lived the last several years trying to fill a God-sized hole with material possessions. So on that day God really began to move in my heart and in my spirit and help me shift my entire life's focus.

So what did you end up doing?

Right on the verge of being hired by the world's largest pharmaceutical company and having my already high salary doubled, I walked away from corporate America and entered full-time youth ministry as an urban youth worker. That meant a cut of approximately $55,000 in my annual salary.

What sacrifices did that mean for you and your family?

It was really tough. I made this decision only five months prior to being married, and my wife and I had our first child within the first couple of years. I'd thought I would never have to depend on my mother or stepfather for financial assistance again, but they ended up having to support my wife and me through such acts of kindness as paying our utility bill. But we never missed a meal, and I would still argue that it was the absolute best decision I could have ever made.

In the midst of your justice journey with your money, what lessons has God taught you?

I've learned the love of money really is the root of all kinds of evil. I've seen so many people who have been driven by money—just as I was—and they will lie, cheat, and steal to get it. When your priorities are out of order, it can really mess up your life.

I once attended a seminar on servant leadership in which Ken Blanchard, world-renowned author of *The One Minute Manager*, commented that an addiction is an ever-increasing desire to fulfill something that has an ever-decreasing ability to satisfy. Looking back, I was addicted to money. I thank God that he has freed me, and that I no longer look to money or what money can buy to satisfy me.

It's been said that when we feel less, we buy more. In other words, when we feel insecure or inadequate, we're more likely to try to find our identity and adequacy in money. Do you think that's true?

Certainly. For me, it started as a teenager. As a young person, I had a lot of insecurities and struggles, and I tried to buy my way out of them. As an adult, I was trying to keep up with the Joneses.

Most folks reading this book are probably not Fortune 500 business people. Instead, they are youth workers—who nonetheless have their

own issues with money. As you have been around youth workers, what do you think our issues are when it comes to money?

I like to remind youth workers that, although we might attempt to live a "normal life," we're not normal. Our calling to justice in our youth ministry means we probably won't live a normal life. Given the time and effort we devote to our ministry jobs, we will probably never get paid what we "deserve."

That's a good point. I think many of us in youth ministry want to experience the joy of obeying God's call to deep justice but still pursue the American Dream.

That's human nature, but the reality is that as youth workers, our wealth is not material. Our wealth comes in being able to contribute to and add value to the lives of others.

Do you ever drive past a really nice car or house and think to yourself, "Man, I could be living like that right now?"

Sure I do. At times, my wife and I ride past gorgeous houses and think to ourselves, "Wow, it sure would be nice to live like that." But the reality is God always brings us back down to earth and helps us be grateful for where he has us.

What types of choices do you and your wife make when it comes to giving your money to kingdom causes?

Whether you have a million dollars in the bank, or whether you have ten dollars in the bank, you can give. I am convinced there is always something you have to contribute to the lives of others. My wife and I have committed never to have a household bill that's more than the amount of money we give. In addition to giving our tithes to the church, we also give financially to other organizations. Plus, we also commit to giving directly to families that are underprivileged. Each year, we identify a family that can directly benefit from us sharing our 3 T's (Time, Talent, and Treasure). Sometimes this is a stretch for us, because every now and again, money gets tight and "life happens." However, our methods of giving have never failed us, and God has continually provided for us.

What would you say to youth workers living "hand to mouth," struggling to pay their bills?

Don't give up. I know it sounds cliché, but truly don't give up and remain faithful to the calling at hand. My philosophy is that if you commit to be 110 percent dedicated to God's call on your life, God will provide. I don't believe there is such a thing as vision without provision. If God has given you a vision for a particular calling, God will surround you with the people and resources you need to make it happen.

I would also encourage folks living paycheck to paycheck to find a mentor—maybe someone who is a financial services professional—and ask that mentor to help you balance your budget and be the best possible steward of the resources God has given you. Begin reading books on financial management and pick three new disciplines related to money management.

What financial disciplines do you recommend for youth workers who want to turn their own checkbooks into tools of deep justice?

There are a lot of simple things we can all do. First, balance your checkbook. Know how much money goes in and out of your accounts each month. Second, surround yourselves with people who are living out the kingdom values you want to live out. Figure out what it is they do with their money that is so attractive to you.

What impact do our choices about money have on the kids in our ministries?

I believe the best sermon we can possibly preach is how we live our lives. As youth workers, we have the chance to be at least somewhat transparent with our students about why and how we make our financial choices. For instance, if we're wrestling with the choice of whether we should buy a house, we can invite them into what it means to have a mortgage and home insurance and all those other fun expenses.

For many of the kids we reach out to, we are the closest thing to Jesus that they'll see. We're the walking, living, breathing example of Jesus that they identify with. So if they see us making mistakes with our money, they are more likely to mimic those mistakes in their own choices. When they see us making kingdom choices with our checkbooks, hopefully they will too.

HOW? (APPLICATION)

STEP 4: HOW?

DEEP JUSTICE APPLICATION QUESTIONS

1. Larry describes an *either/or* extreme relevant to our finances as youth workers: *Either* we live with a sense of comfort *or* a sense of resentment. Which best describes you?

2. For a moment, think about money in light of the Good/Guilt/Grace/ Gratitude kingdom story discussed in chapter 3. How does money have the potential to be used for good? How does sin corrupt the way we use money? How is God gracious to us in the midst of our sin? How can you continue to be grateful for God's faithful provision for your needs?

3. Both Larry and Anthony describe how their upbringings affected their views of money. As we discussed in chapter 1, deep justice means understanding the reasons there are so many wrongs that need to be righted. In what ways have your own family and background affected your ability to use money to right wrongs around you?

4. If someone asked you to describe your students' current attitudes toward money in a few sentences, what would you say?

5. Imagine that, as we discussed in chapter 6, students' needles were pointed toward being kingdom people. How would that change their attitudes toward money?

6. What were your thoughts and feelings as you read about John Wesley's decision to live on limited resources and use the remainder for kingdom justice? Is his example realistic for you (and your family) today? Why or why not?

7. Think about what you have given to others (both in terms of money and specific items) in the last few months. How "sacrificial" was that giving? In other words, did giving the money and items really cost you something, or were you giving from your leftovers? If you were giving from your leftovers, does that make your giving any less significantly or "godly?" Why or why not?

8. Do you agree that all financial decisions are ethical decisions? If you were to live with this conscious awareness every day, how would the way you spend, save, and share your money be different? How would this affect what you're modeling for your students?

9. Of the following list of Deep Justice Recommended Action Steps that flow from this chapter, which would best help you right wrongs as a kingdom follower?

DEEP JUSTICE RECOMMENDED ACTION STEPS:

For Yourself

- Given the examples of Matt and Craig at the start of the chapter, prayerfully consider how God might be calling you to downward mobility. Gather with other kingdom followers who live in a similar context and brainstorm creative ways that your checkbooks can be tools of deep justice.

- In chapter 5, we discussed kingdom shalom as the holistic flourishing that the King intends for all people. Invite to lunch one or more people who use their checkbooks as tools of kingdom shalom. Ask them how they make their financial choices, and how they perceive those choices impacting them and others.

- Take Larry's advice and draft a budget that spends "every dollar on paper before the month begins." If your budget seems out of alignment with your kingdom values, try adjusting it for a few months until you feel at peace about the way you're using your money.

- Make a list of assets you could share with others around you (a car you don't use that often, a spare bedroom, a crock pot, an extra winter coat, a power saw). Add as many items as possible to the list, and try to share generously as you see needs arise around you.

- Meet with the financial administrator of your church or ministry to discuss ways you can start saving for retirement now.

- On a scale of 1-10, with 10 being "very intentionally" and 1 being "not intentionally at all," rate the degree to which you live with an intentional mindset toward using your finances to right wrongs around you. Contrast that with the number you'd like to reach and identify a few ways you could move toward that kingdom goal.

- Establish goals for giving—not just an amount, but also consider the type of justice causes you would like to support. Some possible emphases include local, national, or global; evangelism or discipleship; urban, suburban, or small town. As you have opportunities to give, track your various categories of giving so you can adjust your giving to match your kingdom priorities.

- The next time you consider a big purchase, ask a trusted friend to help you think through all the ethical ramifications of your decision. Is it a want or a need? Can you get by without it? Can you get something cheaper that will work almost as well? Is that purchase a tool of justice, or simply a toy for you to enjoy? Consider inviting a few students in on this conversation as a model of a kingdom decision-making process.

For Your Youth Ministry

We'll be covering this in the next chapter, so turn the page and keep reading...

HOW CAN OUR YOUTH MINISTRIES USE THEIR MONEY SO THE POOR GAIN POWER?

BY LARRY ACOSTA

NOW? (DISCERNMENT)

STEP 1: NOW?

When it comes to the way many youth ministries use money **Now**, the road to shallow justice is paved with good intentions.

I know. I've laid some asphalt there myself.

Odds are good that you have, too.

I recently received this letter from a youth worker who realized his ministry's money had provided only a shallow topcoat of justice:

In the last six months, Danny has become very involved in our youth ministry. He and his friends were especially active in their Tuesday evening small group. Summer camp was fast approaching, which was always a highlight for our small groups to experience together. I was confused, however, because Danny was not yet signed up for camp even though most of his friends were. I asked one of his friends what was up with Danny and camp. He said Danny's mom had been laid off and was doing temp work, but it was not steady enough to pay all the bills. Danny was embarrassed and did not want to ask for help.

I was quick to explain to Danny that we help a lot of kids who need financial assistance by providing odd jobs to earn money for camp and that we even had some scholarships available. I wanted him to know money should not keep him from joining us for camp. As a result of that conversation, Danny was able to join us at camp, and our church even helped his mom with the money for rent one month.

But now I realize that I took the easy way out in that situation. I made quite an effort to find the resources for the rent and a camp scholarship, but truthfully, I spent fewer than five minutes thinking about how to help Danny's mom get a steady job. I changed the short-term situation for Danny and his mom, but did nothing to help alleviate the real problem. Living justly is about using our ministry's money to solve the deeper issues, not just the more immediate or obvious needs.

Why did I think so short term in this situation? Was I really that busy? What would have been a better use of the $1500 it took for rent and camp? What if I had used some of the money to hire someone to help her find a solid job? These questions still haunt me.

Most of us have been in the same boat. And, unfortunately, most of us probably focused on figuring out a quick and convenient way to get some money for camp without thinking about how to paddle through the ocean of injustice that caused the problem in the first place.

When it comes to using our youth ministry's money to right wrongs, youth workers **Now** have a reputation for thinking *short term*. We buy a cheeseburger after youth group for a student whose family is short on cash, or we offer rides to a kid whose family doesn't have a car. Cheeseburgers and car rides are not intrinsically bad. The problem is that our ministry's money **Now** slaps on a short-term Band-Aid while the wound of injustice festers underneath.

Those of us who escape the pitfall of thinking short term often fall into another trap: making *selfish* decisions with our ministry's financial resources. We decide to do another spring break trip to Tijuana, and we mobilize our church to help us raise money to get our kids there for a week. Since we had such a great time playing with the kids at the orphanage last year, we tell the folks there that's what we'd like to do again. Maybe that's what they need; but maybe it's not. The point is we're so busy thinking about *our wants* that we never ask about *their needs*.

> A one-dollar bill met a twenty-dollar bill and said, "Hey, where have you been?
> I haven't seen you around here much."
>
> The twenty answered, "I've been hanging out at casinos, went on a cruise, headed back to the United States for a while, went to a couple of baseball games, to the mall—that kind of stuff.
> How about you?"
>
> The one-dollar bill said, "You know, same old stuff—church, church, church."

Or maybe a few kids in your youth ministry ask if your group could sponsor a child overseas, sending $20-30 per month so she can receive food, clothing, and education, as well as hear about the good news of Jesus Christ. You go online with your kids—but instead of reading the fine print of various international organizations' Web sites to see how they partner with local churches, and ways they support not just that kid but that entire kid's family, you and your students simply pick the girl who looks the "cutest."

The good news is that you can **Now** hang a picture of your "cute" adopted girl on your youth group wall, and that kid will receive spiritual and practical help. The not-so-good news is that you may never know if your youth ministry's money is really giving her—and her family—the tools to escape poverty and oppression for the long haul, or simply offering some solace from the wrongs of poverty and oppression for a few hours each day while she's at school.

When it comes to using our youth ministry's money for justice **Now**, such approaches—though they may be short term or self-centered—are probably better than doing nothing. But they don't give the poor what they really need: a base of power and resources that catapults them forward long term.

It's time for our youth ministries to move beyond service that does little more than make us feel good…

It's time for us to skip past stop-gap solutions that last a few weeks or months at most…

It's time to do the deep work of pouring our ministries' financial resources into kingdom justice that gives power to the poor.

NEW? (REFLECTION)

STEP 2: NEW?

WHO OWNS THE POND?

In my observation, part of the reason some kingdom followers feel reluctant to use their resources to give **New** power to the poor is because they think a commitment to empowering the poor means endorsing an anything-goes approach to social change that may include bloodshed and violence. But that's not the kind of power we're talking about.

> "Power as understood in the kingdom of God will reverse the so-called natural order and the popular understanding of power."
>
> JAYAKUMAR CHRISTIAN,
> *GOD OF THE EMPTY-HANDED*

The kingdom power we're talking about is exemplified by a **New** power twist that Dr. John Perkins (the subject of our **Who** interview in chapter 5) brings to a familiar justice narrative. According to Dr. Perkins, "Some people say 'give a person a fish and he will eat for a day, but teach a person how to fish and she will eat for a lifetime.' Baloney! The crucial question is, *Who owns the pond?*"[54]

The question, *Who owns the pond?* takes us beyond selfish or short-term responses and forces us to ask deeper questions about the unfair power struc-

---

[54] Lowell Noble, "Ownership and Justice," unpublished manuscript, page 2.

tures that perpetuate our world's brokenness. If you want to expand the focus of your ministry's giving and advocacy to *who owns the pond,* you need to lead your students through two **New** shifts—one shift in your theology and one shift in your view of power.

NEW SHIFT 1: JESUS IS NOT WITH THE POOR

What? Jesus is not with the poor? Is that a typo? Well, it's more of a trick statement.

In a sense, Jesus is with the poor. But he's more than just *with* the poor. His image—the image of God—is *in* the poor.

We know this from Jesus' parable of the sheep and the goats in Matthew 25:31-40. We've already looked once at this parable in chapter 3 to better understand the kingdom story of Good/Guilt/Grace/Gratitude, but it's so important to the way our ministry handles our money that we need to look at it again:

> "When the Son of Man comes in his glory, and all the angels with him, he will sit on his glorious throne. All the nations will be gathered before him, and he will separate the people one from another as a shepherd separates the sheep from the goats. He will put the sheep on his right and the goats on his left.
>
> "Then the King will say to those on his right, 'Come, you who are blessed by my Father; take your inheritance, the kingdom prepared for you since the creation of the world. For I was hungry and you gave me something to eat, I was thirsty and you gave me something to drink, I was a stranger and you invited me in, I needed clothes and you clothed me, I was sick and you looked after me, I was in prison and you came to visit me.'
>
> "Then the righteous will answer him, 'Lord, when did we see you hungry and feed you, or thirsty and give you something to drink? When did we see you a stranger and invite you in, or needing clothes and clothe you? When did we see you sick or in prison and go to visit you?'
>
> "The King will reply, 'Truly I tell you, whatever you did for one of the least of these brothers and sisters of mine, you did for me.' "

As Jesus explains in Matthew 25, part of the mystery of deep justice is that when we offer comfort to the needy, we're actually offering comfort to Jesus.

Jesus isn't just standing next to the 16-year-old infected with AIDS in Mozambique or the incarcerated inner-city teenager in Minneapolis. His image is actually *in* them. His image—the image of God—has been present in them since the very second they were conceived.

Because every person is made in God's image, each of us has potential to develop **New** relationships with both God and others. That means that we as kingdom youth workers need to use our ministry's resources to partner with the marginalized in developing transformative relationships with our King as well as meaningful relationships with one another.

So what would this **New** understanding of the image of God mean for your youth ministry? Imagine if Jesus were left alone in a convalescent home, forgotten by his 12 closest friends. You'd undoubtedly invite some youth group kids to swing by on the way to your youth service and sit by his bed with you for a while, right? Even more, you and your students would raise money to offer special outings and opportunities for the seniors in the home, and you'd hire specialists to train the home operators to treat the elderly with the utmost respect and dignity. If you really wanted to move past short-term solutions, you'd also lobby your state officials to improve the healthcare and support systems for the elderly.

Or if Jesus were living in an African village, your youth ministry would never be satisfied with merely sending $30 every month for his food, shelter, and clothing. You'd drop everything, buy plane tickets, and visit him and his friends.

Throughout the history of Christian theology, many leaders and thinkers have equated the "image of God" with a quality or characteristic that is part of our human nature. These "substantive views" describe God's image in us as either a physical resemblance, or a spiritual quality, or even our ability to reason. More recently (in theological terms, "recently" means in the last two centuries), an important additional definition of the image of God has emerged. The "relational view" claims the image lies not in who we are or anything we possess, but in how we relate to God and others.

More and more justice leaders are involved in new international programs that help microenterprises (small, locally owned businesses with less than ten employees). In the last five years, U.S. organizations and donors have supported more than 3.7 million microenterprises worldwide that offer essential services and goods including furniture, footwear, and handcrafted products.

Not only that, but you might also work as a youth ministry to send small loans to villagers so they could earn their own living by making bamboo stools or rattan baskets, thereby creating their own path out of poverty.

Or if Jesus were homeless, you would think it lazy—and probably even downright sinful—to offer him a peanut butter and jelly sandwich and a quick "God bless you" and keep walking. Instead, you'd sit and eat with him and his buddies, asking them to share their stories and giving them opportunity to hear your own stories. After you left, you might raise money to start a job-training center and give Jesus and his friends a ride to the computer seminars the next week. After the center was up and running, you'd become a political advocate for the homeless, sharing the lessons you'd learned with other city officials.

Our broken world shouts from the rooftops (and generally pays a lot of money on eBay) when images of Jesus or the Virgin Mary appear in pancakes, grilled-cheese sandwiches, and potato chips. Ironically, we don't have to look to baked goods to see Jesus' image; his presence is in the homeless woman we pass every day on the way to work.

NEW SHIFT 2: IT'S NOT JUST ABOUT ECONOMIC POWER

Often those who have power in a society are threatened by deep justice, and the parents of some kids in our youth ministries will likely fall right into this fear. To find out more about how to engage parents in your youth ministry's justice work, visit our free resources at www.cyfm.net.

Not only are we blind to the presence of Jesus in the poor, but we're also blind to the variety of ways that poor persons lack power. Sure, we usually recognize that those who are poor lack economic power. Yet the poor also lack other forms of power that are less obvious:

The poor lack powerful geography. In general, poor people are more vulnerable to natural disasters because their jobs are often related to outdoor work (i.e., agriculture), and because their homes are often located in regions more vulnerable to floods, fires, and hurricanes. (Think about who was most affected by Hurricane Katrina in 2005.)

The poor lack intellectual opportunities. It's likely that some of the world's finest minds are among the poor, but most of the world will never know it. Due to lack of good nutrition during childhood and lack of opportunities during adulthood, the ability of poor persons to contribute their innovative ideas to the intellectual capital of the world is squelched.

The poor lack emotional freedom. According to Jayakumar Christian in *God of the Empty-Handed,* poor people are often caught in a "web of lies" about their own ability to solve their problems, robbing them of hope and affirming the status quo.[55]

The poor lack political capital. Few groups lobby on behalf of the poor at your city hall or on Washington, D.C.'s Capitol Hill. Politicians tend to want the votes of those who are poor, but after the ballots are cast, winning candidates usually focus attention on more powerful special interest groups.

DOES MORE POWER FOR OTHERS MEAN LESS POWER FOR ME?

If we're going to move to the Level 3 justice described in chapter 1, we can't ignore this question. It's an especially critical consideration for youth ministers who come from a race or class of position and power, and/or work with students of similarly privileged backgrounds. Will using your ministry's resources to help the poor gain power mean you end up with less power?

If your ministry raises funds to help poor kids apply to and attend college, will this make it less likely that your own students will be accepted at their top college choices? Or if your ministry supports job training that helps the unemployed gain computer skills, will the parents of your kids have greater difficulty finding a job in your town if they are laid off?

Some youth ministries involved in deep justice are using their money to support organizations seeking to help accomplish the United Nations Millennium Development Goals established in the year 2000. This campaign seeks to accomplish the following by 2015:

1. Eradicate extreme poverty and hunger.

2. Achieve universal primary education.

3. Promote gender equity and empower women.

4. Reduce child mortality.

5. Improve maternal health.

6. Combat HIV/AIDS, malaria, and other diseases.

7. Ensure environmental sustainability.

8. Develop a global partnership for development.[56]

"As the oppressors dehumanize others and violate their rights, they themselves also become dehumanized."

PAULO FREIRE, *PEDAGOGY OF THE OPPRESSED*

---

[55] Jayakumar Christian, *God of the Empty Handed* (Monrovia, California: World Vision International, 1999), 161.

[56] http://www.un.org/millenniumgoals/

Maybe. Perhaps even probably.

But let's go back to the view of kingdom shalom presented in chapter 5. The King's deepest desire is that all people experience his full potential for them—relationally, physically, emotionally, and spiritually. If your power can be retained only by ensuring that others stay powerless, do you really want to keep that kind of power?

A SNAPSHOT OF INCREASING POWER

Learning **New** ways to use our ministry's resources to support and sustain the God-given dignity of those who are poor and increase their financial, political, educational, and vocational power has been a 13-year process for me. In my early days of ministry, our ministry channeled much of its financial resources into summer interns who led powerful evangelistic Bible Clubs in four barrio neighborhoods in Santa Ana, California, through our KIDWORKS ministry.

Were people helped by these interns? You bet. But were we using our ministry's resources in partnership with the community to bring about long-term transformation that brought more power and potential to the poor in these communities? Not even close.

So we made a **New** shift that forced our entire team, including my wife and me, to use our time, skills, and resources for more than short-term or selfish responses on behalf of the poor in the Latino community. Instead of offering evangelistic Bible studies during the summer, we became a holistic community development corporation that operated year-round. We continued to meet the spiritual needs of children and families in the neighborhood, but we didn't stop there.

To increase the neighborhood's academic potential, we began to provide an after-school educational program and computer lab.

To find out more about KIDWORKS and the kingdom impact it's making, visit www.kidworksonline.org.

To enhance employment possibilities, we offered English as a Second Language (or ESL) classes for kids' parents and other adults so they could access higher-paying jobs.

To help instill a sense of neighborhood pride and community, our KIDWORKS staff teamed up with a park redevelopment project in the neighborhood.

To increase the political power of those living here, we used our ministry's money to support voter registration campaigns and encourage community organizing initiatives.

Thinking holistically about community development also meant we couldn't start working with kids when they turned 12 years old. We launched our own preschool and school-readiness programs, recognizing that one of the best ways we can use our money to help teenagers is to make sure they get early academic and relational anchors that will help them withstand the storms of gangs and drugs that thunder around them.

> To hear more of Larry's practical insights about fund development, check out a CYFM interview available for free at www.cyfm.net.

None of this was rocket science. It was simply a process of discovering what was wrong, and then increasing the power of the neighborhood to right those wrongs.

By now you're probably realizing that thinking more holistically about power development for the poor might mean more fundraising. In all honesty, fundraising is not my favorite part of justice ministry. But I do love figuring out how to help our ministry—and other ministries like ours—use resources to bring about long-term power transformation on behalf of the least, the last, and the lost.

WHO? (OBSERVATION)

STEP 3: WHO?

To download and hear more of Rudy's insights about justice and leadership, check out a CYFM interview available for free at www.cyfm.net.

Using resources to help the poor gain power drives the mission of Pasadena's Harambee Christian Family Center. Under the leadership of its executive director, RUDOLPHO ("RUDY") CARRASCO, Harambee provides after-school programs and a private, Christian school that emphasizes personal responsibility and indigenous leadership development. As a strategic thinker and gifted communicator, Rudy shares his insights about deep justice regularly through articles in *Christianity Today*, *The Los Angeles Times*, and other publications. Thanks to his hands-on experience with Latino and African-American kids as well as his extensive networking with youth leaders around the country, Rudy has philosophical and practical ideas that can help your youth ministry devote your resources to deeper justice.

Rudy, why are youth ministries prone to use their money for short-term solutions on behalf of the poor?

I think it's usually for pretty practical reasons. Short-term solutions are easier. They don't take as much time, and they don't take as much money. Youth ministries who do short-term work can definitely meet some needs and be transformed some themselves.

The problem is that most injustices and challenges are complex and deep. They've been around for a long time. Effective solutions require an equal response—one that is committed for the long term.

When are short-term solutions most effective?

No question it's when they are partnered with long-term solutions. Here at Harambee, we have youth groups from around the country come and invest their resources in short-term work all the time, but they come to partner with those of us who are living here long term. If short-termers don't have partnerships with long-termers, they can actually make the situation worse. Folks in the community can learn how to manipulate short-termers and tell them sob stories so they give money. No one gains when that happens.

How have you seen youth ministries use their money selfishly in the midst of trying to seek kingdom justice on behalf of the poor?

Usually groups act selfishly when they don't take the time to get to know the real causes of injustice. They are usually well-intentioned, and they think they know what the needs are, so they show up and start addressing the wrong issues.

What difference should it make to us that according to the parable of the sheep and the goats (Matthew 25:31-40), Jesus' presence is in the poor?

It should make a huge difference. In fact, that passage is one of the most important sections of Scripture in my life. It's so dramatic, and even offensive. I'm glad Jesus said it, and I didn't. Now I can just read the Bible and tell folks, "That's what your Lord and Savior says." For many youth ministries, the justice starting point is simply to take a few weeks and reflect on the fact that Jesus' presence is in the poor. He doesn't give us any wiggle room.

Besides economic power, what other types of power do the poor lack?

There are so many types of power that the poor lack, but one major one is they lack connections and access. And even if they somehow end up making some connections and gaining some access, they often don't know what to do with those networks.

What do you mean by "connections" and "access"?

Let me give you an example. Imagine you know a bunch of restaurant owners; perhaps they are in your social circle or you somehow become friends with them. Because of these connections, you get inside information. You learn about hiring trends, which restaurants have job openings, and what types of people they hope to hire. If you gain access to that information, you gain power.

How can privileged youth ministries use their money so the poor gain power?

One of the keys to helping others gain power is giving them sustained attention, probably for at least a year. Maybe you can mobilize your kids to give enough money to provide a one-year scholarship for an inner-city kid to attend a good private school. You can track that kid over the year, get to know him, and even get to know people at the school and in the community.

We've had that happen here at Harambee, and one of the great bonuses is that it's not just dollars that come, but also ideas. As 20 kids in a local suburban youth group decided to stop spending their cash at Starbucks and gave that money to one of our students instead, not only is that kid changed, but the youth group has been transformed as well. The parents of the suburban kids often see this transformation and end up wanting to partner with us in even greater ways.

Besides providing school scholarships, what else can privileged youth ministries do with their resources to increase the power of the poor?

My general answer is that privileged youth ministries need to do a little bit of investigative research and learn what people really need. I'll tell you one thing that most folks need: help getting a job. If youth ministries could use their money to help the unemployed gain jobs, that would definitely increase their power.

I think it would also help if suburban or privileged youth ministries pooled their resources. If six churches got together and combined their money, that would be a much larger chunk of money that could take justice to a deeper level.

What about youth ministries serving in poorer communities?

My answer is going to be controversial, but here it is: almost the exact same thing. I think poorer kids are rarely challenged to give of their resources to right wrongs around them. In our urban neighborhood, kids have never been invited to go on a mission trip, and they've never been challenged to give their own money to others. Our kids tell us they're broke, and often that's true, so we encourage them to be creative. Maybe they have an uncle who has some resources, or maybe they could sacrifice something they have and give it to those who have even less than them. We have to insert a different script into the minds and hearts of urban kids. Even in the midst of the bad stuff they are experiencing, they have capacity.

---

[57] Rudolpho Carrasco, "Protest and Invest," *Prism*, Summer 2004.

Whether you're in a suburban, urban, or small-town youth ministry, how can you do the type of justice work you're describing and maintain the dignity of those you are helping?

You need to find a trusted partner on the other end who can help you know what to avoid, what not to say, and what not to do.

Rudy, in your widely circulated article "Protest and Invest," you write, "From the vantage point of my home, next to a corner store in a black and Latino neighborhood, what I see is a generation carrying picket signs in their hearts but running no businesses, owning no property, creating no wealth, tempted to commit crimes, and doomed to wallow in poverty. The very kids who should be disciplining themselves, saving money, working long hours, practicing how to write a business plan, and learning how to win investor confidence, are instead walking around complaining."[57] What type of responsibility do you think those who are under-resourced have for increasing their own base of power and opportunities?

The primary responsibility is theirs. It's their life. Just thinking about it practically, you can't sit around and wait for others to fix your situation. It's your situation. You know what you need.

If that's true, then what's the role of the church?

The church's responsibility is secondary. As we follow the Lord, the Holy Spirit will reveal injustices we need to be involved with. Suddenly, we'll end up with a real heart for the homeless in our community, or we'll become burdened for children affected by AIDS in Africa.

And it really takes the whole church, not just us as individual believers. In the New Testament, the word that's often translated in English as *you* is actually plural. Many of Scripture's commands related to poverty are meant for a group or a body, not just one individual.

I've seen the importance of the body working together in real life, too. I tried to do what I could as an individual in college and failed spectacularly. Then I had an experience where a group of 15 people worked to help one mother overcome a tragic situation, and you know what? She made it. That has changed the way I think about the role of the church in God's justice. Often it takes a whole bunch of people to help one person. It makes sense both practically and theologically.

Since President George W. Bush first mentioned the "soft bigotry of low expectations" in a 2000 campaign speech, it's become a frequent theme in his comments regarding education and poverty.

I've heard you mention a few times the statement by President Bush regarding the "soft bigotry of low expectations." Why is that statement so significant for you?

Folks who feel victimized often want to lash out and call others "racist" or "oppressors." Frankly, I think calling others racists at every turn isn't all that helpful, and it isn't all that accurate. I think what happens more often is that the rich have low expectations for the poor, and the poor have low expectations for themselves. We assume poor kids won't be able to do their homework, so we don't try to help them get it done.

Honestly, there are days when I think the low expectations we have toward the poor are the number one problem. We're created in God's image, so no matter what our situation or background, we can make it. Sure, it's a challenge, but people are created in God's image. It may take a miracle, but God's in the business of miracles.

HOW? (APPLICATION)

STEP 4: HOW?

DEEP JUSTICE APPLICATION QUESTIONS

1. Is your ministry **Now** more likely to offer *either* short-term *or* selfish help to those who are poor or oppressed? Why do you think your ministry leans to this extreme?

2. In addition to financial power, what other types of power do the poor in your community lack?

3. In both this chapter and chapter 3, we've discussed the relevance of seeing the image of God in the poor for our justice work. If your ministry viewed the needy of the world as Jesus himself, what would you do differently? What prevents you and your kids from viewing the needy this way?

4. After reading this chapter, in what ways is your youth ministry currently seeking holistic justice with and for the poor? How does this goal of holistic ministry relate to God's shalom as described in chapter 5?

5. In Larry's experience, shifting from a summer-only evangelistic Bible study to a **New** year-round holistic community development corporation meant he and his team needed to raise more funds. Do you think the same will be true for you if your group moves toward a more holistic approach? Who from your church or sphere of relationships can partner with you to raise funds that will increase the power of the poor?

6. Of the following list of Deep Justice Recommended Action Steps that flow from this chapter, which would best help your youth ministry right wrongs?

DEEP JUSTICE RECOMMENDED ACTION STEPS:

For Yourself:

Since chapter 9 was dedicated to using your checkbook as a justice tool, skip back to that chapter for a list of ideas.

For Your Youth Ministry:

- Share your youth ministry's budget with your adult leadership team and, if appropriate, your student leadership team. (It might be wise to omit any staff salaries from the figures that you share.) Make a list of ways your ministry's money is currently helping the poor increase their power, and discuss ways you might reallocate your funds to provide a more holistic support system for the poor.

- Teach your kids that the image of God is present in the poor around them. Invite them to consciously view others as Jesus himself for the next week or two, and then discuss how that changed their attitudes and actions.

- Volunteer with your students at a ministry that works with those who are homeless to help them be reintegrated into the community. Keep an eye out for ways your ministry could give money to make a long-term difference, like funding financial literacy classes or providing free babysitting for children whose parents are in these classes.

- Consider asking members of your church or a local foundation for a gift or grant so you have even more resources that can increase the power of the poor.

- Rudy stresses the power that comes to folks who have been unemployed when they are able to get jobs. Jimmy Dorrell, pastor of Church Under the Bridge, an interdenominational church that grew from a Bible study with five homeless men in Waco, Texas, points out that people need job training, job finding, and job coaching.[58] Brainstorm with your students and some influential folks in your church how your youth ministry could use its resources and contacts to meet one or more of these needs.

[58] Jimmy Dorrell, *Trolls and Truth* (Birmingham, Alabama: New Hope Publishers, 2006), 191.

- Instead of serving the homeless or undocumented immigrants directly, mobilize your kids to raise money to serve a meal to those who are advocating for systemic changes that provide long-term transformation.

- Rather than trying to fly your ministry to Darfur, go to Washington, D.C. or your state's capital and try to meet with state and federal officials to call attention to the mass killings in this region of Sudan.

- Take some students with you to meet with the principal of a local public elementary school and offer to raise funds for a computer lab and computer classes for kids who otherwise wouldn't get them.

- Talk with your church leaders about making your church building available to other community organizations (like the YMCA, the Boys and Girls Club of America, or Big Brothers/Big Sisters) when you aren't using it.

- Next Christmas, buy some gifts for kids in an under-resourced neighborhood, but instead of delivering the gifts yourselves, set up a temporary store with dramatic discounts so parents in the community can come and purchase gifts for their kids. That way the parents have picked out and bought gifts for their own kids.

- Help instill in your students a vision for using your ministry's resources to seek justice for those affected by AIDS in Africa by downloading and using the FREE 100-page "One Life Curriculum" (produced in partnership between CYFM, Youth Specialties, and World Vision). It's available at www.cyfm.net.

WHAT'S JUST ABOUT THE RICH GETTING RICHER AND THE POOR GETTING POORER?

BY JEREMY DEL RIO

Jeremy Del Rio, Esq. works as a consultant, providing advice and resources to churches and community groups on youth development, social justice, and cultural engagement. He is the cofounder and director of Community Solutions, Inc. (CSI), a holistic youth-development agency based in lower Manhattan. CSI provides after-school education, summer programs, and community outreach through Generation Xcel, and hosts service learning missions trips nationally through Chain Reaction. Jeremy is the founding youth pastor at Abounding Grace Ministries and has also worked as a corporate attorney in New York.

"I had to say, 'God, I repent, because I can't think of the last time I thought of widows and orphans'... And so I went back and I began to read Scripture, and it was like blinders came off... I've got three advanced degrees. I've had four years in Greek and Hebrew and I've got doctorates. And how did I miss 2,000 verses in the Bible where it talks about the poor? How did I miss that? I mean, I went to two different seminaries and a Bible school; how did I miss the 2,000 verses on the poor?"

—Rick Warren[59]

---

[59] Rick Warren, "Myths of the Modern Mega-Church," The Pew Forum on Religion and Public Life, http://pewforum.org/events/index.php?EventID=R80

NOW? (DISCERNMENT)

STEP 1: NOW?

Is there a city anywhere in America—or, for that matter, anywhere in the world—where the rich do not get richer as the poor get poorer **Now**?

If there is, I don't know of it.

In my own city of New York—the "Capital of the World" and home to some of this planet's greatest financial institutions—the gap between the rich and poor grows wider every year. During Christmas of 1999, the depth of the chasm became especially real for me. I'd been involved in inner-city ministry for seventeen years, since I was eight years old, and five years earlier, I had cofounded a storefront youth group for teenagers living in the low-income housing projects of Manhattan's Lower East Side.

That year, we wanted to do classic "Christmas in New York" stuff—Rockefeller Center, the Lord and Taylor windows, ice-skating in Central Park—so a couple dozen of us took the subway 2.5 miles to 49th Street. We might as well have traveled across the country.

My wife and I took half the group for a walk toward Central Park along the priciest real estate in the world, Fifth Avenue, and ended up stopping at the lobby of the famed Plaza Hotel. The Plaza, legendary for its luxurious décor and clientele, was hosting a holiday party of some sort, with Manhattan's upper crust decked out in tuxedos and evening gowns, and limos lined up for blocks outside. After five or ten minutes, one of our kids, Vanessa, turned to my wife and with a faraway gaze in her eyes, said wistfully, "I could never imagine myself at an event like this."

Two weeks later, I found myself back at the Plaza, this time for my law firm's New Year's party. This time, I was one of the folks wearing a tuxedo and gorging myself on yellowtail sashimi and filet mignon. The open bar was flowing, and my inebriated colleagues were celebrating record bonuses and the still blazing Internet economic bubble.

My head was spinning. As a first-year attorney at a major New York firm, tent-making to support inner-city youth ministry, I knew functions like this went with the territory. But could it really be that some would feel so affirmed in this setting, while others—like Vanessa—would feel so excluded?

Yet this bizarre duality between the very rich and the very poor exists every day **Now** in Manhattan. As 2006 drew to a close, executives for the New York–based global banking company Goldman Sachs enjoyed $16 billion in year-end bonuses, with the highest earners receiving $100 million each. At the same time, gentrification in Manhattan, and increasingly the outer boroughs, displaces the middle class and renders upward mobility for the poor virtually impossible in their own neighborhoods. New York City spends over $14 billion—with another $1.9 billion of state aid on the way—educating its 1.2 million public school students (who, all by themselves, would be the tenth largest U.S. city). Yet statistically, 60 percent of the fourth graders in New York's public schools can't read at grade level and 70 percent fail statewide math exams.

Whether in New York or your own town, whether upper class or lower class, whether rich or poor, none of us chooses the family that births us, the class we are raised in, or the community that surrounds us.

But we as youth ministries **Now** do have a choice. What is our kingdom response to the widening canyon between the rich and the poor? Unfortunately, we **Now** tend to fall into *either/or* extremes that keep us from offering deep justice to all, regardless of class.

Extreme 1: Denial

It's easy for youth workers in the middle or upper classes to avoid or deny the class canyon that **Now** fractures our world and our relationships. As long as we are comfortable and taken care of, we keep our blinders on and ride the wave of wealth as high and far as we can.

Whether by actively withholding good or through passive indifference or neglect, our youth ministries often fail to take seriously the mandate to act on behalf of the lower classes. But concern for the poor is a priority God takes very seriously. We know this because his Scripture includes more than 2,000 verses about the poor, among them the famously misunderstood story of Sodom.

Why did God destroy Sodom? Instinctively, we evangelicals think we know the answer. It's been ingrained in us since Sunday school, and popular words—*sodomy, sodomite*—express our notion of Sodom's fatal flaw. We believe God destroyed Sodom because of homosexuality and related sexual behaviors. But is our conventional understanding correct?

Although the Genesis account of Sodom's destruction refers to homosexuality and other passages reference "sexual immorality," the prophet Ezekiel identifies Sodom's greater sin:

> Now this was the sin of your sister Sodom: She and her daughters were arrogant, overfed and unconcerned; they did not help the poor and needy. They were haughty and did detestable things before me. Therefore I did away with them as you have seen. (Ezekiel 16:49-50)

Arrogant.

Overfed.

Unconcerned.

Failing to help the poor and needy.

FACTS ABOUT POVERTY **NOW** IN THE UNITED STATES THAT MIGHT SURPRISE YOUR STUDENTS:

- At age 20, more than one in ten Americans live in poverty.

- By age 40, more than 1/3 of all Americans have experienced at least a year of poverty.

- In just the four years between 2000 and 2004, the number of children in poverty in the U.S. increased 12.4 percent.

- In America today, children are just as likely to be poor as they were 40 years ago.

- According to U.S. Census Bureau figures, the income gap between the top 20 percent of households and the bottom 20 percent of households is the widest ever.

- The median incomes of black and Latino families are 62 percent and 70 percent of white family incomes, respectively.

- A full-time minimum-wage paycheck, which until the 1980s would have kept a family of three above the poverty threshold, now provides an income equivalent to only 75 percent of the poverty line.

- Of female-headed households with no husband present, the percentages of families falling below the poverty vary by race: 18.0 percent for Asian families, 22.6 percent for white families, 37.4 percent for black families, and 39.0 percent for Latino families.[60]

---

[60]See "Income, Poverty, and Health Insurance Coverage in the United States," U.S. Census Bureau, and "State of America's Children, 2005" by the Children's Defense Fund.

We know from the story of Lot that not even ten people in Sodom cared (Genesis 18:16-33). As a result, God destroyed the entire city by raining down fire from heaven.

Yet how many of our evangelical leaders and youth workers are speaking out against the injustice of the rich getting richer and the poor getting poorer **Now**? Some of our most outspoken voices rant about "sodomy" and mobilize costly crusades against the politics of "sodomites." Yet they often ignore completely the problem the Bible identifies as Sodom's greatest sin—the same inhospitality that can so easily befall us in America.

Fast forward to the New Testament and Matthew 25's parable of the sheep and the goats, which we've considered earlier in the book. Notice that the "sheep" in the parable, the ones the King gathers to himself on the last day, are those who feed the hungry; offer a drink to the thirsty; welcome the stranger; clothe the naked; and visit the imprisoned—for in doing so, Jesus says, they have ministered to Christ himself. By contrast, the "goats"—those who see others in need and fail to respond—are damned "into the eternal fire prepared for the devil and his angels" (Matt. 25:31-46). It's the only parable that speaks of judgment as eternal fire, and it reserves that judgment for those who neglect economic and social justice.

Extreme 2: Despair

When Vanessa told my wife the Plaza party was out of her reach, what came through most clearly wasn't her distaste for evening gowns and fancy food or a preference for one party style over another. Her prevailing emotion was one of despair. Hopelessness. Like she'd just viewed the pinnacle of some mountain she could never climb, no matter how much she might want to.

Feeling stuck without options and powerless to change things is the worst aspect of generational poverty **Now**. When mom is poor and grandma is poor and dad is absent and big brother dropped out of school and the school is on probation because of abysmal performance and unemployment pushes toward record highs and community leaders play politics with hunger, kids feel hopeless. Why study if two plus two doesn't equal four? Why cultivate character and competence if all the opportunities are reserved for someone else and all the doors remain closed?

NEW? (REFLECTION)

STEP 2: NEW?

A BOY IN THE GHETTO

Let me tell you about a teenage boy I know. He appears ordinary enough, with nothing much to distinguish him—except that he's studious and works with his stepdad in construction. Like many teens, he's struggling to find his place.

Living in the ghetto is hard, especially since he just immigrated to the neighborhood in the last few years. Try as he might, he hasn't mastered the accent and local customs. And forget the slang; that's like learning a third language. Worse, the old-timers all seem to know something about him that he still hasn't figured out yet. He gets the distinct impression that they talk about his family, reinforced by the name-calling he's overheard. His peers can be especially cruel, teasing him to his face and instigating fights after school.

Sometimes the mocking gets to him. He wants desperately to fight back, but mom forbids it, promising that someday the rejection will make sense. He tries to take comfort in her words, but for now his heart just hurts, and the unfairness makes him angry.

So he sneaks off to the outskirts of town and hides behind a gnarly old sycamore tree. There he remembers the hunger and loneliness of the refugee camp, and recollects vague memories of a midnight flight from the small town where he spent his childhood. The details are sketchy, but he recalls stories of bloodshed and murder that he barely escaped. Not fitting in has been a recurring struggle for him.

Then those memories fade, and he hears the echo of his mom's voice telling him about his birth. No way he'll ever let his schoolmates find out he was born in a barn. The ammunition that would give them! They already call him choice animal names.

Perhaps you know this friend of mine.

No longer a nameless and faceless teenager, his name is both revered and reviled around the world, and artists have imagined his likeness for centuries. In case you missed it in Sunday school, this boy we call Jesus Christ.

When the King of Kings decided to usher his kingdom "on earth as it is in heaven," he penetrated class lines to do so—not as a well-intentioned outsider but from within the community. He "became flesh and blood and moved into the neighborhood," (John 1:14, *The Message*) and his manner of doing so invited scorn. He was born into straw poverty made worse by political exile, and lived as an immigrant teenager in the ghetto. He worked his ministry with no place to lay his head (Matthew 8:20); made his last trip on a borrowed donkey; spent his last evening alive in a borrowed room; watched his lone possession, a robe, become a gambler's prize at his death; and was buried in a borrowed tomb.

JESUS' INCARNATION MEANS DENIAL OR DESPAIR ARE NO LONGER OPTIONS

If you are one of our society's "haves," Jesus' birth, life, and death mean you can no longer live in denial about the injustice of the class canyon. If the King of Kings chose—I repeat, *chose*—to enter the world through the lower class, then we simply cannot ignore those who enter through it today. He spent his whole life rubbing elbows with members of all classes, even when he was soundly criticized for it.

If you are one of our society's "have nots," Jesus' birth, death, and resurrection mean you can no longer live in despair. Jesus knows—really *knows*—your every thought and fear, your every fulfilled and unfulfilled dream, because he lived them firsthand. He knows what it's like to grow up feeling disconnected, rejected, exposed, and exploited. He's been there, done that, and overcome it—so that he can meet you and love you and empower you toward deep justice. And now he offers **New** hope by restoring options.

JESUS' TEACHINGS ON JUSTICE AND JUBILEE CALL US TO COMPASSIONATE ACTION

Jesus' **New** lessons about class for our youth ministries don't stop at his birth. He began his ministry and teaching by declaring his heart for justice—not in some abstract cliché but in concrete statements about his mission and his anointing. "The Spirit of the Lord is on me," he announced, "because he has anointed me to preach good news to the poor. He has sent me to proclaim freedom for the prisoners and recovery of sight for the blind, to set the oppressed free, to proclaim the year of the Lord's favor" (Luke 4:18-19).

Jesus defined his mission as jubilee on behalf of the poor and oppressed, quoting the first two verses of Isaiah 61 and invoking for Israelites the promises of Leviticus 25 and Deuteronomy 15. Isaiah 61 describes a God who provides comfort for those who mourn, exchanges beauty for ashes and praise for despair, rebuilds ancient ruins, and restores places long devastated. "Instead of your shame," Isaiah concludes, "you will receive a double portion, and instead of disgrace you will rejoice in your inheritance... and everlasting joy will be yours. For I, the Lord, love justice" (Isaiah 61:7-8).

> "Action with and for those who suffer is the concrete expression of the compassionate life and the final criterion of being a Christian. Such acts do not stand beside the moments of prayer and worship but are themselves such moments."
>
> DONALD P. MCNEILL, DOUGLAS A. MORRISON, AND HENRI J. M. NOUWEN, *COMPASSION*

The "year of the Lord's favor" is a reference to the Year of Jubilee, which occurred every fifty years (Leviticus 25). Jubilee was an even more extreme "year of canceling debts" (as described in Deuteronomy 15) in which debts were forgiven, new loans were granted without interest, property was returned to its original owners, and slaves were set free.

The year of canceling debts occurred every seventh year. Richard Townsell, executive director of Lawndale Christian Community Development Corporation in Chicago, offers Deuteronomy 15 as a timeless model of the kingdom's fight to offer deep justice to the rich, the poor, and everyone in between. The Law of Moses established that every creditor, without exception, would cancel any loan made to a fellow Israelite every seven years. Why? Because the kingdom rejects systemic poverty and provides opportunities for the economically disadvantaged to break free. "There need be no poor among you ... if only you fully obey the Lord your God and are careful to follow all these commands I am giving you today" (Deuteronomy 15:4-5).

Deuteronomy warned the Israelites about being reluctant to make loans as the year of canceling debts approached:

> Be careful not to harbor this wicked thought... so that you do not show ill will toward your needy among your people and give them nothing. They may then appeal to the Lord against you, and you will be found guilty of sin. Give generously to them and do so without a grudging heart; then because of this the Lord your God will bless you in all your work and in everything you put your hand to. (Isaiah 15:9-10)

The passage concludes by echoing a line Jesus would ultimately repeat when rebuking Judas' self-righteousness toward helping the poor (Matt. 26:6-13). "There will always be poor people in the land. Therefore I command you to be openhanded toward your brothers and toward the poor and needy" (v. 11).

JUBILEE JUSTICE FOR ALL CLASSES: THE SERMON ON THE MOUNT'S COMPASSIONATE ACTION

Youth ministries trying to bring about **New** justice in a broken world can't escape the ramifications of Jesus' jubilee justice for all classes. The good news is that Jesus does not leave us guessing about how to right the wrongs that imprison us, wherever we fall on the economic spectrum. He's given our youth ministries some **New** snapshots of kingdom justice for all classes through the compassionate action he describes in his famous Sermon on the Mount.

Compassionate Act 1: Recognize Your Own Poverty

The formerly corrupt tax collector Matthew recounts that Jesus began the Sermon on the Mount—his longest recorded sermon and the one that best defines his kingdom values—with an unsettling premise: "Blessed are the poor in spirit, for theirs is the kingdom of heaven" (Matthew 5:3). The kingdom doesn't belong to the wealthy, powerful, and self-reliant, but to those who recognize their poverty.

From a kingdom perspective, no matter what class you are in, you are poor. You are a sinner saved by grace, and the knowledge of your destitution apart from Jesus Christ should keep you humble.

Now's probably a good time to point out that on the flip side, in the kingdom economy, we are also all rich. We have been saved, redeemed, and reconciled to God and to one another. Even if you have just a few dollars to your name, you have the priceless treasure of relationship with God and his kingdom community.

Since each of us is simultaneously *both* rich *and* poor, we have much to teach one another, and we have much to learn from one another. That homeless person you walk by on your way to church—she's got something to teach you. That city mayor you're meeting with to talk about high-risk kids in your community—he's got something to teach you. That family displaced by hurricanes in Central America—they've got something to teach you. And as someone *both* poor in spirit *and* rich in grace, you have something to teach them, too.

> Luke is even more explicit. In his retelling of the same story, Luke quotes Jesus this way: "Blessed are you who are poor, for yours is the kingdom of God. Blessed are you who hunger now, for you will be satisfied...But woe to you who are rich, for you have already received your comfort. Woe to you who are well fed now, for you will go hungry" (Luke 6:20-21, 24-25). In the broader context of Jesus' entire sermon, it's clear that Jesus is emphasizing that, whether we are financially poor or spiritually poor, we are all dependent on him.

Compassionate Act 2: Change Your Goals

Matthew's account of Jesus' most famous sermon continues with a number of other counterintuitive descriptions of what his kingdom represents. Jesus declares blessed those who mourn, the meek, those who hunger and thirst for righteousness (Matthew 5:4-6). His kingdom upends all that we regard as valuable—wealth, happiness, knowledge, self-assuredness, strength, and security—and provides a new range of aspirations.

The concept of shalom expresses this best. In his book *Simply Christian: Why Christianity Makes Sense*, British theologian N. T. Wright describes biblical justice as "putting the world to rights." It's the fulfillment, as Paul wrote, of all creation's waiting "in eager expectation" to be "liberated from its bondage to decay" (Romans 8:19-23)—what the Old Testament calls shalom. More than the absence of strife, shalom is the kind of peace that holds the far reaches of the universe together. It's what the Prince of Peace came to reestablish: the interdependency of healthy communities; the intricacy of our physiology; the manifold mysteries of a parent's love; the splendor of the cosmos; and the microscopic details of subatomic matter.

Dr. Tim Keller, founder and senior pastor of Manhattan's Redeemer Presbyterian Church, describes shalom as the webbing together of God, humans, and all creation in a state of universal flourishing, wholeness, and delight. It's an intricately woven garment that diminishes when things unravel physically, psychologically, and economically. Social unraveling comes when people who "have" hold on to their blessing rather than sharing and interweaving it with those who "have not."

The condition of sin robs us of shalom, but kingdom justice restores it. The catch is that justice isn't forced upon us. It comes as we change our priorities, as we begin to hunger and thirst after justice with a poverty of spirit that allows us to mourn its absence. Then we can pursue it with meekness, mercy, and a pure heart.

> "Jesus ties his being with those who are hungry, thirsty, naked, alien, imprisoned, and ill. Whatever Jesus may look like, he can be found in the struggle of the disenfranchised, not because they are holier but because they struggle for the abundant life. If we want to describe Jesus' appearance, we need to describe the appearance of those who reside in the margins of society. If we want to commune with Christ, if we want to look into the eyes of the one we call Lord, then we can access him when we walk in solidarity, when we accompany the outcasts of society. For whatever is done or not done to one of these is done or not done to Jesus."
>
> MIGUEL A. DE LA TORRE, *READING THE BIBLE FROM THE MARGINS*

Compassionate Act 3: Give, but Give Quietly

The same sermon offers guidance on giving to the needy—"Do not announce it with trumpets, as the hypocrites do" (Matthew 6:2)—and perspective on the true value of earthly wealth—"Do not store up for yourselves treasures on earth, where moth and rust destroy, and where thieves break in and steal. But store up for yourselves treasures in heaven...For where your treasure is, there your heart will be also" (6:19-21).

The Western idea of justice revolves around protecting individual rights, but the biblical idea is the opposite: We owe one another what we have. Righting wrongs through our youth ministries means sharing our power and possessions with those around us to enable their social flourishing.

Dr. Keller again offers a convicting warning for our youth ministries: "The way you treat the poor and the way you treat [God] are absolutely linked. If you don't treat the poor as you ought to it's because you aren't treating [God] as you ought to. If you have a bad relationship with the poor it's because you have a bad relationship with [God], whether you know it or not."[61] Or, to paraphrase Proverbs: If you insult the poor you insult their Maker; but if you are kind to the poor you lend to the Lord, and he will reward you (Proverbs 14:31, 19:17).

Compassionate Act 4: Forgive

Jesus also stresses kingdom economics within the prayer he teaches his disciples, the one we call the Lord's Prayer (Matthew 6:9-13). In it, he tells us to ask for personal forgiveness only "as we also have forgiven our debtors" (v. 12). It's not a coincidence that the fundamentals of kingdom faith—sin, its wages, redemption, forgiveness, and even people who hurt us—are described here and throughout Scripture in economic terms. Because our heart lies where our treasure is, Jesus speaks directly to the hearts of his listeners. Sinning, he says, is like racking up debts that get increasingly difficult to repay. Being sinned against is like holding a worthless promissory note that can't be repaid. Forgiveness, whether extended or received, is like an economic transaction that relieves the debtor of his obligation to repay. But redemption comes after the price has been paid in full. Because Jesus paid the price of shalom in full, he expects nothing less than forgiveness from those who follow him.

Compassionate Act 5: Don't Worry about Stuff

Jesus further says not to worry even about sustenance—"what you will eat or drink... or wear"—but to seek his kingdom first, and everything else will fall into place (vs. 25-34). For Americans raised on a culture of rugged individualism and Puritanical self-reliance, what could be more contrary than that? Yet God's upside-down kingdom overturns even those things we consider most basic to our survival—food, drink, clothing. It's the same impulse that allowed Jesus to resist the temptation to eat during his 40-day fast in the wilderness by reminding himself: "People do not live on bread alone, but on every word that comes from the mouth of God" (Matthew 4:4). Justice, kindness, compassion, and the everyday incarnational realities of the Word made flesh and living among us—these are the things that sustained Jesus throughout his ministry. And he says these are the things that must become most important for us.

We're so busy pursuing the American Dream that the pursuit itself can keep us from seeing what really matters to the kingdom. Even within many churches, we're told that our best life now includes material booty that comes to those who call forth blessings from on high. But Jesus says not to concern ourselves with such things. *Seek God's justice,* he tells us, *and all those things that keep you awake at night and preoccupy your thoughts during the day will be take care of.*

---

[61] Dr. Tim Keller, Resurgence Conference, 2006, http://jeremydelrio.com/blog/2006/11/21/thanksgiving-for-justice/

COMPASSIONATE ACTION THAT CHANGED A TEENAGER

Mei-Ling is a woman whose life was transformed by the compassionate action of kingdom leaders. I first met Mei-Ling when we were teenagers. She visited our youth group with a friend and kept attending because she developed a crush on one of the boys. Over time I learned that her father was absent, and her mother was dying of AIDS, which she'd contracted in the 1980s through intravenous drug use or the unprotected prostitution that supported her addiction. Mei-Ling had recently returned to New York after several years living with various foster families in Puerto Rico. Odds were that Mei-Ling would drop out of high school and stay stuck in generational poverty.

Instead, kingdom justice came knocking on her door.

But Mei-Ling was not destined to end up a casualty of a war she didn't start and couldn't finish. In her final weeks, Mei-Ling's mother approached my parents, who were also the pastors of our church, Abounding Grace, and asked them to take in her daughter when she passed away. They agreed, and Mei-Ling became my sister. She grieved her mother's passing, and became mildly rebellious for a while. But her adoptive family wouldn't let her go. We understood that deep justice for Mei-Ling was worth a fight.

During high school, Mei-Ling joined 12 other young people from the same storefront church in cofounding a youth center to provide their peers refuge from the streets. Ten years later, Generation Xcel—the ministry she and her friends started without money, space, equipment, or paid staff—continues to provide opportunities for kids like Mei-Ling through after-school and summer tutoring, arts programs, athletics, and mentoring.

Because a few church leaders decided to do something about the poor getting poorer, Mei-Ling is now crossing the class canyon. She went on to complete high school and then became the first college gradu-

A comprehensive youth development agency in Lower Manhattan, Generation Xcel exists to empower young people so they can transform their cultures and communities. It was founded in 1996 by 13 young people who defied the stereotypes about their generation and overcame the absence of money, space, equipment, or paid staff to open two youth centers, build a theater in the heart of the East Village, serve hundreds through after-school and summer-camp programs, employ dozens of neighborhood teens, invest in a retreat center upstate, and touch thousands through extensive outreach activities.

To download and hear more about indigenous leadership development in urban youth ministries, check out our free additional Deep Justice resources available at www.cyfm.net.

ate in her biological family when she got her degree from New York University. Mei-Ling remains a vital part of our church and now works as a registered nurse at NYU Medical Center, where she helps the infirm find shalom in their physical bodies.

WHO? (OBSERVATION)

STEP 3: WHO?

Thanks to justice advocates like Bono, awareness efforts like the One Campaign, and (increasingly) evangelical leaders like Rick Warren from Saddleback Community Church—whose public repentance for neglecting the poor and needy was a watershed moment for evangelical America—combating global poverty has become a priority for many in the United States. The language of grace and jubilee are hallmarks of the movement. Bono, for one, is fond of saying: "Rather than ask God to bless what you're doing, find out what he's doing among the poor because it's already blessed."

As the founder and executive director of the New York-based Youth Ministries for Peace and Justice, ALEXIE TORRES-FLEMING is doing just that. The mission of Youth Ministries for Peace and Justice is twofold: First, they work to rebuild the neighborhoods of the South Bronx that were decimated in the late 1960s and early 1970s by the crack epidemic and the divestment of the city resources. Second, they mobilize young people to be prophetic voices for peace and justice. Given that Youth Ministries for Peace and Justice is located in the poorest congressional district of the United States, Alexie and her team have endless opportunities to partner with people of all classes to right wrongs.

Alexie, in thinking about deep justice when it comes to class, can you help us understand some of the reasons poverty exists in our country today?

Poverty exists in this country for one simple reason: greed. When the highest paid CEOs in this country make a base salary of $1,273,978 and the average worker makes around $36,000, you can see there is no grand or complicated reason for poverty—except that some people in this country accumulate wealth. Jesus said the equality of the kingdom of God will be made manifest when we love one another as we love ourselves. Given the gap between the rich and the poor, it is quite clear that we are not treating one another by the commandment Jesus set forth to those who call themselves his disciples.

To download and hear the full audio interview with Alexie, check out our free additional Deep Justice resources available at www.cyfm.net.

From a kingdom justice perspective, what mistakes do youth workers in middle- and upper-class communities make when it comes to seeking justice for all classes?

I've observed that middle- and upper-class youth ministries that want to "empower" the poor often forget that people in poor communities are *already* empowered, and that they do not require the assistance of their well-to-do counterparts to empower them. My poor brothers and sisters have the talents, skills, and ideas necessary to challenge the structures of injustice that benefit from their oppression. This is one of the main reasons Youth Ministries for Peace and Justice has been so successful in our organizing campaigns; we partner *alongside* our brothers and sisters, rather than judging them or giving them the answers. I think folks from middle- and upper-class communities need to stop doing what they think needs to be done in poor communities and start listening to those closest to the problem. The poor know what changes need to be made in their communities. We need to start trusting their analysis and then have the courage to take action against those in the seat of oppression—which is, ironically, usually found in middle- and upper-class communities.

Given that, what advice would you give youth ministries that want to start seeking justice for all classes?

As someone who believes in the community-organizing model of social change, I believe it is inappropriate for me to give any solutions for another community. I would suggest that it is important to first look at yourself and truthfully assess your own level of involvement in maintaining structures of inequality. Don't automatically assume it is someone else's fault. The places we shop, the things we consume, the cars we drive, how we treat our employees, and so much else greatly contribute to our existing structures of inequality. Too often, middle- and upper-class folks come to the poor with the idea that the poor need to change. I truly believe people in well-to-do communities need to first take a long and honest look at themselves and come to their own conclusions about what they need to do to live the gospel of Jesus Christ faithfully.

"Four main assets can be identified in any neighborhood: (1) the capacities and gifts of local residents, (2) the power of local associations and organizations, (3) the potential of local public institutions, and (4) the diverse streams of local economic activity, including the neighborhood's land and other physical assets."

MARK R. GORNIK, *TO LIVE IN PEACE*

When you think about youth ministries that have transcended their biases and preconceptions about folks in other classes, what exactly did they do?

Youth ministries that have transcended these biases and preconceptions have learned the difference between charity and justice. When young people realize that charity work (homeless shelters, food kitchens, clothing drives) deals only with the effects of injustice, while justice deals with the underlying structures or causes of injustice, they can begin to see that justice is what is necessary to have an honest and faithful relationship with people living in poorer communities.

Can you give an example of what you mean?

I work with a coalition of youth groups around the country doing extraordinary work for social change. They train their young people in community organizing by raising social consciousness and then stepping back as the young people themselves lead campaigns for environmental justice, economic justice, education reform, immigration reform, gender equity, and so much more. They are courageous and are transforming the oppressive systems of this country, block by block.

It's pretty clear this type of kingdom justice will only come as our youth ministries build relationships that cross the class divide. I know a lot of youth ministries want to build those types of relationships, but they don't do it very well. Why do you think it's so hard?

Relationships between well-to-do communities and poor communities of faith are hard to establish and maintain because they require deep levels of honesty and sincerity. These relationships need to be based on mutual respect, not on a charity model in which the wealthy are coming to save their "poor and impoverished brethren." I think it is very hard for people to give up the inherent power and privilege that comes from being situated in the middle or upper class.

Another difficulty that arises in maintaining these relationships is that most poor communities are hesitant to deal with wealthier communities because they believe wealthy communities are not in it for the long haul. Poor communities are well aware of the fact that these relationships rarely reach the point of tackling systemic change. So people begin to question the point of forming these relationships if they are not going to be true and honest partnerships in the struggle for justice. I believe these relationships will only work when both parties are truly committed to the quest for peace and justice, rather than seeing the work as an opportunity to log a few community service hours.

In all honesty, some youth ministries probably won't be able to make the type of long-term commitment you're describing. Is doing a little bit better than doing nothing?

Unfortunately, I think sometimes a half-day in the inner city or a short-term mission trip can do more harm than good for suburban kids, because they can feel like they've done their "justice thing," and then they become complacent.

As you've seen youth workers lead their ministries into deep justice, what separates those who "get it" from those who don't?

Those who "get it" don't assume the goal is to make all of us middle class. The work of the church is not to make people middle class. When I turn to the Acts of the Apostles, and I read what the early church did to care for the poor, the widows, and the orphans, nowhere does it say they were working with them to make them wealthier.

Our mission is not to turn poor people into capitalists who make lots of money and consume more and more. In the end, that will only make poor people here richer at the expense of poor people somewhere else.

The hope is that we all critically look at ourselves and understand the broken values within middle- and upper-class communities. We're all guilty, and we all need to work together to create a society that is truly economically just.

HOW? (APPLICATION)

STEP 4: HOW?

DEEP JUSTICE APPLICATION QUESTIONS

1. Which of the two *either/or* extremes best describes your ministry's response to the class divide: denial or despair?

2. If you were to ask God why he had Jesus enter the world through a poor family, what do you think his answer would be? How does that answer impact your view of the Good/Guilt/Grace/Gratitude kingdom story? What are the implications of his answer for your youth ministry?

3. What would happen if you tried to launch Jubilee in your church?

4. Of the five compassionate acts, which do you think would be most effective in taking your youth ministry into deep justice? What can you do in the next few months to try to make progress in that area?

5. How do you think your youth ministry would be enriched by bringing justice to all classes?

6. Alexie asserts that "the work of the church is not to make people middle class." What is your response to that? If you were to ask your students to react to this statement, what would they say? How about your students' parents?

7. In light of chapter 5's portrayal of the kingdom as encompassing both personal salvation and social reform, what exactly is the work of the church when it comes to class?

8. Of the following list of Deep Justice Recommended Action Steps that flow from this chapter, which would best help you as a kingdom follower right wrongs? Which would best help your youth ministry?

DEEP JUSTICE RECOMMENDED ACTION STEPS:

For Yourself

- Jeremy describes the duality between rich and poor he sees every day in Manhattan. Identify places you've seen this duality, noting how it makes you feel, especially in light of all you've read up to this point about kingdom justice.

- Alexie comments, "I would suggest that it is important to first look at yourself and truthfully assess what your level of involvement is in maintaining structures of inequality. Don't automatically assume it is someone else's fault. The places we shop, the things we consume, the cars we drive, how we treat our employees, and so much else contributes greatly to our existing structures of inequality." Make a list of the choices you make that could perhaps be perpetuating structures of inequality. Reflect on whether you feel God inviting you to make different choices that better reflect kingdom justice.

- The city of Sodom was condemned by Ezekiel for being arrogant, over-fed, unconcerned, and uninvolved in helping the poor and the needy. Identify ways that you share in Sodom's sin, and prayerfully confess them to the Lord.

- Jesus begins his Sermon on the Mount by teaching, "Blessed are the poor in spirit, for theirs is the kingdom of heaven" (Matthew 5:3). Make one list of the ways you are already poor in spirit, and a second list of ways you'd like to become more aware of your own poverty.

For Your Youth Ministry

- Reflect (ideally with your adult leadership team) on the socioeconomic backgrounds of the kids in your youth ministry. Compare your kids' backgrounds with those of the kids in the surrounding community. Identify ways you can more effectively reach out to kids of all classes.

- Both in this chapter and in chapter 5, we encourage your ministry to view justice through the concept of shalom. Talk with your youth ministry about Jeremy's and Chap's descriptions of shalom, and ask your students to create poems, pictures, spoken-word pieces, stories, or songs that depict the part the King wants us to play in seeking shalom with and for the poor.

- Scripture's teachings about Jubilee make it clear that God intended society to be structured in such a way that the poor were not disadvantaged. Brainstorm with your students the ways the poor in your city, or in our country, are at a disadvantage. If your students seem particularly passionate about any one or two sources of injustice, make that a focus for your justice work in the next six to twelve months.

- Teach about the Old Testament practice of Jubilee, inviting your students to identify one way they could forgive the financial debts of others. It could be as simple as not making a friend pay back the $4 she borrowed for a blended coffee.

- Challenge your students to give, but to give *quietly*, without anyone knowing they were the ones doing the giving. A week or two later discuss with them not only how it felt to give, but how it felt to give anonymously.

- Invite some students and their parents to come with you to meet with local officials to discuss class dynamics in your town. Afterward, brainstorm ways your ministry could help right wrongs created by class.

- Give your kids some time during a youth group meeting to write letters to local, state, or federal officials, encouraging them to act on behalf of the under-resourced. Do an online search ahead of time and print up some sample letters so kids have examples they can follow.

- Meet with the principal of an elementary school in a poor neighborhood, expressing your youth ministry's desire to serve that school. Suggest that your kids serve as tutors and/or mentors (ideally in pairs with an adult leader) for the high-risk kids at that school, or possibly raise money for the school's library or special after-school activities.

- Alexie highlights the importance of authentic relationships between upper- and lower-class folks who partner together in a mutual quest for God's justice. Before your next service or justice experience, brainstorm with students what they'd like to learn or receive from those in the community where they serve, and then spend some time afterward identifying what they truly did learn and receive.

- Schedule a youth ministry field trip to a job-training center geared to help those in the lower classes find work. Afterward, debrief with your students using the Joplin model described in chapter 6.

12

WHO IS MY NEIGHBOR?

BY JEREMY DEL RIO

"Charity begins at home, and justice begins next door."
—Charles Dickens (1812-1870)

NOW? (DISCERNMENT)

STEP 1: NOW?

The knots in my stomach tightened. As the distance between us grew, I could feel the color leave my face. "You hypocrite," I thought. "So busy with ministry that you pretend not to notice?"

Truthfully, I had noticed. In fact, I saw her so vividly that I crossed the street so she wouldn't see me ignoring her. Not that it would have really made a difference. She didn't know me from the thousands of others who ignore her every day, and we'd never even seen each other before then as far as I knew. That wasn't the point.

The point was that I felt guilty—and I didn't want her judging me like I was judging her. It was just shameful, especially since we'd been praying for her for weeks. Not her specifically, but for teens like her—with matted, green hair, body piercings, and unshaven armpits.

It was July 1996, and I was one of thirteen inner-city young people ages 14-22 who had joined together to open a youth center called Generation Xcel in one of the country's oldest housing projects in Manhattan's Lower East Side. At 21, I was the unqualified youth pastor and the oldest cofounder involved in our day-to-day activities. Like the rest of the neighborhood, we were mostly Latino, with two white girls and a black guy thrown in for good measure.

But that summer, a change had come to the neighborhood. Suddenly, there were lots of white kids hanging around, and not just the Range Rover teens and college students who liked to party at night and leave before the sun rose. Homeless and dirty, this wave of newcomers did strange things to their hair and wore funny clothes. They slept in parks and banded together for protection.

A couple of our youth leaders asked why none of the green-haired kids came to our new youth center. Good question. I suggested that we should pray for them and maybe then they'd come. So as a group, that's what we did.

Now I found myself walking away from one of the people our youth ministry was praying for. Even worse, I was walking away from the chance to be an answer to those very prayers.

There she was, one of *those* girls, panhandling on a stoop across the street from the entrance to the park. And I was too busy for her. Worse, I was a phony, pretending not to notice.

I tried to justify my actions internally.

I've got things to do, places to go. The youth center. The interns. The kids we're already serving.

It didn't work, so I tried excuse-making.

Too late now. I already passed her. It wouldn't make sense to waste more time and go backward.

Not good enough. As an aspiring attorney, I even appealed to precedent.

I've ignored homeless people before without feeling like this. Surely she'll survive just as the others did.

The jury was close to reaching a verdict. And then the kicker came.

You Levite. You Pharisee. Where's the Samaritan in you?

Conviction fell, so reluctantly I went back, wondering as I walked: *What am I going to say? "I'm sorry for ignoring you?" How weird is that?*

Weird, maybe, but appropriate. A couple of false starts later, I finally walked over. "God, help me," I muttered under my breath.

I squatted beside her, introduced myself, and awkwardly apologized for being a hypocritical youth pastor. She looked hungry, so I invited her to breakfast. She told me she hadn't eaten in several days because her last meal—scraps from someone else's garbage—had made her sick. She was just starting to feel better.

We went to a diner a few doors down from where she'd been sitting. She ordered French toast, as I recall, and saved half the portion for "her" stray dog, who hadn't eaten, either. She ate. We talked.

She had run away from family problems at home and hitchhiked to the city. She said she was waiting for some friends to take her to California. She claimed to have just made an appearance on an episode of *The Montel Williams Show* about teenage runaways.

How much of her story was true, I don't know. But for an hour that morning, I did everything I could to make her feel important. Like she mattered. Nothing special, really, I just tried to treat her with the dignity that God our Father gave her. Like I'd want someone else to treat my sister.

I told her about the youth center a few blocks away that we'd started "by youth for youth," and about our church, Abounding Grace. If she or her friends ever needed anything, I promised they could visit anytime. She was grateful, but said she didn't think she'd stick around the city long enough to take me up on the offer. Before she ate, we prayed. Before we said goodbye, I prayed for her again. That was the only time we ever met, but periodically God reminds me to pray for her some more.

I often wonder why God sent me back, why he valued the delay on my walk to work. What really happened that day? Did anything change for her?

Maybe, maybe not.

But something changed for me. That day God saved me from myself, and in the process introduced me to kingdom shalom for all classes. Hopefully, she experienced it, too.

> "The dominant reality of...suffering is that people are wasted: wasted by hunger, torture, deprivation of rights. Wasted by economic exploitation, racial and ethnic discrimination, sexual suppression. Wasted by loneliness, nonrelation, noncommunity."
>
> MORTIMER ARIAS, *ANNOUNCING THE REIGN OF GOD*

Salvation visited me in the person of a homeless runaway who forced me to confront my tendency, even as a youth worker, to live for myself instead of for those around me. The most marginalized and vulnerable among us, like the homeless, are easiest to overlook now. The circumstances of those in lower classes are so foreign to many of us that it's hard even to try to understand.

As a youth worker, I had felt trapped in the *either/or* lenses through which we **Now** view the homeless.

Either we avoid them as a nuisance *or* we fear them as a menace.

Either we pity them as perpetually less than human *or* we hope that treatment for their addictions will restore at least some of their human dignity.

Either we wish they'd get a job and contribute to society *or* we wish they'd disappear from our society altogether.

As if it's our job to diagnose their problems and dictate prescriptions.

But that day I experienced a bigger kingdom reality, one that transcended my selfish *either/or* myopia. Regardless of how or why people may have found themselves homeless, the kingdom requires that I not view them as inconveniences or threats or somehow less than human. The kingdom requires that I love them as neighbors.

NEW? (REFLECTION)

STEP 2: NEW?

THE SCANDAL OF LUKE 10

"What must I do to inherit eternal life?"

The question sounds innocent enough, but its questioner, a lawyer, was attempting to test Jesus. Jesus deftly turned the tables. "How do you read it?" he asked. The man replied simply: "'Love the Lord your God with all your heart and with all your soul and with all your strength and with all your mind'; and, 'Love your neighbor as yourself.'"

"You have answered correctly," Jesus replied. "Do this and you will live" (Luke 10:25-28).

Do this, and you will live. Coming from Jesus, those six little words burst with meaning. The unending life he offers brings joy and peace and abundance, and its citizenship rests in his kingdom. If that's the **New** life our youth ministries want, we must first understand the "this" that Jesus requires us to do.

Curiously, the "this" Jesus speaks of is not the salvation formula we evangelicals describe. There's nothing in the lawyer's response about repeating a prayer or responding to an altar call or attending a 12-week discipleship class. Instead this **New** life he promises grows in proportion to obedience to three commands:

Love God.

Love your neighbor.

And, perhaps most difficult of all, love yourself.

In these three commands, we're given four **New** steps that help us walk down the road of deep justice. Whether we spring or crawl, these four **New** steps are essential to the path of deep justice for the rich, the destitute, and everyone in between.

New Step 1: Receiving Personal Justice

As our youth ministries think about deep justice for all classes, it's easy to overlook Jesus' command to love ourselves, and focus only on loving God and others. Still, this third command is there as the standard by which the other two are measured. It's there when Jesus explains how we love God: with all our heart, soul, strength, and mind. If we resent who we are—if we think we're not smart enough or we're too weak or too unattractive or too emotional—then we're withholding our love for him. He wants us in our entirety, withholding nothing.

If we confuse who we are—who God has made us to be—with the circumstances which have landed each of us in a certain class, we end up bringing him the wrong gift. If we define ourselves by our economic status or the people with whom we associate—I'm rich or poor or cool or nerdy—then we hide behind those associations rather than probing deeper to see what God really cherishes in us. Every day our culture attempts to define us by our material surroundings—the trappings of wealth, or poverty, or middle-class striving. The American Dream teaches us to aspire to more and more stuff—the cliché white picket fence in a safe subdivision with a high-def plasma flat screen. Music, movies, and fashion moguls all tell us last year's hot list needs to be replaced with this year's even hotter list.

> Therefore, I urge you, brothers and sisters, in view of God's mercy, to offer your bodies as a living sacrifice, holy and pleasing to God—this is true worship. Do not conform to the pattern of this world, but be transformed by the renewing of your mind. Then you will be able to test and approve what God's will is—his good, pleasing and perfect will.
>
> For by the grace given me I say to every one of you: Do not think of yourself more highly than you ought, but rather think of yourself with sober judgment, in accordance with the faith God has distributed to each of you.
>
> ROMANS 12:1-3

But when we allow our socioeconomic class and possessions to define us, we miss out on the richness of receiving justice for ourselves. The Apostle Paul tells us in his seminal letter to the church in Rome not to conform to the world's standards of beauty and value but to be transformed by the renewing of our minds. Receiving personal justice means learning to see what God sees in us and to appreciate what God appreciates so we don't think of ourselves "more highly than (we) ought," but "with sober judgment." Instead, Paul invites each of us to offer our whole self as "a living sacrifice, holy and pleasing to God, which is our spiritual act of worship." Everything else, including the capacity to view our neighbors through the prism of heaven, flows through that.

New Step 2: Justifying Ourselves by Extending Justice to Others

The lawyer who questioned Jesus in Luke 10 understood the self-love part of the equation. Brimming with self-confidence, he was, after all, attempting to trap the incarnated Word in a battle of words. But "wanting to justify himself," he comes back for more and asks the critical question: "Who is my neighbor?"

Jesus responds with a parable about a man on a journey. On an isolated stretch of road, thieves rob him, beat him, and leave him battered and bloodied in a ditch. In time, the local priest (or, in our context, the pastor) passes by on his way to the synagogue (the church). Too hurried to stop, he crosses the street and pretends not to notice. Then a Levite (the worship leader) also approaches, perhaps on the way to the same church. He follows the pastor's lead and similarly ignores the man.

> "The true fellowship of the poor is of more value than all the alms and development aid of the rich...the fellowship of the poor and suffering Christ is the secret of the 'holy church' and the 'communion of saints.'"
>
> JÜRGEN MOLTMANN, *THE CHURCH IN THE POWER OF THE SPIRIT*

Then a Samaritan rounds the corner. Unlike the pastor and worship leader, he doesn't pretend not to see. Kingdom compassion compels him to right wrongs for all classes, so he rolls up his sleeves and prepares to get dirty.

Why did Jesus make the "neighbor" in his story a Samaritan? Why not the priest or the Levite? Why not a Jewish layperson? The reason has everything to do with the race and class issues of Jesus' day. The Jews to whom Jesus was preaching, even his own disciples, reviled Samaritans. Most infamously, in Luke 9—the chapter before this parable—Jesus rebuked James and John (the disciple whom "he loved") for praying that fire would consume a Samaritan village.

Samaritans were hated because they descended from Assyrian soldiers who centuries earlier had conquered Israel and marched all the able-bodied survivors across the desert as slaves. The infirm and vulnerable who were left behind—the elderly, women, and children—were plundered and raped. When exiled Jews returned years later, they found children fathered by the Assyrian conquistadors. These they called Samaritans—and their presence in Israel reminded Jews of slavery, colonialism, and injustice.

Yet this Samaritan's love mirrors God's kingdom love. "Go and do likewise," Jesus tells the lawyer. Learn to love like this Samaritan loved. Then you'll truly live.

> To find out more about how neighborhoods and "space" foster identity, check out our free Deep Justice resources available on www.cyfm.net.

The Samaritan's love for his Jewish neighbor, even though the broken man likely would have disdained him under different circumstances, was made possible because the Samaritan, who had been marginalized his entire life, had learned how to love.

New Step 3: Moving Beyond Compassion to Justice

It was compassion that compelled the Samaritan to respond to the bloody mass of human flesh beside the road. But it was justice that kept him there. Kingdom justice required him to get dirty, and restoring shalom meant overcoming the absence of adequate remedies for the battered man's need. There was no 911 operator to call. There were no EMTs to provide urgent care and high-speed transports to a hospital. There wasn't an appropriate health care facility nearby, and no insurance or Medicaid to finance treatment.

Yet shalom came to the battered man because the Samaritan was willing not only to sit with him in the ditch, give him water, and bandage his wounds (a compassionate response), but also to transport him to an inn, personally care for him overnight, and prepay his medical expenses. Compassion, as commonly practiced in youth ministries today, would have served the beaten man but stopped short of healing him. But Christ's kingdom justice brought healing and reconciliation and restoration.

New Step 4: Being Kind

Finally, righting wrongs on behalf of the least among us requires rejecting oppression of those in any class and replacing it with kindness. Proverbs 14:31 reads, "Whoever oppresses the poor shows contempt for their Maker, but whoever is kind to the needy honors God." The word *kind* in this verse is the Hebrew word for *grace*. The gospel tells us that, because of grace, God loved us despite our inability to love him back. The price of sin, which corrupted humankind and disrupted shalom, was death. But God's grace—his infinite

> "Revolutions begin when people who are defined as problems achieve the power to redefine the problem."
>
> JOHN MCKNIGHT, *THE CARELESS SOCIETY*

kindness—paid the price of that sin so we wouldn't have to die.

When our youth ministries remember this, then looking down on the poor becomes repulsive. If we realize when we see those who are poor that we're looking in the mirror because we're "poor in spirit," then we won't feel superior. Their economic need matches our spiritual need. Just as the remedy for spiritual poverty began with someone else's kindness, so too the remedy for economic poverty begins with kindness.

FAITH, NOT WORKS, BUT FAITH WITHOUT WORKS IS DEAD

Amidst all this talk about justice for all classes, I can hear the time-honored clatter of skeptics who would remind us that we've been saved by grace through faith—not by works (Ephesians 2:8-9). But God's saving grace demands a response. When Jesus instructed us to love him and others as ourselves, he wasn't urging passive acceptance of something that would be imposed on us externally. Instead, he imbues his invitation to love with everything that makes the act of loving someone meaningful. Love that is coerced or otherwise manipulated is no love at all. But love that is voluntary and active demonstrates itself in how we choose to treat others.

Evangelicals esteem John 3:16 as our credo for personal salvation: "For God so loved the world that he gave his one and only Son, that whoever believes in him shall not perish but have eternal life." The ubiquitous reference is everywhere, from bumper stickers and gospel tracts to sporting event banners and altar calls. Sometimes we even quote verse 17 for good measure: "For God did not send his Son into the world to condemn the world, but to save the world through him."

But what about another passage most likely written by the same author: 1 John 3:16? "This is how we know what love is: Jesus Christ laid down his life for us. *And we ought to lay down our lives for one another.*" (Emphasis added.) In case laying down our lives for one another is too vague a concept, John elaborates again in verse 17: "If any one of you has material possessions and sees his brother or sister in need but has no pity on them, how can the love of God be in you?"

We live in a culture where our economic class dictates where we can live, who our friends are, which educational and career options we have, and how we view the world. Some would argue that class is even more important than race, religion, and ethnicity, because in a who-you-know world, wealth associates with wealth and begets more wealth. But 1 John requires that even in this culture, the poor and rich alike are siblings, and kingdom justice requires that we and our youth ministries lay down our very lives for the benefit of all classes.

WHO? (OBSERVATION)

STEP 3: WHO?

The good news is that evangelicals are starting to reconcile John 3:16 and 1 John 3:16 by righting wrongs for all classes. In the tradition of Saint Francis of Assisi—who spent his life serving the poor and urged his fellow Christians to preach the gospel always (and even use words if necessary)—SHANE CLAIBORNE is a modern exemplar **Who** embodies the kind of selfless self-love to which Christ calls us. Shane lives out this love as part of an Acts 2 community called the Simple Way in Philadelphia.

Shane, for those who haven't read your book *The Irresistible Revolution*, what is the mission of the Simple Way?

We sort of stumbled into all this. I am from the Bible Belt in East Tennessee, but when I was a student at Eastern University, some friends and I heard about a group of 40 poor and homeless families who were living in an abandoned cathedral in North Philadelphia. The archdiocese was trying to evict them from the cathedral; if the families didn't leave, they were facing arrest for trespassing on church property. That didn't add up for us, so we decided to do something about it.

I remember the first night we drove down to the cathedral to meet the people. On the front of the cathedral, they had hung a banner that said, "How can we worship a homeless man on Sunday and ignore one on Monday?" We knocked on the cathedral's front door and the families just wrapped their arms

To download and hear the full audio interview with Shane, check out our free additional Deep Justice resources available at www.cyfm.net.

"I remember hearing about an old comic strip... Two guys are talking to each other, and one of them says he has a question for God. He wants to ask why God allows all of this poverty and war and suffering to exist in the world. And his friend says, 'Well, why don't you ask?' The fellow shakes his head and says he is scared. When his friend asks why, he mutters, 'I'm scared God will ask me the same question.'"

SHANE CLAIBORNE,
THE IRRESISTIBLE REVOLUTION

To find out more about how the multiple layers of our neighborhoods shape us and our kids, check out our free resources available at www.cyfm.net.

around us, poured out their stories and struggles, and invited us in. We went back to Eastern really stirred up, and we organized students to come alongside those families. Eventually 100 of us were involved in that housing crisis. Thanks to the attention of other kingdom-minded people as well as the media, the families received housing.

About two years later, we started the Simple Way. Simple Way is simply a community trying to live like the early church. We see the kingdom of God as something that we are to live out incarnationally in neighborhoods that are struggling as well as in neighborhood that are beautiful.

As you have spent time with the poor in Philadelphia, in other cities in the U.S., as well as in countries like India and Iraq, what have you learned about the causes of poverty, and how we as kingdom people should respond?

Mother Teresa said, so well, "Poverty is not created by God, but by you and me because we haven't figured out how to love." It's clear in Scripture that God never intends for people to be poor, but that our ignorance and our indifference allow poverty to continue. I think in God's eyes it's an absolutely heartbreaking reality that there are people on the streets while other folks have extra bedrooms in their houses. That there are kids starving while others have extra food in their cupboards. Our justice work flows from a real love of God and of neighbor that recognizes that these blessings of God are too good to keep for ourselves. God created enough stuff for all of us, but when we take more than our share and insulate ourselves from our neighbors, it creates poverty. Gandhi was right when he said there is enough for everyone's need, but there is not enough for everyone's greed.

You just mentioned love for our neighbor. When Jesus said, "Love your neighbor as yourself," who is our neighbor?

When I was in East Tennessee, "love your neighbor as yourself" meant Southern hospitality. It meant sharing sugar with the person who lived next door.

That's beautiful, but it's not enough. Our neighbor is also the person who is sleeping on the streets. Our neighbor is the refugee in Iraq. Our neighbor is the person who is deeply suffering in this world.

Jesus could have said, "Love your neighbor as much as I love you," or "Love your neighbor a whole bunch," but he said, "Love your neighbor as yourself." What does it mean to love our neighbors *as ourselves*?

Grounding our love for others in our love for ourselves is so essential because it's so important to know we are loved. We all deeply long to know we are loved. We try to prove we are lovable in so many heart-wrenching ways. We try to fill our longing for love with stuff and with addictions and with forms of love and intimacy that are unsatisfying. In the middle of that, if we hear that whisper that we are loved, it fills us with love and compassion for other people, because just like us, they are created in the image of God.

When you think of youth workers who are seeking God's justice for all classes, what makes them effective?

They model it. I think we replicate who we are. So it's impossible to develop students who care about the poor if we don't care about the poor. It's impossible to produce disciples if we're not following after Jesus. The youth workers I know who are having incredible fruit in this area of justice are people who are living with integrity—and their students are magnetized toward that.

Mother Teresa was so insightful when she said, "Of course we care about the poor. Everybody cares about the poor. But if we really care about the poor, we can name them."

What would you say to a youth worker who wants to be involved in deep justice for all classes but is doing ministry in a church where that sort of thing isn't all that welcome?

I would say get ready to get in trouble. So many of the things that are at the core of the gospel are in conflict with our culture that there comes a point where they collide and we realize, "Oh my gosh. My kingdom really is not of this world." If we don't have some collision with the culture, then are we really imagining what it means to follow Jesus and be a part of another kingdom?

> "The reality of our rebirth should mess with us."
>
> SHANE CLAIBORNE, *THE IRRESISTIBLE REVOLUTION*

My mom has taught me this well, because my mom has been on the journey of figuring this out with me, and she was not always supportive. A few years ago my mom said to me, "I used to pray that you'd be safe. Now I'm not sure that's the best prayer, because I look at Christians throughout history, and they're not safe. I'm not sure that we're called to safety, but we're promised that if we're where God wants us to be, then there is no place better to be than that. So I pray that you would be where God wants you to be. Maybe there is no more dangerous place to be as Christians than to be in comfort and detached and isolated from the suffering of our neighbor."

I would also say that I have such deep admiration for youth pastors who are trying to gently open up these questions, because it has to be done with so much humility and grace. Jesus was so wise. He asked a lot of questions. He didn't go around hammering the answers down people's throats. In fact, when people would figure it out—"Oh, you're the Messiah!"—he'd respond, "Shhh. Let everybody figure that out. Let people ask the questions and enter into this, and then it's their journey."

What advice would you give a youth worker who's passionate to help kids love their neighbors and seek God's justice for all classes, but doesn't know how to start?

Dr. Martin Luther King Jr. would say we're called to be the Good Samaritan—but then after we've lifted so many people out of the ditch, we start to wonder if the whole road to Jericho needs to be repaved. We want students to reach that point, but they only get there by lifting a lot of people out of the ditch. It comes from getting our hands dirty. It comes from beginning to feel some discomfort and pain with the things that are wrong with the world. Feeling the pain of people who are suffering in the systems and the principalities and powers stirs up the bigger questions around justice like, What is the dream God has for this creation and how are we a part of incarnating that?

In the midst of getting our hands dirty, how do we help our service be more than a placebo that alleviates our students' guilt? How can our justice work instead change the way our students view their role in our world?

I once heard someone say that this whole adventure is not just about having better vision but about having new eyes. Youth pastors who are living out kingdom justice are starting to have kids who have new eyes. These kids begin to look at people of all classes differently and wonder, "Maybe my neighbor is the high school lunch lady or the person who's cleaning my bathroom. Maybe that person has a story that I want to know." Those kids often come from ministries where the leaders are asking, "Who is it that's making our clothes? Where did this coffee come from? Let's try to trace some of the products we use every day to their sources and figure out who those invisible people are." When we start to see that this is a global neighborhood where we're all interdependent on one another, we end up wanting to make sure the people who make our jackets and shoes are treated fairly.

> "There is a movement bubbling up that goes beyond cynicism and celebrates a new way of living, a generation that stops complaining about the church it sees and becomes the church it dreams of."
>
> SHANE CLAIBORNE, *THE IRRESISTIBLE REVOLUTION*

I've received letters from youth groups who are now making their clothes together as a way of doing something creative to identify with people who are making clothes and to make sure their clothes are made in ways that don't suppress other folks. Another youth ministry went out to pick cotton and vegetables so they could identify with the folks who do that every day to provide things we need. I know some teenage girls who have committed to visiting senior citizen homes and painting the nails of elderly women who never have guests. They just sit and listen to their stories. There are so many questions that rise up from this type of justice work.

What type of impact do those types of justice experiences have on kids long term?

Creative justice work stirs up all kinds of bigger questions around vocation. Maybe I'm going to be a doctor or a lawyer, but what kind of doctor or lawyer am I going to be? How am I going to use my gifts for kingdom justice and for my neighbors?

Shane, any last thoughts for youth workers trying to seek deep justice with and for all classes?

When we settle for something short of the dreams God has for us then everybody loses. I think that if young people turn away from the gospel and the church, it's not going to be because we didn't entertain them well. It's because we didn't dare them to risk. We didn't dare them to try the gospel as a way of life. I think it's a fun time to be alive, and I'm excited to be a part of this conversation. I'll be praying for all the youth pastors who will be entering into this conversation, and for those who lose their jobs because of it.

HOW? (APPLICATION)

STEP 4: HOW?

DEEP JUSTICE APPLICATION QUESTIONS

1. What's the difference between compassion and justice? When does compassion lead toward justice? When might it hinder it?

2. How would your youth ministry look different if your kids were familiar with both John 3:16 and 1 John 3:16? How do those two verses help answer the question posed in chapter 5's title: Is the gospel about Personal Salvation or Social Reform?

3. The Good Samaritan knew there was no 911 operator to call, and no ambulances that would transport the injured man to a hospital. How can these services, which we certainly value and wouldn't want to eliminate, make us less likely to help those in need?

4. Shane tells youth workers who want to seek God's justice with and for all classes they should "get ready to get in trouble." How might your justice work get you in trouble? Who can support you in the midst of whatever negative reactions you might face?

5. Shane says, "If young people turn away from the gospel and the church, it's not going to be because we didn't entertain them well. It's because we didn't dare them to risk. We didn't dare them to try the gospel as a way of life." Do you agree? How can you help your students embrace the gospel and kingdom justice as a way of life?

6. Of the following list of Deep Justice Recommended Action Steps that flow from this chapter, which would best help you as a kingdom follower right wrongs? How about for your youth ministry?

DEEP JUSTICE RECOMMENDED ACTION STEPS:

For Yourself

- Jeremy writes of ignoring a homeless teenager and then thinking to himself, "You hypocrite, so busy with ministry that you pretend not to notice." For the next month, note the times when you similarly ignore those in need, and then confess that sin before the Lord.

- Shane paraphrases Mother Teresa as saying, "Of course we care about the poor. Everybody cares about the poor, but if we really care about the poor, we can name them." Make a list of the poor people you can name, and contemplate how you feel about the number of names on that list and the depth of relationship you have with each.

- According to Shane, youth workers who effectively seek God's justice with and for all classes are effective because they model it. Make a list of the ways students see you seeking kingdom justice with and for the least, last, and lost. Make a second list of new ideas you have to seek kingdom justice with and for others. Choose two or three of those ideas to focus on during the next month.

- Memorize 1 John 3:16.

For Your Youth Ministry

- Whenever you share John 3:16 with students, commit to sharing 1 John 3:16 with them also.

- With your students, make a list of the "neighbors" you and your ministry are called to serve, both locally and globally. Spend some time brainstorming ways you could love them as you love yourselves. Ask a few students to work with you to make sure you follow up on some of your ideas.

- Make that list even more practical for students by identifying "neighbors" they see at school, like kids who don't have many friends, or kids with developmental disabilities, or the adult cafeteria workers and janitors. Invite students to love those neighbors in the next week and then come back and share what happened.

- Remind students of the Good/Guilt/Grace/Gratitude kingdom story in chapter 3 and ask them how our neighbors play a part in each movement. What does it mean that our neighbors are created as good? How has sin affected our relationships with our neighbors? If we embrace the truth that Jesus' grace is available to our neighbors, how will that change the way we interact with them? How can we serve our neighbors out of gratitude for all the King has done for us?

- In Shane's early justice work, he read a banner that asked, "How can we worship a homeless man on Sunday and ignore one on Monday?" Discuss this ironic question with your students

- Schedule times for your youth group to feed the homeless in your town, but instead of handing someone a sandwich and then walking away, make it a priority to sit with that person, ask questions, and listen to his or her stories.

- Based on what you have heard from the homeless (see the prior action step), bring students and their parents with you to meet with local officials to talk about how your town can better respond to the homeless in your community.

- Invite your students to talk with their parents about their families' budgets, and how much they spend on housing, utilities, food, transportation, clothing, and health care. Send your students' families to this Web site, http://www.nccbuscc.org/cchd/povertyusa/tour2.htm, to help them understand the almost impossible choices a U.S. family living in poverty must make every month.

- Invite some adults from various vocations to share (through testimonies, talks, or a panel) about how their jobs give them unique opportunities to love their neighbors and seek kingdom justice for all classes.

- Invite some students to join you in meeting with a few influential leaders in your church to explain your vision for deep justice for all classes. Enlist their help in identifying ways your entire church might partner with you and your kids to right wrongs by identifying the root causes and solving them.

CONCLUSION
HOW CAN WE WORK TOGETHER TO BRING ABOUT JUSTICE FOR ALL?

BY KARA POWELL

As you seek the kingdom, does your youth ministry have the potential to bring deep justice to a broken world?

You bet.

Does the King intend for you to bring deep justice to a broken world by yourselves?

Don't bet on it.

Our world is simply too broken for us to try to right wrongs on our own. From the high school dropout rate in Detroit to alcoholism among rural teens outside Des Moines to the genocide in Darfur, there are just too many broken and brokenhearted for us to do Lone Ranger justice work.

Plus, that's not how the King wants it done.

In John 13:34-35, Jesus taught his first and twenty-first century disciples, "A new command I give you: Love one another. As I have loved you, so you must love one another. By this everyone will know that you are my disciples, if you love one another."

Every single believer has something to offer to the least, last, and lost.

So does every church.

Yesterday, I had lunch with two youth workers in East Palo Alto, a community of almost 30,000 halfway between San Jose and San Francisco. In the midst of the wealth of Silicon Valley and neighboring communities like Palo Alto and Menlo Park, East Palo Alto (or EPA) has the unenviable reputation of being a hotbed of crime, gangs, and violence. Sadly, this reputation is probably deserved; in 1992, EPA had the highest per capita murder rate in the entire United States. Although these crime problems have lessened in severity more recently, EPA remains a struggling community.

But the kingdom is alive in East Palo Alto. And deep justice is breaking through. Largely because kingdom churches and ministries are working together to right wrongs.

> To read the findings of recent study on violence conducted by Fuller Seminary, check out our free additional Deep Justice resources available at www.cyfm.net.

Two large churches near East Palo Alto—one mostly white and one ethnically diverse—are starting to partner with the people of that city, sending their kingdom believers out of the suburban environment and into the urban hood for a few hours at a time to mentor high-risk kids at the public high school.

Students from different church and parachurch ministries at nearby Stanford University are working together to launch "Extreme Makeover" weekend projects to renovate homes for families.

Young adults who feel called to live incarnationally have relocated themselves to EPA, setting up homes in the community where any kid who needs a place can stay. These same young adults, many of whom are part of either Young Life or For Youth/By Youth (a local ministry extending justice to high-risk kids) are considering joining the EPA Housing Commission or the EPA public school board, to help Latino and African-American kids and families gain equal access and equal opportunities.

The justice model is beautiful. Some can give an hour, some can give a day, and some can move into the neighborhood.

Some who come to work as tutors are billionaires, and others who work alongside them are barely scraping by.

Teenagers, young adults, married couples, and retired business leaders are making the marginalized a front-and-center opportunity in their churches.

Maybe the same can happen in your community. Maybe your first step toward deep justice is to meet with other leaders and youth workers to pray and dream together about how you could bring your respective gifts and resources together to right the wrongs around you.

Please don't try to bring deep justice by yourself. Even the Lone Ranger had Tonto.

As we link arms together—across our cities, our nation, and our world—maybe we'll experience the power of Amos 5:24 and "let justice roll on like a river, righteousness like a never-failing stream!"

May our youth ministries dive deeply into God's justice river together.

Whether you're struggling to make anything work in your youth ministry or finding that most things are clicking along, this book will help
you develop a practical theology—to ask what is happening, what
should be happening, and how you can make it happen. Each chapter
is followed by discussion questions to help you process in a group or
on your own.

Deep Ministry in a Shallow World
Not So Secret Findings About Youth Ministry
Kara Powell and Chap Clark
RETAIL $18.99
ISBN 0-310-26707-2

youth
specialties

Many people think teenagers aren't capable of much. But Zach Hunter is proving those people wrong. He's only fifteen, but he's working to end slavery in the world—and he's making changes that affect millions of people. Find out how Zach is making a difference and how you can make changes in the things that you see wrong with our world.

Be the Change
Your Guide to Freeing Slaves and Changing the World
Zach Hunter
RETAIL $9.99
ISBN 0-310-27756-6

We may nevr fully understand teenagers, but we can learn more about them with *Youth Culture 101*. Cultural analyst and adolescent expert, Walt Mueller, shares research and trends to help you better understand yours students and minister to them more effectively in their ever changing world. It's an invaluable resource for youth ministry teams and parents of teenagers.

Youth Culture 101
Walt Mueller
Author Name
RETAIL $19.99
ISBN 0-310-27313-7

Contemplative Youth Ministry is a more organic approach to youth ministry, allowing you to create meaningful silence, foster covenant communities, engage students in contemplatice activities, and maximize spontaneity—and to help your students recognize the presence of Jesus in their everyday lives.

Contemplatice Youth Ministry
Practicing the Presence of Jesus
Mark Yaconelli
RETAIL $12.99
ISBN 0-310-26777-3

youth
specialties

Ever wish youth group fun and games could accomplish more than burning off students' high-octane energy? It can—if you have the right tools at your disposal. And your number-one tool is *Experiential Youth Ministry Handbook 2*. This innovative resource provides intentional activities with a purpose, specific program sequences, and adaptable templates for making games resonate with your students' minds and hearts.

Experiential Youth Ministry Handbook 2
How Intentional Activity Can Make the Spiritual Stuff Stick
John Losey
RETAIL $16.99
ISBN 0-310-25532-5

visit www.youthspecialties.com/store
or your local Christian bookstore

We all know that burnout is a major reason churches post openings for new youth pastors every 18 months or so. Sadly, many of these men and women walk away from their jobs, their callings, and their passion because their interior worlds are falling apart. That's why *Soul School* is essential for developing an effective and healthy you(th) ministry. Because while your ministry might look healthy to outsiders, only you know that something is lacking. It's easy to get so busy caring for the external parts of your ministry that you forget the most important part—your soul. And it's only when you're truly connected to the Giver of Life that you can offer real hope and love to your students. So spend some time going beneath the surface, to the core of who you are. In the pages of this book, you'll learn to receive God's love and actually love yourself.

Soul School
Enrolling in a Soulful Lifestyle for Youth Ministry
Jeanne Stevens
RETAIL $15.99
ISBN 0-310-27496-6

Whether you're crafting a five-minute devotional or a 30-minute sermon, *Speaking to Teenagers* is essential to understanding and preparing great messages. Doug Fields and Duffy Robbins show you how they craft their own messages and give you the tools to prepare and deliver meaningful messages that effectively communicate the gospel to your students.

Speaking to Teenagers
How to Think About, Create, and Deliver Effective Messages
Doug Fields and Duffy Robbins
RETAIL $18.99
ISBN 0-310-27376-5

youth
specialties

In *Teenager Guys*, author Steve Gerali breaks down the stages of development that adolescent guys go through, providing stories from his own experiences in ministry and counseling, as well as practical research findings to equip youth workers (both male and female) to more effectively minister to teenage guys. Each chapter includes advice from counselors and veteran youth workers, as well as discussion questions.

Teenage Guys
Exploring Issues Adolescent Guys Face and Strategies to Help Them
Steve Gerali
RETAIL $17.99
ISBN 0-310-26985-7

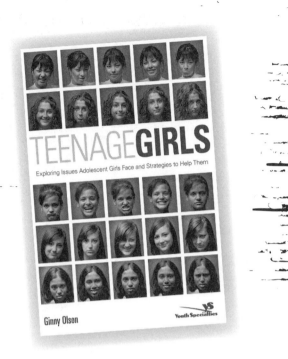

In *Teenager Girls*, you'll find advice from counselors and veteran youth workers, along with helpful suggestions on how to minister to teenage girls. In addition to the traditional issues people commonly associate with girls (eating disorders, self-image issues, depression, etc.), author Ginny Olson will guide you through some of the new issues on the rise in girls' lives.

Teenage Girls
Exploring Issues Adolescent Girls Face and Strategies to Help Them
Ginny Olson
RETAIL $17.99
ISBN 0-310-26632-7